Star Wars
and Philosophy

Popular Culture and Philosophy™

Series Editor: William Irwin

Star Wars and Philosophy

*More Powerful Than You
Can Possibly Imagine*

Edited by
KEVIN S. DECKER
and
JASON T. EBERL

OPEN COURT
Chicago and La Salle, Illinois

Volume 12 in the series, Popular Culture and Philosophy™

To order books from Open Court, call toll-free 1-800-815-2280, or visit our website at www.opencourtbooks.com.

Open Court Publishing Company is a division of Carus Publishing Company.

Printed and bound in the United States of America.

Library of Congress Cataloging-in-Publication Data

Star wars and philosophy : more powerful than you can possibly imagine / edited by Kevin S. Decker and Jason T. Eberl.
      p. cm. — (Popular culture and philosophy ; 12)
   Includes bibliographical references and index.
   ISBN-13: 978-0-8126-9583-0 (alk. paper)
   ISBN-10: 0-8126-9583-6 (pbk. : alk. paper)
   1. Star Wars films—History and criticism. 2. Philosophy in motion pictures. I. Decker, Kevin S. II. Eberl, Jason T. III. Series.
   PN1995.9.S695S76 2005
   791.43'684—dc22
                                  2005002396

To Suzanne and Jennifer,
You're the brains, sweethearts!

Contents

Part I
"May The Force Be with You":
The Philosophical Messages of *Star Wars*   1

Part II
"Try Not—Do or Do Not":
Ethics in a Galaxy Far, Far Away   55

Part III
"Don't Call Me a Mindless Philosopher!": Alien Technologies and the Metaphysics of The Force

Part IV
"There's Always a Bigger Fish": Truth, Faith and a Galactic Society

Heroes of Rogue Squadron

It takes three years to make a *Star Wars* movie, from script to screen. Fortunately, it didn't take nearly as long to put this volume together, and the credit for that achievement goes to a number of persons. First of all, our contributors, who raced full-throttle down the Death Star trench of writing and editing to score bulls-eyes with the chapters they produced. Next, of course, are the good people at Open Court who saw the Force-potential in our proposal and supported us all the way: David Ramsay Steele, Carolyn Madia-Gray, and Grand Master Bill Irwin.

As the volume progressed, a number of colleagues and friends took time from their bounty-hunter training seminars to review drafts of various chapters or influenced the volume in myriad other ways: Dave Baggett, Susan Bart, Greg Bassham, Gregory Bucher, Seetha Burtner, Donald Crosby, Keith Decker, Mario Intino, Jr., Jennifer Kwon, Chris Pliatska, William Rowe, Scott Rubarth, Charlene Haddock Siegfried, James South, Kevin Timpe, C. Joseph Tyson, and Wayne Viney. An extra special "thank you" goes to Carlea Alfieri and Andrew Clyde for reading and offering their insights on each chapter as it neared completion.

Obviously, our families, including the secret twin sisters we don't know about yet, deserve a great deal of credit for their inspiration and patience with our other life in that galaxy far, far away. We dedicate this *opus* to our wives Suzanne and Jennifer, and wish to express our love and devotion to our children Kennedy, Ethan, Jack, and August, through whose eyes we see the *Star Wars* saga and life itself in whole new ways.

The Force Is with You . . . but You're Not a Jedi Yet

Now this may shock you, but there's an arcane, little-known quotation, one rich in meaning, that appears in every *Star Wars* movie: "I've got a bad feeling about this." In each episode of George Lucas's "space opera," one of the main characters expresses this basic existential anxiety.[1] It's an intuitive response to an undefined problem. Yet it has its root in the essentially *philosophical* thought that our relationship to the world is one of questioning. Questions sometimes emerge from wonder, sometimes from doubt. We stare up at the heavens, much as Luke did on Tatooine, and wonder about the extent of the universe, its origin, and its meaning. In a crisis of faith, much as Luke had when confronted by his parentage on Cloud City, we may doubt many of our firmly-held beliefs and preconceptions. We search our inner selves, as did Leia when Han was being lowered into the carbon-freezing chamber, and wonder about what it means to love or be virtuous. Sharing Han's skeptical worldly point of view, we may doubt that we have any existence as a mind or soul after our bodily processes are nullified by death. We comb through our junkyard, much as Watto constantly does, and wonder whether there are formulas describing the variances of the value character of the products of labor.[2]

But philosophy doesn't have a monopoly on wonder or doubt. You could be in a state of wonder reflecting upon the birth of your twin children, or while viewing the new piece of art on your favorite Hutt's wall. Similarly, you could be in doubt whether the modifications to your podracer are sufficient to allow you to be competitive in the Boonta Eve Race. In these cases, no philosophical questioning needs to occur. Philosophy

---

[1] Although known to only a few, even Chewbacca voices this sentiment in the Boba Fett-driven cartoon segment of the infamous *Star Wars Holiday Special*.
[2] Actually, this is a wonder entertained *only* by Marxists studying *Das Kapital*. And so we doubt that it applies to many of you.

begins with wonder but leads to *thinking*. The need to think things through, to change our mind and our environment, arises only because we get into sticky situations. Simple problems disclose their solutions almost immediately, like young Anakin's uncanny ability to fix machines. More difficult ones require us to search among alternatives for a solution: Should Obi-Wan tell Luke the truth about his father from the start or wait until he matures? Should Qui-Gon use Jedi "mind tricks" on Boss Nass to secure transport from the Gungan city? Philosophical problems are often distinguished by the fact that *the problem itself is unclear*—we need to settle certain things about the world and ourselves, sometimes at the deepest levels, before we can "blow this thing and go home."

Now *Star Wars* doesn't wear its philosophy on its sleeve—it doesn't make clever allusions to Alice in Wonderland or the Kabbalah in an effort to jump-start the mind of the average viewer. Although these movies are primarily vehicles for action scenes and fantasy themes, they still involve characters reaching out and deeply within to solve problems that are significantly larger than themselves. In *Star Wars*, conflict is a constant, but it's not fighting in the "wars" of the title that spurs the development of the main characters' personalities—after all, "wars not make one great." Instead, it's the struggle to understand and overcome deep problems of identity, truth, freedom, and the tragic side of life that defines the rise, fall, and rise again of the Skywalker family and the impact they have on allies and enemies alike.

Essentially, the *Star Wars* movies tell a simple story of tragedy, courage, and redemption. But under this simple guise the ageless questions of philosophy—many of which are examined in this book—derive new meaning when held against the background of its plot, colorful situations, and memorable characters. For example:

- Are the virtues good because they are appreciated by the Jedi, or are they appreciated by the Jedi because they are good? (Plato)
- Is Yoda a Jedi Master so great that a greater one can't be conceived of? (Anselm)
- Can Anakin commit himself as a chaste, unattached Jedi Knight, but just not yet? (Augustine)

- As absolute ruler of a galaxy-wide Empire, is it better to be loved or feared? (Machiavelli)
- Am I a mind, a body, or an overweight glob of grease? (Descartes)
- How do we know the sun will rise on Alderaan tomorrow, even if it has done so every day since the beginning of time? (Hume)[3]
- If Vader looks into the abyss, doesn't the abyss also look back into him? (Nietzsche)
- Is hell other Sith lords? (Sartre)
- Who's scruffy-lookin'? (Solo) *heh heh*

Here, you'll encounter thoughtful and lively discussion of these questions, but not hard-and-fast answers to them—don't blame us, some of these questions have gone unanswered for over two thousand years! Judith Barad takes on the most ancient of these while exploring the virtues of the Jedi Order. Yoda is conceived of as a both a great Jedi Master and a wise Stoic sage by William Stephens. For Chris Brown, Anakin's fall and redemption may be unavoidable if evil is needed for good to exist. Emperor Palpatine, in the eyes of Kevin Decker, is the galaxy's most masterful practitioner of Machiavellian political arts. Robert Arp finds Descartes's question about mind and body just as intriguing to ask about C-3PO and R2-D2 as of ourselves, and Jerome Donnelly concurs that droids may be more "human" than the humans in *Star Wars*. While we know the answer to the Alderaan question, Jan-Erik Jones finds similar cocktail party discussions about expected cause-and-effect relationships still unresolved on our planet—just what makes gravity work anyway? Of course, Darth Vader's entire life is spent looking into the metaphorical abyss of darkness and evil, and occasionally into the literal abyss of space station reactor shafts; what this says about his moral character and capacity for redemption is the fascination of many in what follows. And while Sartre's question regards three strangers trapped in a room with "no exit" for all eternity, Brian Cameron notes that it takes only two? Sith to dance the *pas de deux* Hegelian "dialectic" that leads to mutual self-destruction.

---

[3] This question was much entertained at cocktail parties on Alderaan right up until the tragic and unexpected events of *A New Hope*.

These are by no means the only philosophical questions raised and addressed by our Force-sensitive contributors. Using nature and other sentient beings merely as means to one's own ends, valuing deception as a tool to bring about the greatest good, avoiding the dehumanizing influence of technology, finding the balance between love and duty, taking a leap of faith, and achieving the enlightened mind of "no mind" are also defining philosophical issues in Lucas's galaxy and our own.

This book came together with Socrates's thought that wisdom, for humans as well as R5 droids, begins when we discover our own "bad motivators." The preceding questions and the issues they raise are deep and challenging, but thinking about them can be rewarding and even fun to those whose thinking is slightly more precise than a stormtrooper's aim. Consider this book a "Kessel Run" for your brain, and enjoy—you get bragging rights if you read the whole book in less than five parsecs!

Part I

"May The Force Be with You"

The Philosophical Messages of *Star Wars*

1

"You Cannot Escape Your Destiny" (Or Can You?): Freedom and Predestination in the Skywalker Family

JASON T. EBERL

In *The Phantom Menace*, Jedi Master Qui-Gon Jinn brings a nine-year-old boy, recently released from slavery and separated from his mother, before the Jedi Council to ask that he be trained in the ways of the Force. When the Council refuses to permit the boy's training, Qui-Gon declares, "He *is* the Chosen One. You must see that." To which Master Yoda replies, "Clouded this boy's future is."

The boy is, of course, Anakin Skywalker—the future Darth Vader—and his being "the Chosen One" is based on a Jedi prophecy that refers to Anakin "bringing balance to the Force." Approximately thirty-five years (*Star Wars* time) after this exchange, Anakin's son, Luke, has nearly completed his training to become a Jedi Knight. After the deaths of Obi-Wan Kenobi and Yoda, Luke will be the "last of the Jedi" and the "last hope" for the galaxy to be saved from the tyrannical power of the Dark Side of the Force exercised by Darth Vader and Emperor Palpatine. Yoda tells Luke, however, that he will be a Jedi only if he faces Darth Vader in battle a second time (their first battle having ended badly for Luke and his extremities!) Luke balks at the idea of killing his own father. But the apparition of Obi-Wan responds, "You cannot escape your destiny. You must face Darth Vader again."

These scenes raise particularly interesting philosophical questions concerning freedom and moral responsibility.[1] What

---
[1] The fact that George Lucas recasts what *Star Wars* is really about with the

does it mean for Anakin to be the Chosen One? Is it possible for him to fail to fulfill the prophecy? Is Anakin *predestined* to fall to the Dark Side and become Darth Vader? Must Luke unavoidably shoulder the burden of saving the galaxy? Or, does Anakin *choose* to ally himself with the Emperor? *Could* Luke have chosen to remain on Tatooine and live out his life tending his uncle's moisture farm instead of going with Obi-Wan?

"Clouded This Boy's Future Is"

Anakin Skywalker's destiny seems to have been set for him since before he was even born. "Who was his father?" asks Qui-Gon after sensing Anakin's incredible Force-potential. His mother, Shmi, replies, "There was no father. I gave birth to him, I raised him . . . I can't explain how it happened." The realization then dawns on Qui-Gon that Anakin may be the Chosen One of Jedi prophecy. Qui-Gon is a true believer in Anakin's destiny from that moment on and, with his dying breath, insists that Obi-Wan train Anakin to become a Jedi Knight. Qui-Gon's belief in Anakin, however, is just that—a *belief*—and Master Yoda points out the uncertainty of Anakin's future.

For us, the future is also clouded. Typically—despite some people's belief in crystal balls or Tarot cards—we don't have visionary insights into what's to come. Even gifted Jedi don't have *certainty* about future events. When Luke has a vision of Han and Leia suffering on Bespin, he asks Yoda, "Will they die?" If any Jedi is able to see clearly into the future, it should be the oldest, wisest, greenest, and most powerful of all of them. But even Yoda can only reply, "Difficult to see. Always in motion is the future." Perhaps it's this lack of certainty about our knowledge of the future that allows us to *freely* choose what actions we'll take to determine the future for ourselves—as Luke courageously, but perhaps also foolishly, chooses to end his training early and leave Dagobah to help his friends. Of course, we typically don't equate ignorance with freedom. Suffering under the delusion that you're free because you don't know your own

---

three prequel films—from the mythic hero-journey of Luke Skywalker to the fall and redemption of Anakin Skywalker—is evidence of Lucas's own fascination with issues of fate and moral responsibility.

future isn't nearly as good as actually having an *indeterminate* future—a future not already set in stone.

But at least one individual in the *Star Wars* galaxy seems to have had a pretty clear idea of what lay ahead in the future: whoever wrote the Jedi prophecy that Anakin fulfilled when he, as Vader, killed Emperor Palpatine in *Return of the Jedi*. This visionary, at least in this case, had a "God's-eye view" of the future and it's this perspective that raises questions regarding Anakin's freedom as well as our own.

In our galaxy, many religious believers—particularly those in the Jewish, Christian, and Islamic traditions—conceive of God as omniscient (all-knowing) and understand God's infinite knowledge to include infallible knowledge of the future.[2] If God knows from all eternity that I would be writing this chapter right now, it might seem that there's no way it could be false that I'm now writing this chapter. When I was sitting in my Lay-Z-Boy chair about thirty minutes ago wondering whether I should work on my chapter or watch *Attack of the Clones* on DVD with my 5.1 surround sound system on full-blast (because my wife is out with her girlfriends tonight), God already knew what I was going to choose and, since God can't be wrong, it seems I couldn't have chosen to watch my DVD instead of working on my chapter. Was I free in my choice to work on my chapter?

To approach this question, we have to understand a little more about God's nature. Both St. Augustine (354–430) and St. Thomas Aquinas (1225–1274)—two very influential Christian philosophers of the Middle Ages—reason that there isn't much we can definitively say about God's nature, since it is far beyond our comprehension. Nevertheless, there are certain things they're sure that God is *not*. For example, both hold that God is not "in time." Aquinas relies on Aristotle, who argued that time is the measure of motion. There can be no time if there's no motion; and there can be no motion if there is no universe with things in it that are in motion—just as the Force requires living things in order to exist. God, though, must exist outside the universe, because God *created* the universe. This also means that

[2] See Linda Zagzebski, *The Dilemma of Freedom and Foreknowledge* (New York: Oxford University Press, 1991), pp. 33–34.

God could exist even if no universe existed. Since time requires the existence of a universe that contains things in motion, and God could exist without such a universe existing, God must exist outside of time—God is *eternal*.[3]

What would eternal existence—living outside of time—be like? We experience the passage of time in a *linear* fashion—one moment passes to the next, which passes to the next, and so on. When Han Solo makes the Kessel Run in less than five parsecs (a measure of distance, not time), he must travel the first parsec, before he can travel the second, before he can travel the third, and so on. This, of course, requires that he travel for one period of time, before he can travel for a second period of time, before he can travel for a third . . . you get the idea. This is the nature of time from our perspective. From the eternal perspective, though, every moment in time occurs *at once*. Imagine seeing every frame of all six *Star Wars* films at the same instant, not one after another—like scenes on the page of a comic book; you would see Han shooting Greedo and being frozen in carbonite at the same time!

If someone could see from this eternal perspective, he would know the future, because, from this perspective, the past, present, and future are all equally *present* to the observer. For us linear observers, the future doesn't exist. Neither does the past, which we simply recollect. We can perceive only the present. Aquinas writes:

> God knows future events still undetermined . . . Now God knows such events not only in their causes but also as actual happenings. Though they happen one after another, God's knowledge of them happening is not itself successive (like ours), but instantaneously whole. His knowledge, like his existence, is measured by eternity, which in one and the same instant encompasses all time; so his gaze is eternally focused on everything in time as on something present and known to him with certainty, even though it is future and undetermined in relation to its cause.[4]

---

[3] See Aquinas, *Summa Theologiae: A Concise Translation*, edited and translated by Timothy McDermott (Allen: Christian Classics, 1989), p. 23; Eleonore Stump and Norman Kretzmann, "Eternity," *Journal of Philosophy* 78 (1981): pp. 429–457.

[4] Aquinas, *Summa Theologiae*, p. 41.

Does the eternal observer's knowledge of the linear observer's future *determine* that future? Assuming that the eternal observer can't be mistaken in his perceptions, it would seem that it does. How can I change the future that is already known by someone who can't be wrong about it? Assuming that the prophecy is true and Anakin is indeed the Chosen One, it seems he can't avoid bringing balance to the Force. He couldn't freely choose not to kill the Emperor.

Some philosophers would answer that Anakin does not freely choose to throw the Emperor down the second Death Star's reactor shaft. They assume that the eternal observer's knowledge determines his fate; whatever has been correctly prophesied must happen. But what determines the eternal observer's knowledge? What causes the prophecy of the Chosen One to exist in the first place?

When Anakin, as Vader, is watching his son being tortured and slowly killed by the Emperor, it's evident that he's wrestling with a moral choice between devotion to his master and love for his son. John Williams's dramatic score reaches a dark crescendo as it seems all hope for saving the galaxy from tyranny is about to be lost. But then the music suddenly shifts to the triumphal "Force Theme" as Anakin *makes his choice* and destroys the Emperor—thereby saving his son, restoring freedom to the galaxy, and bringing the Force back into balance— all at the cost of his own life. It may be that Anakin's choice determines the eternal observer's knowledge of what he'll do, not the other way around. If Anakin hadn't chosen to destroy the Emperor and thus fulfill the prophecy, the prophecy might not have existed in the first place. The prophecy that *seems* to determine the ultimate course of Anakin's future may itself be determined by the ultimate course of Anakin's future that results from his choices.

This possibility implies "counter-temporal causality"—that, in this case, a future choice causes past knowledge, whereas we typically think of past events causing future events. But, from the eternal observer's perspective, Anakin's choice and the knowledge expressed in the prophecy are both *present*. So this isn't a case of counter-temporal causality. Anakin's choice causes the eternal observer's knowledge in the same way that my pushing a ball across the floor causes the ball's movement— both events occur *simultaneously*.

Augustine compares the eternal observer's knowledge of the future to our mundane knowledge of the past:

> Why cannot [God] justly punish what He does not force to be done, even though He foreknows it? Your recollection of events in the past does not compel them to occur. In the same way, God's foreknowledge of future events does not compel them to take place. As you remember certain things that you have done and yet have not done all the things that you remember, so God foreknows all the things of which He Himself is the Cause, and yet He is not the Cause of all that He foreknows.[5]

This is not the only way of responding to the problem of the eternal observer. We've been assuming that the eternal observer—personified by the classical theistic notion of God—has infallible knowledge of the future. But maybe there are no such eternal observers and there's no time beyond the present moment that we linear observers are currently experiencing. When Yoda asserts, "Always in motion is the future," he may not have been speaking merely from a linear perspective, but reflecting a metaphysical fact: The future isn't set, because it doesn't yet exist. When it does, we call it "the present," so nothing called "the future" really exists.

"Everything Is Proceeding as I Had Foreseen"

Even if the future doesn't exist until it becomes the present, a powerful person in the present may attempt to determine what the future will be. In *The Phantom Menace*, Darth Sidious puts into motion a plan to take revenge on the Jedi and gain tyrannical control of the galaxy. In *Revenge of the Sith*, the plan comes to fruition as Sidious becomes the Galactic Emperor and, in *Return of the Jedi*, he prepares to sweep away for good the Rebellion that threatens his Empire and convert the last of the Jedi to the Dark Side of the Force. After arriving on the second Death Star and seeing his vast Imperial army and fleet amassed, he boasts to Vader, "Everything is proceeding as I had foreseen" [insert evil cackle]. But in *The Empire Strikes Back*, he warns

---

[5] Augustine, *On Free Choice of the Will*, translated by Anna S. Benjamin and L.H. Hackstaff (New York: Macmillan, 1964), Book III, §4.

Vader that Luke "could destroy us." Vader shares this prediction with Luke when he first tries to persuade him to the Dark Side, but obviously has slightly different designs, saying, "You could destroy the Emperor. He has foreseen this. It is your *destiny.*"

We all know how the story goes. Things don't proceed as the Emperor had "foreseen," otherwise he would not have laughed in such a gleefully wicked manner after boasting to Vader. The Emperor tries his best to act as the grand "puppet-master" pulling everyone's strings. But people aren't marionettes and the Emperor appears truly shocked and chagrined when Luke, striking down his father in rage, then throws away his lightsaber and declares that he'll never turn to the Dark Side: "You've failed, Your Highness. I am a Jedi, like my father before me." Caught off-guard by this sudden assertion of free choice, the Emperor can only declare solemnly: "So be it, *Jedi.*"

For some religious believers, God can pull certain strings in the world to make it turn out as he wills. God designed the universe with all the physical causal laws that we live by everyday, such as gravity, inertia, centrifugal force, the fact that all "lite" beers are tasteless, and so forth. But does God also pull the strings of human will? Does he, for example, truly "harden hearts" as the Bible says he did to the Egyptian Pharaoh (*Exodus* 4:21)? This is an important question for religious believers who also think that human beings are morally responsible for their actions: Do good and you go to Heaven, do evil and you go to Hell. If God hardened Pharoah's heart so that he wouldn't let the Israelites leave Egypt, does he deserve his punishment when God drowns the Egyptians in the Red Sea?

For religious philosophers, such as Augustine and Aquinas, God may infuse "grace" into the minds and hearts of those who invite it, and deny it to those who refuse it. And this grace may influence a person's will, usually toward goodness. But the reception of grace requires the compliance of the person's own will. The only way to receive God's grace is not to reject it, and someone can avoid being infused with grace by willing against it. Thus, by creating human beings with freedom of will, God limits his own power to control our lives; God can pull only those strings in our will that we let him—though he can still pull the strings of everything around us.

In this sense, God has about as much power over us as the Emperor does over Luke and Vader. The Emperor believes he has a power over others' wills that he can't have, because, although he's a powerful Sith Lord, he's ultimately a limited, mortal being. God, on the other hand, is omnipotent (all-powerful) and thus could have exercised total control over everything he has created—including us! For example, God could have designed us as mindless automatons just as the Kaminoans modified the genetic structure of the Republic's clone troopers to make them "less independent" and "totally obedient, taking any order without question." But God chose to create us with freedom of will and thereby elected to limit his own power to pull our strings. Though omnipotent, even God can't control us because of the way he created us. This allows us to be responsible for our moral choices and merit whatever reward or punishment we deserve.

But even if there might be no future to be determined and also no infallible cosmic puppet-master, we haven't escaped the possibility of *fate*. It could be that the mere truth of what philosophers call "future-contingent propositions"—statements about the future—requires that events unfold in a determinate fashion. Various views of fate actually predate much of the religious philosophy we've been talking about—the ancient Sumerian culture, the Homeric epics (*Iliad* and *Odyssey*), and the best Greek tragedies all concern themselves with fate.

In his *De interpretatione*, Aristotle raises the issue of fate by noting that one can truthfully say at any time that "Either there will be a sea-battle tomorrow or there won't be." Now this is about as uninformative as a statement can get—imagine a Rebel strategist telling Admiral Ackbar and Lando Calrissian "Either you will destroy the Death Star when you reach Endor or you won't." Nevertheless, Aristotle continues, if someone says "There will be a sea-battle tomorrow," she may be right, for there may indeed be a sea-battle tomorrow. But she may also be wrong, for there may not be a sea-battle tomorrow.

Let's say there is a sea-battle and the person who says so is right even though she lacks the benefit of omniscient foreknowledge. The fact that the proposition "There will be a sea-battle tomorrow" is true today seems to determine that there will indeed be a sea-battle tomorrow. How could there not be unless the proposition is false? If it was true at the time of *The Phantom Menace* that Obi-Wan would later die at Vader's hands in *A New Hope*, then Obi-Wan must die at that time. But Obi-Wan ceased

fighting, held up his lightsaber, and *allowed* Vader to kill him—
an apparently free, but mysterious, action.

One way to answer this apparent fatalism is by noting once
again where the chain of causality starts. If the proposition
"Obi-Wan will die at Vader's hands" is true thirty-plus years
before it happens, it doesn't necessarily cause Obi-Wan's death.
Rather, Obi-Wan's choice to allow Vader to cut him down is
what makes the proposition true and also makes the proposition "Obi-Wan will live to see the Emperor defeated" false.
Another way is to deny, as Aristotle does, that future-contingent
propositions have any truth value whatsoever—they are neither
true nor false when they are spoken. Such propositions become
true or false only when the event to which they refer occurs or
fails to occur.

"He's Got to Follow His Own Path"

But what if Obi-Wan did not freely choose to allow Vader to kill
him, because he had no real *alternatives?* Many philosophers—
typically referred to as "libertarians"[6]—would agree that Obi-
Wan isn't free if he can't choose to do otherwise. Vader seems
to suffer from this lack of freedom in a sympathetic scene from
Return of the Jedi when, after Luke makes a valiant effort to
reach the goodness he still senses in his father, Vader declares,
"You don't know the power of the Dark Side, I *must* obey my
master . . . It is too late for me, son."

And, indeed, the Force seems to work this way. Qui-Gon
argues, with reference to Anakin, "Finding him was the will of
the Force, I have no doubt of that," and he later explains to
Anakin how the midi-chlorians present in all life-forms are "constantly speaking to us, telling us the *will* of the Force." If the
"will of the Force" determines the fate of the universe, perhaps
even directly intervening to cause Anakin's conception as Qui-
Gon surmises, then it doesn't seem as if Anakin or any other
being subject to the Force has alternative possibilities of action.
They must act as the Force wills.

If true, then the only possibly free beings in the *Star Wars*
galaxy are those who don't subject themselves to the will of the

---

[6] Note that *free-will* libertarians are not the same as *political* libertarians.

Force[7]—the paradigmatic example being Han Solo, who emphatically asserts, "No mystical energy field controls *my* destiny." Han has lived his entire life as a "free spirit," wandering the galaxy carrying spice shipments for Jabba the Hutt, breaking speed records in the Millennium Falcon, and trying to "avoid any Imperial entanglements."

Han exercises his freedom of choice most assertively when he decides to take his reward for rescuing Princess Leia and leave the Rebel Alliance behind instead of helping them destroy the Death Star. Luke confronts him, but Han's will to leave is strong and he simply gives Luke a half-hearted "May the Force be with you." Luke's less naïve sister, Leia, is equally disappointed with Han's decision, but understands that there's nothing they can do to stop him: "He's got to follow his own path. No one can choose it for him." We know, of course, that Han eventually changes his mind and chooses to come to Luke's rescue at the last instant, freeing him to use the Force to destroy the Death Star.

Han, unlike Anakin and Luke, appears to have alternative possibilities in determining his own future, which most libertarian philosophers take to be fundamental to the definition of "freedom." Enlightenment-era philosopher John Locke (1632–1704), however, notes that freedom may not require having alternative possibilities:

> Suppose a Man be carried, whilst fast asleep, into a Room, where is a Person he longs to see and speak with; and be there locked fast in, beyond his Power to get out: he awakes, and is glad to find himself in so desirable Company, which he stays willingly in, *i.e.* prefers his stay to going away. I ask, Is not this stay voluntary? I think, no Body will doubt it: and yet being locked fast in, 'tis evident he is not at liberty not to stay, he has not freedom to be gone.[8]

What makes the person in Locke's story free, despite having no alternative to staying in the locked room, is that he *desires* to be there. He perceives the pleasurable company he's in and desires

---

[7] No one is *completely* free, because we're all subject to the laws of gravity and inertia, the impulse to satisfy our hunger and thirst, the drive to seek pleasure and avoid pain, and so on.

[8] John Locke, *An Essay Concerning Human Understanding* (1695), edited by Peter H. Nidditch (Oxford: Clarendon, 1975), Book II, Chapter 21, §10.

to stay in that pleasurable company. So long as he desires to stay in the room, his remaining there is freely chosen, so says Locke. If, however, he decides to leave the room and finds the door locked, then his remaining in the room has been forced upon him against his will to leave and he's thereby not free. Freedom, then, may ultimately depend upon a person's will—whether he desires to do one action or another, whether he desires to do good or evil—and his ability to do whatever he wills.

In demonstrating why human beings act freely when they commit evil, and aren't caused to do so by God's will or eternal foreknowledge, Augustine contends that desire is the foundation of all evil that results from a person's disordered will: "Each evil man is the cause of his own evildoing."[9] Augustine describes a person as having an "inordinate desire" when he focuses too much on "temporal" things. Good persons live by "turning their love away from those things which cannot be possessed without the risk of losing them." While evil persons "try to remove obstacles so that they may safely rest in their enjoyment of these things, and so live a life full of evil and crime, which would be better named death."[10] This description certainly fits Anakin, who is unable to turn his love away from his mother and from Padmé, both of whom he loses. When he expresses his frustration at being unable to save his mother from the Sand People, he vows to become "the most powerful Jedi ever" and to "learn to stop people from dying." George Lucas, the man who knows the most about Anakin's psychology, notes:

> The problem that Anakin has in this whole thing is he has a hard time letting go of things. As he sought more and more power to try to change people's fate so that they're the way he wants them, that greed goes from trying to save the one you love to realizing you can control the universe.[11]

It is Anakin's desire to control things that are ultimately outside of his control, in defiance of the natural order of the

---

[9] Augustine, *Free Choice*, Book I, §1.

[10] *Ibid.*, Book I, §4. Augustine is setting quite a high standard for morality here.

[11] Interview in "The Return of Darth Vader" documentary included on the bonus disc of the original *Star Wars Trilogy* DVD release (2004).

universe established by the will of the Force, which leads to his moral downfall. And this desire stems from Anakin himself: "What each man chooses to pursue and to love lies in his own will."[12] On this view, it doesn't matter whether Anakin has the possibility to *act* as he wills. Even if something prevents Anakin from, say, marrying Padmé on Naboo—imagine that their ship blows up on the way there—he has already freely willed to violate the Jedi Code and is morally responsible for that volition. So, despite the appearance that Anakin has no alternative possibilities with regards to being the Chosen One and destroying the Emperor, he's nonetheless free in his choosing to ally himself with the Dark Side, because that choice stems from his own will, his own inordinate desires.

"This One a Long Time Have I Watched"

Luke, like his father, carries the burden of future expectation on his shoulders. While Anakin is the child of prophecy, Luke is both the new and last hope for restoring freedom to the galaxy. But to restore galactic freedom, Luke must first exercise his individual freedom. As he discovers in the cave on Dagobah, Luke has the same potential to allow inordinate desire to control his will and turn him to the Dark Side. Both Vader and the Emperor attempt to tap into Luke's desire to destroy, and each try to turn that desire to their own advantage. But, ultimately, only Luke can give into that inordinate desire; only he can turn his own will to the Dark Side: "After all, what cause of the will could there be, except the will itself?"[13]

And while both Yoda and Obi-Wan have put great faith in Luke from the time he was born, even they can only watch Luke's life unfold and help train him as a Jedi. Despite their good intentions, neither has the power to bend Luke's will, as we see in *The Empire Strikes Back* when they plead with him not to leave Dagobah before his training is completed. Luke is much like his father, as he's inclined to allow inordinate desire to control his will. But he's also like Han Solo, because he's not wholly subject to the will of the Force. When he asks Obi-Wan

---

[12] Augustine, *Free Choice*, Book I, §16. For more on the origin of evil according to Augustine and others, see Chapter 6 in this volume.
[13] *Ibid.*, Book III, §17.

if the Force "controls your actions," Obi-Wan responds, "Partially, but it also obeys your commands." In a <u>deleted scene</u> ✓ from *Attack of the Clones*, Mace Windu counsels Obi-Wan regarding Anakin, "You must have faith that he will take the right path." Anakin has control over his own destiny and even the Jedi Masters are powerless to prevent what he wills. Unfortunately, Anakin doesn't take the right path, but his son does despite similar obstacles.

In our own lives it's important to ask which "forces" are ⟩ attempting to bend our will. What desires have the potential to become "inordinate" and be allowed to take over our will? And we must also be conscious of the control we have over our own will and desires. Even if there's an eternal observer keeping watch over us or a puppetmaster pulling the universe's strings around us, we can pull our own strings and thereby determine what the eternal observer knows and limit what <u>the puppet-</u>   *ital* <u>master can accomplish</u>. We are *radically free* and thus *responsible* for what we choose to will. And since my wife is still out with "the girls," I think I'll exercise my radical freedom to watch *Attack of the Clones* and wake up the neighbors, comfortable in the knowledge that *Que sera, sera . . . Whatever will be, will be.*[14]

---

[14] I'm most grateful to Jennifer Vines, Kevin Decker, Kevin Timpe, Greg Bassham, and Bill Irwin for helpful comments on an earlier draft of this chapter.

2

Stoicism in the Stars: Yoda, the Emperor, and the Force

WILLIAM O. STEPHENS

Stoicism is the ancient Greek philosophy that originated in the third century B.C.E. in the "Stoa" or porch where Zeno of Citium taught in Athens. Stoicism counsels acting virtuously and without emotional disturbance while living in harmony with fate. But why care about Stoicism today? For one thing, Zeno's followers, the Stoics, exerted enormous influence on Roman culture, Christianity, and Western philosophy for centuries. Today, Stoicism continues to receive a lot of attention from philosophers,[1] novelists,[2] soldier-politicians,[3] and psychologists.[4] This is because Stoic ideas provide an effective strategy for addressing conflicts and kinds of adversity faced in the real world. *Star Wars* fans too can benefit from some Stoicism.

Understanding the Force is key to understanding the *Star Wars* universe since how the Force is conceived, used, or ignored by the characters goes a long way to determining their identities, allegiances, and goals. What is it that makes the Force and the discipline necessary to master it so compelling to figures

---

[1] Check the internet for *The Stoic Voice Journal*, The Stoic Registry, The Stoic Foundation, The Stoic Place, and the International Stoic Forum.

[2] See Tom Wolfe, *A Man in Full* (New York: Farrar, Straus, and Giroux, 1998).

[3] Vice Admiral James Bond Stockdale is one of the most highly decorated officers in the history of the U.S. Navy. He credited Stoicism for his survival while a prisoner of war in Vietnam. He was Ross Perot's Vice Presidential running mate in 1992.

[4] Dr. Albert Ellis's Rational Emotive Behavior Therapy is inspired by a Stoic approach to emotional problems.

like Luke, Yoda, and the Emperor? Stoicism helps reveal both the logic of the Light Side of the Force and the logic of the Dark Side. How Yoda and the Emperor understand the Force radically shapes their moral characters and drives their actions. A brief study of Stoicism will allow us to understand why Yoda and the Emperor can each be so devoted to contrary sides of the Force.

Appearance versus Reality: Jester or Jedi Master?

When Luke and Artoo arrive on Dagobah in *The Empire Strikes Back*, Luke instinctively brandishes his blaster when they are startled by an unthreatening, wizened, olive-skinned dwarf clad in rags. "Away put your weapon! I mean you no harm," the cringing dwarf pleads. With his quirky sense of humor, Yoda remarks that Luke has *found* someone, though Luke doesn't realize he has found the very Jedi master he is *looking for*. But while this puny goblin assures Luke he can help him, Luke doubts him. Luke explains that he is looking for a great warrior. Laughing, Yoda responds: "Wars not make one great." This remark is ironic since "yoda" is Sanskrit for "warrior." Yoda certainly *looks* nothing like a great warrior.

Yoda then *acts* like a silly beggar. He finds, nibbles on, and discards an untasty snack bar in Luke's supplies. When he fights over a tiny power lamp with Artoo, Yoda looks even sillier. Luke is impatient to find the Jedi master, but the goofy goblin wants to eat first. So our first impression of Yoda is of a solitary, harmless, vulnerable, shabby, hungry geezer with a quirky sense of humor and an odd manner of speech. Yoda's *appearance* inspires no awe at all.

Contrast this image with the first appearance of Darth Vader in *A New Hope* and the Emperor in *Return of the Jedi*. Moments after the first wave of stormtroopers, all clad in white armor, have blasted their way onto Princess Leia's ship, a tall, dominating figure in a face-concealing helmet, cape, and armor, all in black, strides confidently amidst the victorious stormtroopers. He issues commands in a deep, rasping, mechanical, monotone voice. Vader appears menacing, invulnerable, and powerful, surrounded by his minions, who instantly obey his every command. This dark, imposing man-machine inspires awe. He is obviously a great warrior and a very powerful leader. As the saga unfolds we discover that this great warrior obeys an even *more* powerful master. Massed ranks of Imperial officers and stormtroopers honor the arrival of the almighty Emperor on the second Death Star when he first appears in the flesh.[5]

Luke's first impressions of Yoda are of a jester, not a Jedi. Luke fails to see past appearances to the reality of Yoda's virtues. Yet the virtues that emerge from Yoda's words and actions reveal him as a Jedi master. Similarly, the virtues of the Stoic wise man are precisely what enable him to be happy no matter what. What specific virtues does Yoda display? When Yoda offers to take Luke to the Jedi master he seeks, Luke insists that it be done immediately. Instead, Yoda suggests that they first eat. When Luke objects, Yoda replies "For the Jedi it is time to eat as well." *Timeliness* is a virtue for Yoda. Why is it a virtue? Because just as *what* one does and *how* one does it matters, so too *when* one acts matters. Whereas Luke often doesn't act appropriately for the moment, Yoda's acts are timely. Timeliness is a key virtue for a Jedi, as it is for the Stoic wise man.

While Yoda prepares their first meal together, Luke is impatient to be brought to the Jedi master. Yoda urges Luke to have *patience*—a virtue Yoda has cultivated over centuries. Luke's impatience turns into frustration and vexation. Disappointed, Yoda addresses Obi-Wan Kenobi's disembodied presence, "I cannot teach him. The boy has no patience." It finally dawns on Luke that this weird, elderly goblin is the Jedi master himself. Appearance had blinded Luke to reality.

Yoda criticizes Luke for his inability to focus on his present situation. Yoda says, "All his life has he looked away . . . to the future, to the horizon. Never his mind on where he was . . . what he was doing." Yoda dismisses Luke's lust for adventure and excitement as things a Jedi does not crave. Yoda is never distracted by frivolous desires for adventure or excitement, nor does he worry about things beyond his control. This too is characteristic of the Stoic, who enjoys equanimity and peace of mind. Yoda focuses on the task at hand and how to act in the present, whether consulting with other Jedi, eating, training Luke, or resting. Focus on the present is another Jedi virtue, and one which is shared by the Stoic.

---

[5] As opposed to the hologram in *The Empire Strikes Back*.

Yoda cautions the young Anakin that "A Jedi must have the deepest commitment, the most serious mind." This warning is repeated decades later to Luke. Yoda's mental seriousness, deep commitment to the lifelong Jedi pursuit of mastering the Force, and rejection of frivolity, however, do not mean that he's humorless. Yoda indulges his sense of humor in allowing Luke to be blinded by his presumptions about what a Jedi master looks like.

Yoda observes in *The Empire Strikes Back* that there is much *anger* in Luke, like there was in his father. Yet Yoda, in contrast, never gets angry. As he says, "Fear is the path to the Dark Side. Fear leads to anger. Anger leads to hate. Hate leads to suffering." Wiser words are never spoken in all of *Star Wars*. Later Yoda tells Luke: "Anger . . . fear . . . aggression. The Dark Side of the Force are they." This is the logic of the Light Side of the Force: (1) Fear leads to anger, then to hate, then to aggression. (2) Aggression leads to the suffering of *both* aggressor *and* victim. That Yoda is never seen to *suffer* implies that he is never fearful, angry, hateful, or aggressive. The Stoic wise man, just like Yoda, lacks the vices of fear, anger, hatred, and aggression. But does rejection of aggression require pacifism? When can a Jedi fight? Yoda says, "A Jedi uses the Force for knowledge and defense, never for attack." Although Yoda actively defends and protects when necessary,[6] he lacks the vice of aggression.

Yoda wisely knows that fear, anger, hate, and aggression lead to suffering and the Dark Side of the Force, and his wisdom allows him to tell the difference between the Light Side and the Dark Side of the Force. Yoda explains to Luke that he will know the difference between the two when he is "calm, at peace, passive."

Stoicism and the Virtues of the Sage

Several elements of Stoicism help us to better understand Yoda's virtues. The Stoics believed that the goal of life was to live in agreement with Nature. This meant several things. First, Nature,

---

[6] In *Attack of the Clones* Yoda, hobbling forward on his cane, uses the Force to defend himself from Count Dooku's telekinetic attacks. Yoda and Dooku, his former padawan, duel with lightsabers and Yoda protects his wounded comrades Obi-Wan and Anakin.

that is, the cosmos as a whole, is structured and well-ordered through and through according to *Logos*, reason. As I will explain more fully below, *Logos* is akin to the Force. Second, to live in agreement with Nature requires embracing and making good use of all events that unfold in this rationally structured universe. So living in harmony with cosmic events entails living in agreement with our distinctive human nature. While we have various functions in common with other animals, the Stoics believed that reason is our special, distinctive natural endowment. So to live well is to harmonize our distinctive human reason as individuals with the larger rational structure of the universe. The Stoic Epictetus (*ca.* 55–*ca.* 135 C.E.) says:

> God has introduced humans into the world as spectators of himself and of his works; and not only as spectators, but interpreters of them. It is therefore shameful that humans should begin and end where irrational creatures do. We ought rather to begin there, but to end where nature itself has fixed our end, and that is in contemplation and understanding and a way of life in harmony with nature.[7]

The Stoics understood the perfection of reason to be virtue itself. So the successful, good human life is the life in agreement with virtue. Virtue is the one and only necessary and sufficient condition for the happy life, according to the Stoics. Vice guarantees misery. Because of this, they believed that virtue is the only thing that is really good, and that vice is the only thing that is really bad. Knowledge of what is really good, what is really bad, and what is neither, they thought, is crucial to living well. Moreover, the Stoics believed that all the virtues—wisdom, justice, courage, self-control, piety, and generosity—were really just perfected reason applied to various spheres of conduct.

Reason leads the Stoic to concentrate his mind on what is up to him and under his control rather than worrying about, fearing, anticipating, or being distracted by anything that is beyond his control and not up to him. Timely behavior, for example, is under one's control and is a virtue of the Stoic. This mindful concentration on what is within one's control allows the Stoic to

---

[7] *Discourses* I.6.19–21; translation adapted from *The Discourses of Epictetus, The Handbook, Fragments*, edited by C. Gill (London: Dent, 1995), p. 17.

be calm and even-tempered no matter what happens, and to be high-minded and noble of heart by rising above trivial or frivolous matters that plague non-Stoics.

In addition, the Stoic seeks to free himself from all passion, excitation, and frivolity in order to be able to apply his reason reliably. The Stoics understood "passion" (*pathos* in Greek) to be a disturbing, unhealthy movement of the soul. That is why a sickness (of the soul) is called a *pathology*. The Stoic who has succeeded in freeing himself from all disturbances to his "reason" has become good. The Stoics believed that there are no degrees of goodness. Until a man is good, he is bad. For the Stoics, the good man thus functions as a prescriptive ideal known as the perfect wise man or "sage." The sage's soul is steady, orderly, completely virtuous, and it does not suffer from any "passion." However, the Stoic sage is not devoid of all emotion. The Stoics believed that there were three "good emotional states" that were not pathological movements of the soul, namely, benevolence (wishing someone good things for his own sake), joy (in virtuous deeds), and caution (reasonable wariness).

Clearly Yoda has many Stoic traits. Yoda is free from the emotions that subvert reason. Yoda is not reckless or impatient, as Luke is at first. Nor is Yoda frivolous. Like a Stoic, Yoda never becomes perturbed or excited. Most significantly, Yoda does not succumb to anger. The ancient Roman Stoic Seneca (*ca.* 3– *ca.* 65 C.E.) called anger "the most hideous and frenzied of all the emotions." Seneca thought angry people were insane, saying of anger:

> Oblivious of decency, heedless of personal bonds, obstinate and intent on anything once started, closed to reasoning or advice, agitated on pretexts without foundation, incapable of discerning fairness or truth, it most resembles those ruins which crash in pieces over what they have crushed.[8]

Yoda also exhibits the positive emotions allowed to a Stoic. Since Yoda doesn't fear, get angry, or hate, he doesn't *suffer*. Yoda concentrates on what is up to him and what he can do in the present. He thus enjoys impassivity, the lack of disturbing

---

[8] *On Anger* I.1.2, in *Seneca: Moral and Political Essays*, translated by J.M. Cooper and J.F. Procopé (Cambridge: Cambridge University Press, 1995), p. 17.

passions the Stoics called *apatheia.* Yoda is calm and even-tempered. He can tell the difference between the good and bad
sides of the Force, and knows what is good, what is bad, and
what is neither. Knowing that only virtue is good, only vice is
bad, and everything else is really indifferent to one's happiness
is the heart of Stoic wisdom.

Yoda is also benevolent and cautious. His quirky humor displays a quasi-Stoic joy. His odd wit and unusual pattern of
speech humanize him by tempering his seriousness. One of the
ancient Greek names for the Stoic sage is *spoudaios*, which
means "serious person." Perfecting one's mind by conditioning
it to make only rational judgments about all things that occur is
a very serious business that requires commitment. The Stoics
called this arduous training and disciplined practice *askêsis*
(from which we get the word "ascetic," a person devoted to
austere self-discipline). Yoda too displays the virtue of commitment and lives an ascetic lifestyle in both his sparse quarters in
the Jedi Temple on Coruscant and his simple mud-hut on
Dagobah.

The Stoics believed that the wise man, the virtuous person,
was as rare as the phoenix, due to the difficulty of disciplining
oneself to make consistently rational judgments. Such mental
discipline, they thought, required an entire life to cultivate. That
is why the Stoics distinguished between those who are simply
vicious and those who are making progress toward virtue,
though still suffering from vice. Even if becoming a sage turns
out to be unachievable over the course of an entire life, progress
toward this ideal state is possible. Someone who is progressing
toward virtue they called a "progressor." Similarly, Luke can be
seen as a "progressor." He is an apprentice—first of Obi-Wan,
then of Yoda—as he strives to learn the ways of the Force and
become a Jedi.

To recap, the virtues the Jedi shares with the Stoic sage are
patience, timeliness, deep commitment, seriousness (as opposed
to frivolity), calmness (as opposed to anger or euphoria), peace-
fulness (as opposed to aggression), caution (as opposed to recklessness), benevolence (as opposed to hatred), joy (as opposed
to sullenness), passivity (as opposed to agitation), and wisdom.
Given all these virtues, Yoda certainly resembles what the
ancient Stoics described as the sage—the ideal person who has
perfected his reason and achieved complete wisdom. In contrast

with Luke's youth and inexperience, Yoda has had over eighty
centuries to study and attune himself to the Force.

The perfection of the Stoic sage's character in his human reason mirrors the perfection of all of Nature, which the Stoics
believed was coherently structured through and through. The
sage acts in accord with and accepts events that occur in the
world since his personal reason and his will harmonize with
cosmic reason and fate. The sage understands the principles of
regularity by which the universe operates. His knowledge of
Nature thus guides his conduct. Is this similar to following the
Force?

Yoda says that life creates the Force and makes it grow, and
that the energy of the Force surrounds people and binds them,
and that it pervades the entire physical world. This description
resembles the ancient Stoics' idea of the "breath" that pervades
all objects in the cosmos. This "breath," composed of the elements air and fire, is the sustaining cause of all bodies, and it
controls the growth and development of all living bodies. It
holds the cosmos together as the passive principle of all matter.
The active principle pervading the cosmos is the "reason" that is
one and the same as Nature, fate, providence, and the Greek
god Zeus. When Yoda uses the telekinetic power of the Force
to lift Luke's X-wing fighter from the swamp on Dagobah, he
uses the power of his mind to move matter. A Jedi master, it
seems, while not omnipotent, can use the active power of reason to move passive matter. In this modest way, Jedi who use
telekinesis act something like Zeus or providence, as understood by the Stoics. Telekinesis, psychic perception of events
that are distant in space and time, and the luminous afterlife of
dead Jedi constitute the mystical side of the Force.

The Stoics emphasized that ethics, physics (the study of
Nature), and logic (the study of speech, language, and argument) are the three *interconnected* branches of philosophy. So
does Stoic philosophy allow for the mystical? The mystical element of the Force conflicts with the Stoics' understanding of the
physical world. Yoda tells Luke: "Luminous beings are we . . .
not this crude matter." This is confirmed by the scenes that show
the deceased Obi-Wan, Yoda, and Anakin as non-physical, yet
luminous, visible disembodied spirits. Since the Emperor was a
master of the Dark Side, would he too continue to exist as a
luminous, disembodied spirit? Or would he be a dark, shadowy

disembodied spirit? For the Stoics, these kinds of metaphysical quandaries are ludicrous. The Stoics were physicalists who believed that souls (minds) were just as physical as flesh and blood bodies. They reasoned that since one's soul causally interacts with one's body, and one's body is physical, then one's soul must be physical too. So the Stoics rejected the notion of nonphysical souls (or minds or spirits) that are the "luminous beings" Yoda claims to be the real Luke and Yoda. For the Stoics, a person is destroyed when his body is destroyed, whereas deceased Jedi apparently enjoy an afterlife which allows them to speak with, see, and be seen by, the living.

While the naturalism of Stoicism rules out supernatural, disembodied spirits, the sage's understanding of Nature is amazingly profound and total. In fact, the Stoic sage has *infallible* knowledge of what should be done in every situation. The sage takes the right steps at the right times and does them in the right way to accomplish the right goal. But is Yoda a Stoic who acts from *reason* in every situation? No, Yoda *feels* the Force guiding his actions and the counsel he gives. Qui-Gon says to Anakin, "Feel, don't think, use your instincts." Obi-Wan tells Luke, "Trust your feelings." So the character traits that make reason possible for a Stoic resemble the traits that make it possible for Jedi like Yoda to feel and harness the Force.

In *Star Wars*, of course, there is also a Dark Side of the Force. Darth Vader and the Emperor also harness the Force to achieve their goals. How does the Dark Side shape Darth Vader and the Emperor? What makes them evil if Yoda is supposed to be good?

The Logic of the Dark Side

To answer these questions we must reconstruct the logic of the Dark Side of the Force. Here again the contrast between appearance and reality reveals clues. In Qui-Gon's first meeting with the Jedi Council, Yoda observes: "Hard to see, the Dark Side is." Is this double entendre intended as a joke or a serious insight? In any case, it well describes how the Emperor appears. His head and face are hidden inside a dark, hooded cloak. Like the Dark Side itself, the *Emperor* is hard to see and an obvious foil to Yoda. Both Yoda and the Emperor are ascetic devotees of the Force. Both wear simple robes. Neither is tempted by bodily pleasures. Both appear to live monkish lives of religious devotion. Is the Emperor merely evil or is his character more complex?

The Emperor does seem to have several virtues. Like Yoda, the Emperor has a serious mind and the deepest commitment, though his is to the Dark Side. The Emperor is *the* Master of the Dark Side, and this surely must count as a kind of supremacy. Moreover, in *Return of the Jedi* the Emperor urges patience on Vader in his search for Luke, a virtue Yoda shares. In these respects, the Emperor and Yoda *appear* to be similar. How are they *really* different?

A few scenes later the Emperor says that Luke's compassion for his father will be his undoing. The Emperor sees compassion as a weakness, not a strength, a vice, not a virtue. The Stoics rejected compassion as irrational. Taking on the "disturbing passion" (*pathos*) of someone who is miserable makes you miserable too, so it's foolish to be misery's company by *feeling* compassion. Unlike the Emperor, however, the Stoics thought that it's virtuous to *show* compassion to others by acting to help them. Doing things to help others is beneficence. Beneficence can be motivated by philanthropy, kindness, or simple recognition of one's fellow beings as members of the community of rational persons in the cosmos we all inhabit. The ancient Greek Stoics originated this idea of a citizen of the universe or "cosmopolitan." The Emperor clearly has no such inclusive vision of the subjects populating *his* Empire.

So while the Emperor is correct, from a Stoic perspective, to reject the *feeling* of compassion as a weakness, he is wrong to be cruel by failing to *show* compassion to those he can help. From the Stoic perspective, his logic is twisted. But what twists it? What makes the Dark Side of the Force *dark*? Why think the Emperor is evil rather than simply eccentric or illogical?

The logic of the Dark Side is glimpsed in the moving conversation between Luke and Vader. Vader wants to turn Luke to the Dark Side, so that he will join Vader and the Emperor. Luke senses the moral conflict within Vader, and wishes to turn his father back to the Light Side. Vader tells Luke "You don't know the power of the Dark Side.[9] I must obey my master."

---

[9]Yoda, in contrast, denies that the Dark Side of the Force is stronger. He tells Luke it is quicker, easier, and more seductive than the Light Side. Greg Bucher has suggested to me that the partisans of the Light and the Dark Sides of the

The Force is power that can be directed toward good or bad ends. Obi-Wan, Yoda, and all the "good" Jedi use the Force to achieve their goals. Vader and the Emperor do the same. Yoda says that the Force is his *ally*. Vader, however, is a *servant* of the Dark Side. Vader is in its power, because he must obey his Master, the Emperor. So the essence of the Dark Side is mastery over others, or tyranny. But the Dark Side limits the masters to only two Sith at a time—the Master and the Servant.

When Vader brings Luke captive to the Emperor, the Emperor says he looks forward to completing Luke's training as his new master and gloats about the trap he has set for Luke's friends on the moon of Endor. The Emperor goads Luke by urging him to take his lightsaber:

> You want this, don't you? The hate is swelling in you now. Take your Jedi weapon. Use it. I am unarmed. Strike me down with it. Give in to your anger. With each passing moment you make yourself more my servant.

The Emperor continues to torment Luke, basking in his suffering: "Good. I can feel your anger. I am defenseless. Take your weapon! Strike me down with all your hatred and your journey toward the Dark Side will be complete." When Luke is fighting Vader, the Emperor is pleased. He congratulates Luke for using his aggressive feelings and letting the hate flow through him: "You, like your father, are now *mine*."

So in contrast to the logic of the Light Side, the logic of the Dark Side is this: (1) Anger leads to hatred. (2) Hatred leads to aggression aimed at the mastery of others. (3) Mastery of others is true power. (4) True power is irresistibly desirable. When Luke slashes off Vader's right hand with his lightsaber, the Emperor applauds Luke: "Your hate has made you powerful." But Luke refuses to kill Vader, as the Emperor wishes: "You've failed, Your Highness. I am a Jedi, like my father before me." If mastery of others and enslavement to evil fails, then the Dark

---

Force speak at cross-purposes, neither understanding the motivations of the other. In the end the Light Side prevails because they have better *people* in their ranks, not because the Light Side is superior in *power* to the Dark Side. The vision of the empire which Vader and the Emperor champion, while neither desirable nor good, is not inherently unworkable.

logic demands destruction: "If you will not be turned, you will be destroyed."

Consequently, the Emperor is a propagator of terror, hatred, and cruelty. He gloats and takes pleasure in the distress of others. The ancient Stoics were quite familiar with tyrants like Cambyses of Persia, Hippias of Athens (both sixth century B.C.E.), and Gaius Caligula (first century C.E.). These tyrants, along with the evil Emperor Palpatine, can be usefully contrasted with the Stoic Marcus Aurelius (121–180 C.E.), who ruled the Roman empire from 161 to 180 C.E. The benevolence and rectitude of the Emperor Marcus is plain in his *Meditations*. The Stoic does not seek to exploit others. Rather, the Stoic aims at emotional self-sufficiency and cultivating his own mental discipline. This means that the Stoic sage has succeeded in mastering himself by having mastered his desires and having eliminated vice from his character.

Luke is therefore urging Stoic wisdom upon Vader when he tells him to let go of his hate. Unfortunately, hatred has had such a viselike hold on Vader for so long that he tells Luke: "It is too late for me, son.[10] The Emperor will show you the true nature of the Force. He is your master now." For servants of the Dark Side, the true nature of the Force is servitude to evil, enslavement to hate. Like virtues, vices tend to control one's behavior. Vader has used fear and hatred to achieve his ends for so long that now the superior hatred and aggression of the Emperor use him. That is how Vader's mastery of the Dark Side is at the same time servitude to it.

The reality behind the monkish appearance of the Emperor is the soul of a monster afflicted by vice. On the other hand, the Emperor's hatred follows a cool logic of its own. His cruelty is calmly calculated, not haphazard. The Emperor shows an icy rationality and self-possession that is a shallow reflection of the Stoic's passionlessness. His is an arrogant[11] rationality which

---

[10] Vader's admission underscores the Stoic idea that it takes a lifelong commitment to stand a chance to become good. Vader has grown too old to reverse his evil course, apparently.

[11] When Obi-Wan expresses his concern that the talented Anakin Skywalker is becoming arrogant, Yoda concurs: "Yes, yes, a flaw more and more common among Jedi. Too sure of themselves they are, even the older, more experienced ones."

seeks to dominate, exploit, and enslave people through careful planning and use of the Dark Side of the Force. As Luke warns him, "Your overconfidence is your weakness." According to Stoicism, however, the Emperor's cleverness, devotion, and self-possession are not virtues. As a tyrant, the Emperor's goal is to master things and people that are in fact beyond his control rather than to master himself by becoming virtuous. Since the Emperor fails to understand what is really good, namely virtue, and what is really bad, namely vice, he lacks Stoic wisdom. Since he lacks wisdom, he lacks all the virtues, and so he is full of vice. Since he has no desire to gain wisdom, his mind is fundamentally flawed and his vice is incurable. As a consequence, when Vader throws him into the reactor shaft, he appears to die suffering.[12]

"Control, Control, You Must Learn Control"

Yoda and the other Jedi use discipline, commitment, and training to control themselves, thereby harnessing the power of the Force. Vader and the Emperor, on the other hand, stoke their anger and hatred to empower themselves with the Dark Side of the Force. They feed, rather than overcome, the negative emotions within themselves. They seek to control not themselves, but others, in an ultimately doomed attempt to fill the cold, black void behind the mask or the hood with the false satisfaction that arises from domination and oppression of others. A Stoic could never be seduced by the Dark Side, but might well feel at home among the calm, self-disciplined, virtuous Jedi. But a Stoic indulges in none of the supernaturalism or mysticism expressed in some aspects of the Force in *Star Wars*. The wisdom of Yoda and the vices of the Emperor are illuminated nicely by the plain light of natural reason provided by the Stoic philosophy.[13]

---

[12] Note that Obi-Wan and Yoda do not die suffering.

[13] I thank Gregory S. Bucher, Susan T. Bart, and Scott Rubarth for their excellent, generous comments on this paper. I also thank the editors and the series editor for their suggestions.

3

The Far East of *Star Wars*

WALTER (RITOKU) ROBINSON

The "Force" is central to the *Star Wars* mythology. In *A New Hope* Obi-Wan Kenobi describes it as "an energy field created by all living things. It surrounds us and penetrates us. It binds the galaxy together." This is an extremely good description of what is known in Chinese as "ch'i," or in Japanese as "ki."

In the *Star Wars* galaxy, the Jedi use the Force in their fighting arts. "A Jedi's strength flows from the Force," Yoda teaches Luke. In the martial arts of the Far East, ch'i is cultivated to give special fighting advantage over someone who relies only on physical strength. Eastern philosophy, most especially philosophical Taoism and Zen Buddhism, plays a major role in the *Star Wars* mythology. This is most true in relation to the martial-arts philosophy of the Jedi. The historical development of this philosophy begins with a Buddhist synthesis with Taoism producing Zen and Kung-fu. This synthesis spread to Korea and Japan, and with it the knowledge of ch'i. The philosophy of the Force is thus best understood by way of understanding the nature of ch'i and the wisdom of Zen.

"Looking? Found Someone You Have"

The origin of ch'i-oriented martial arts in China is found in the teachings from the Shaolin Temple. It was here that Bodhidarma, who came from India to China in the sixth century, founded Ch'an (known in Japanese as Zen) and Kung-fu, a discipline that cultivates and directs the flow of ch'i, applying it to fighting techniques.

29

(ch'i)

The Shaolin Temple was founded as a Buddhist monastery in 497 C.E. When Bodhidarma arrived he found that the monks were weak and in ill health and tended to fall asleep during meditation. China at this time was in a state of disunity with competing military powers fighting with one another and bands of bandits wandering the countryside. Buddhist monks in central Asia had evolved a system of self defense based in Yoga and utilizing "prana"—a Sanskrit term the meaning of which approximates ch'i. Bodhidarma came out of this tradition, integrating it with Taoist practice, and taught it to the Shaolin monks to promote heath, mental discipline, self-defense, and spiritual awareness.

The origin of Buddhism goes back a thousand years before Bodhidarma to the teachings of Gautuma Sakyamuni in Northern India. As an advanced student of Yoga, Gautuma was principally concerned with liberation from the bonds of karma, which causes suffering. The idea is that one is subject to innumerable incarnations due to the conditions of karma—that is, past actions produce the conditions of the present moment, and what one does now determines the conditions of the future. In this there is suffering due to ignorance of reality. With enlightenment (which is the meaning of the word "Buddha") one comes to know reality and thus liberation from the chains of karma. Bodhidarma was in a lineage of mind-to-mind transmission through twenty eight generations beginning with Sakyamuni Buddha. At Shaolin, he transmitted this wisdom, which is the essence of Zen.

The character of Yoda was created with Zen in mind. George Lucas envisioned a character one would find in traditional fairy tales or mythologies, like a frog or a wizened old man on the side of the road. The hero meets this character thinking him to be insignificant, yet he holds the very wisdom the hero needs to fulfill his quest.

Lucas learned from Joseph Campbell that underlying religious mythologies are archetypal patterns which reflect univer-

sal truth.[1] Dig deeply enough into any of the great spiritual traditions and one comes upon a reservoir of truth common to all
and the source of each. *Star Wars* mythology is an intentional
expression of archetypal truth. This truth is known through mystical experience. Campbell maintained that the Zen experience
is the mystical wisdom which springs forth from the great reservoir of universal truth. Thus Yoda is intended to be a motif for
universal wisdom. When Luke Skywalker enters into Jedi training, he undergoes what Lawrence Kasdan (screenwriter for *The
Empire Strikes Back*) envisioned as Zen education. He tells us
that "the stories I find most interesting are stories of Zen education and the Zen master teaching a pupil how to transcend
physical prowess into some kind of mental prowess. That's what
all the training sequences are about."[2] spiritual

"Don't Give In to Hate: That Leads to the Dark Side"

When Buddhism was introduced to China, it entered into dialectic with Taoism and the synthesis of Buddhism with Taoism produced the Zen philosophy. The notion of ch'i is rooted in
Taoism, which teaches that the ch'i is manifested as yin and
yang, the light and the dark, and that one must harmonize with
this energy which requires balance. Lucas said that "The idea of
positive and negative, that there are two sides to an entity, a
push and a pull, a yin and a yang, and the struggle between the
two sides are issues of nature that I wanted to include in the
film."[3]

The word "tao" literally translates from the Chinese as "way"
and the philosophy of Tao is about the Way of nature. Everything
in nature exists in the field of opposites: up-down, left-right, in-
out, male-female, light-dark, positive-negative, yang-yin, and so
forth. The Way of nature has a tendency toward balance which
is the Great Harmony know as Tai Chi, which literally means
"Supreme Ultimate." The so called "yin-yang symbol (a circle the

---

[1] See Joseph Campbell, *The Hero With a Thousand Face* (New York: Princeton University Press, 1949).

[2] Laurent Bouzereau, *Star Wars: The Annotated Screenplays* (New York: Ballantine, 1997), p. 180.

[3] *Ibid.*, p. 36.

inside of which is divided by a wavy line, one half being light with a dark dot, and the other half dark with a light dot) is properly called the emblem of Tai Chi. The white dot in the dark side and the dark dot in the light side symbolize the interdependence of opposites.

In *The Phantom Menace,* Qui-Gon Jinn refers to "the prophecy of the one who will bring balance to the Force," believing the "one" to be Anakin Skywalker. This implies something other than a duality of good versus evil. In Taoist thought there is neither absolute good nor absolute evil, but rather good and evil are relative conditions of one another. As Obi-Wan puts it, "You're going to find that many of the truths we cling to depend greatly on our own point of view." From a Taoist point of view, it is not possible to have the light without also having darkness, or in the language of *Star Wars*, one cannot exist without the Dark Side being ever-present. When Anakin Skywalker becomes Darth Vader, he is seduced by the Dark Side, but in *Return of the Jedi,* his son, Luke, draws him back to goodness. Anakin thus bring balance back to the Force in himself as well as to the galaxy by destroying the Emperor.

Is it possible to be out of balance with too much goodness? The short answer is "yes." The prequel trilogy outlines just such a condition where the Jedi Order finds itself in the smugness of complacency as the Dark Side is active right under their noses. The Jedi are living so much in the light of morality, that the shadow of unconscious desire, symbolized by the Sith, takes on a life of its own and, like an unsupervised child, becomes delinquent. If one is out of touch with the shadow side of one's nature—one's Dark Side—it become pathological, like feeling lust or greed and living in denial or otherwise becomes unconscious, such that it only magnifies itself in the repressed unconsciousness. This, it seems, is the lesson that Luke learns in the depths and darkness of the cave on Dagobah in which he confronts his own Dark Side.

Yoda teaches Luke that "a Jedi's strength flows from the Force. But beware of the Dark side. Anger . . . fear . . . aggression. The Dark Side of the Force are they. Easily they flow, quick to join you in a fight."

Luke asks if the Dark Side is stronger. "No" answers Yoda, but it is "quicker, easier, more seductive."

Luke then asks, "How am I to know the good side from the bad?"

"You will know. When you are calm, at peace, passive. A Jedi uses the Force for knowledge and defense, never for attack."

According to Buddhist psychology, there are three poisons which produce the karma of suffering: attraction, repulsion, and ignorance. Attraction includes desire to have or possessiveness, greed, lust, and any other emotions of holding on or clinging to what is wanted. Anakin's excessive clinging attachment to his mother leads him into self-destructive hate and rage. The problem is not that he loves his mother, for that is good and natural; but his attachment, rooted in the fear of losing her, leads him to aggression when her death sends him into a rage and he slaughters a tribe of Sand People, including women and children. Following this is his fear-based, ego-centered drive to be strong enough never to lose what he is attached to again, blaming his own weakness for his mother's death. He promises Padmé, "I will be the most powerful Jedi ever."

Anakin thus suffers repulsion toward his own perceived weakness. Out of repulsion are generated fear, anger, hate, violence, and other such emotions. In *The Empire Strikes Back,* Vader prompts Luke to use his hate. And in *Return of the Jedi,* the Emperor goads "Use your aggressive feelings, boy. Let the hate flow through you." Acting out of such emotions leads to the Dark Side. Luke knows this and so encourages his father to "let go of your hate," as doing so will lead Anakin back to the good that Luke has faith must still exist in him.

Both attraction and repulsion are rooted in ignorance, which is the illusion of being an isolated individual ego. Buddhism teaches that there is no inherently substantial self. Everything is impermanent. All is in process, with everything changing, always flowing. Nothing is in isolation from the whole of this ever changing process. Existence is not made of parts, but is a relative process of interdependence. As Obi-Wan says, "The Force binds the galaxy together." And it's interesting to note that the one hero character who explicitly professes to not believe in the Force is named Han "Solo," derived from the Latin for "alone."

The ignorance of egotism produces the negative karma of suffering. When one is constricted by one's ego, the emotions characteristic of the Dark Side are generated. In *The Phantom Menace* Yoda warns Anakin, "Fear is the path to the Dark Side . . . Fear leads to anger . . . anger leads to hate . . . hate leads to suffering." Fear is the clinging of ego, of not realizing the oneness of life. Anger and hate follow. Sakyamuni Buddha said that he taught one thing and one thing only, how to be free from suffering. This freedom is the letting go of clinging to the ego. With this letting go, negative emotions dissolve into nothingness.

When Yoda teaches Luke to know by way of being calm, at peace, passive, this is the teaching of Tao. In Taoism, and in the Tao of Zen, there is the practice of letting go and emptying. Lao-tzu writes in the *Tao Te Ching*, the core text of Taoism, that the Tao is to unlearn and to undo. Yoda says to Luke, "You must unlearn what you have learned!" In Chinese this directive is called "Wu Wei," which literally means "no action"; but a better translation would be effortless action or ego-less spontaneity. When Yoda says to be passive, he does not intend for Luke to become inactive, for the Force is ever in motion, like water flowing in a river—passively in action without effort.

In the Japanese martial art of Aikido, effortless action is of the essence. The name "Aikido" means the way (do) of harmonizing or unifying (ai) the ch'i (ki). In order to use the ki, one must let go of effort. In the prequel trilogy one Jedi Master is named "Ki-Adi-Mundi," which seems to be inspired by the name "Aikido." When Obi-Wan begins to teach Luke the Way of the Force, he says, "A Jedi can feel the Force flowing through him." When Luke asks if "it controls your actions," Obi-Wan answers: "Partially, but it also obeys your commands." This is an important teaching in all of the ch'i/ki-oriented martial arts and what differentiates them from gross fighting techniques.

"Great Warrior? Wars Not Make One Great"

Buddhist monks traveling throughout China, Korea, and Japan shared their martial arts with worthy students. About a half-century after the founding of Shaolin Kung-fu, the king of Silla on the Korean peninsula invited Buddhist warrior monks to begin training an elite order of warriors to be known as Hwa Rang. This order was to serve the kingdom, uphold justice, and maintain social order. They were a monastic order trained in not only martial arts, but also the healing arts, Taoist Ch'i kung, the arts of political leadership and diplomacy, as well as Buddhist philosophy. Like the Jedi, the Hwa Rang were chosen at a young age, trained to be pure of mind, and to follow a strict ethical code of loyalty, honor, and service. They were also given authority over the regular military in much the same way the Jedi are in *Attack of the Clones*.

Buddhism was first introduced to Japan through Korea, and with it also the Buddhist martial arts forming the basis of Jujutsu. In Japan, the Sohei, an order of warrior monks much like the Hwa Rang, was developed. They lived in mountain monasteries surrounding the Imperial capital of Kyoto. Their considerable political power eventually put them at odds with the Shogun (military ruler over the warrior class, the samurai), culminating in the fifteenth century when samurai destroyed the Sohei monastic complex, killing most of its monks; parallel to the way in which the Jedi are practically wiped out in *Revenge of the Sith*. A few Sohei went into hiding, blending in with non-militant monks, and over time they taught their martial arts to other monks and a few worthy samurai. Eventually, Buddhist martial arts became the core of samurai training.

The indigenous religion of Japan is Shintoism, which centers around reverence for the ancestors and worship of the Japanese Emperor as a divine incarnation. Traditional Japan was hierarchical with the Emperor and his family on top, then the nobility, and then the samurai. The common people were subordinate and submissive to this social structure. The word "samurai" means "to serve." It was the role of the samurai to serve the good of the nation with honor and loyalty to the Emperor, and with absolute obedience to his master even unto death. The samurai had a strict code of conduct known as Bushido, which means "the way of the warrior." The code consists of general precepts which are open-ended and fluid. Over time it would integrate into itself much of the ethical teaching of Buddhism.

The sword is the soul of a samurai. The relationship that a samurai has to his sword is much like a Jedi's relationship to his lightsaber. The name "Jedi" is derived from the samurai era of swordsmen called "Jidai geki," which literally means "the era of play," referring to samurai-inspired settings or themes used in Japanese drama. The Jedi's kimono-style dress is loosely based on samurai clothing with the addition of a medieval hood to give a more monkish motif. Vader's helmet and armor are based on those used by the samurai as well. Swordplay in the original *Star Wars* trilogy reflects the way of sword called Kendo, as derived from the samurai tradition. In the prequel trilogy we see sword styles based more on Kung-fu.

Zen master Takuan Soho wrote to a sword master giving advice on Zen and the art of swordsmanship. He advised to have a "no-mind" mindfulness. Do not let the mind stop, but keep it flowing. As soon as the mind stops it localizes itself, thus becoming limited. Rather than localizing the mind, "let it fill up the whole body, let it flow throughout the totality of your being . . . Let it go all by itself freely and unhindered and uninhibited."[4] Soho goes on to say that when the mind is nowhere— that is, when it does not stop at any location—it is everywhere. In Zen practice one is with one's original mind, which is no-mind. A mind that stops and localizes is a delusive mind that is divided against itself, thus interfering with the free working of original mind. When Obi-Wan tells Luke to let go of his conscious self and act on instinct, he is essentially advising to let go of the divided delusional mind and go with the original mind which is the mind unconscious of itself: "A mind unconscious of itself is a mind that is not at all disturbed by affects of any kind . . . the mind moves from one object to another, flowing like a stream of water, filling every possible corner."[5]

There is a story of a centipede that was asked how with so many legs he was able to walk. When the centipede began to think about it he was not able to walk. The act of walking is simple without thought, but think about it and it become impos-

---

[4] D.T. Suzuki, *Zen and Japanese Culture* (New York: Bollingen, 1959), p. 107.
[5] *Ibid.*, p. 111.

sibly complex. To master is to simplify. The sword master must act on no-mind spontaneity. Takuan tells his student that his actions must be like sparks flying off flint struck by metal. There can be no delay, no hesitation. Attack and response must be in the same moment, such that no space and no time divide one thing from another. Zen sword master Tesshu calls this the "sword of no sword." in which, as he says, "I naturally blended with my opponent and moved in unhindered freedom."[6] Aikido is founded on this same philosophy. In fact, it is literally the art of the sword without the use of a sword. There is a story told about Morihei Ueshiba, the founder of Aikido, being unarmed, defending himself from a sword attack by a high-ranking swordsman, by avoiding the cuts and thrusts until the swordsman gave up.

In *The Empire Strikes Back*, when Luke is confronted with a task that he perceives as difficult, he declares, "Alright, I'll give it a try." To which Yoda responds, "No! Try not. Do or do not. There is no try." So long as there is effort, that very effort divides the mind against itself. When "I" try, the mind is divided between "I" and trying. With effort there is division between the actor and what's acted upon. This division is a psychological fabrication that fragments the whole into parts, thus removing one from original mind. In Zen enlightenment, known in Japanese as "satori," there is the experience of undivided wholeness. Satori is what Zen is all about.

Tesshu was one of the greatest sword masters. After his early training, he went for many years undefeated. Then he met Yoshiaki whom he was not able to defeat. Although Yoshiaki was older and much smaller, he repeatedly forced Tesshu to retreat. Tesshu began to suffer from the image of this master as a great mountain bearing down upon him. This was for him like Luke's vision of Darth Vader inside the cave on Dagobah. And just as the real obstacle for Luke was his own mind (as revealed in the severed head of Vader exploding into the likeness of Luke's face), so it was for Tesshu. Thus he went to a Zen master for help. "If an opponent frightens you or confuses you," advised Zen Master Ganno, "it means you lack true insight." Ganno gave Tesshu a koan for his zazen (Zen mediation practice). A koan is

---

[6] John Stevens, *The Sword of No Sword* (Boston: Shambhala, 1984), p. 26.

problem to work on with zazen that cannot be solved on the level of thought. Some classic koans are: "Show me your original face before your parents were born," and "What is the sound of one hand clapping?" To answer a koan, one must demonstrate insight which comes out of satori. After years of Zen training Tesshu entered into a satori, after which the threatening image of Yoshiaki vanished. When next he encountered Yoshiaki and they crossed swords, Yoshiaki withdrew his sword and declared, "You have arrived." There was no further need to fight for there was "no-enemy." When Luke says to Yoda, before he knows it is Yoda, that he is looking for a "great warrior," Yoda asserts that "Wars not make one great." In like manner Tesshu only became truly great warrior when he realized that in truth there is "no-enemy."[7]

As a novice monk studying with Taizan Maezumi Roshi (a Japanese Zen master), I worked on a koan attributed to Bodhidarma: "If you use your mind to study reality, you will understand neither reality nor the mind. If you study reality without using your mind, you will understand both." Axiomatic to Zen philosophy is the insight that conceptual understanding is illusory. A core assumption of Western thought is that one can use intellect to understand mind and reality. Zen asserts that this is not the case. True understanding is beyond all conceptualization. The mind is endlessly active in effort to achieve that which is impossible for it. Zen is a philosophy to undo philosophy, to study mind and reality with no-mind. There is no end to asking why and no way to give an intellectual answer that will be fully satisfactory. When Luke asks the "why question," Yoda answers, "No, no, there is no why. Nothing more will I teach you today. Clear you mind of questions. Mmm. Mmmmmmmm."

---

[7] *Ibid.*, p.18.

4

Moral Ambiguity in a Black-and-White Universe

RICHARD H. DEES

The moral universe of *Star Wars* has two colors: black and white. In the opening moments of *A New Hope*, we find Darth Vader, dressed all in black, confronting Princess Leia, dressed in virginal white. Every identifiable character in the six movies works either for the Light Side of the Force or for the Dark Side. It's a world with very few shades of gray, much less of brighter, more interesting moral colors. In this galaxy, unlike our own, there seems, at first glance, to be no room for moral tragedy, for choices where no answer is morally correct, or for plain moral ambiguity.

Nevertheless, moral ambiguity can be found lurking in the *Star Wars* universe, if we look for it. Often, important characters are first presented to us as morally ambiguous. When we meet them, we do not know whose side they are on in the war, but later, their true natures reveal themselves. We can, I think, learn some important moral lessons by looking at the ways characters like Han Solo or Lando Calrissian reason when we first meet them and at the ways in which they turn towards one side or the other. There are also a few cases that are closer to real ambiguity, like Count Dooku and Anakin Skywalker. From both kinds of cases, we can learn how to think about moral problems more deeply and more intelligently.

"What Good's a Reward if You Ain't Around to Use It?"

When we first meet Han Solo in *A New Hope*, he's a smuggler caught in the web of the crime lord Jabba the Hutt. He's arrogant and cocky, a "scoundrel," as Leia puts it. His moral philosophy is unmitigated egoism: he only looks after himself. "I take orders from just one person—*me*," Han proclaims. He accepts the mission to Alderaan only for the exorbitant fee that Obi-Wan offers him, and he helps to find Princess Leia in the Death Star only because Luke promises him a large reward. Indeed, even after he rescues Leia, Han tells her, "I ain't in this for your revolution, and I'm not in it for you, Princess. I expect to be well paid. I'm in it for the money." As soon as he delivers the Princess to the Rebel Alliance, Han takes his reward and departs, leaving Luke to observe bitterly, "Take care of yourself, Han. I guess that's what you're best at, isn't it?" Han sees no reason to accept any authority, moral or otherwise, outside his own self-interest.

In his egoism in *A New Hope*, Han is equaled only by Jango Fett in *Attack of the Clones*, who is, as he puts it, "just a simple man, trying to make my way in the universe." But Jango is clearly a mercenary for hire, willing to assassinate a senator for a price and even to sell his own genetic code for profit. His one act of apparent altruism is his obvious love for his son, Boba, the clone of himself that he insisted that the Kaminoans create for him. Although many parents love their children because they see themselves perpetuated in them, Jango's love for Boba carries this sentiment one step further towards mere narcissism.

Han and Jango's view is a form of *ethical egoism,* the view that morally what I should do is what is in my interest to do. As the seventeenth-century philosopher Thomas Hobbes argues, "whatsoever is the object of any mans Appetite or Desire, that is it, which he for his part calleth *Good*: And the object of his Hate, and Aversion, *Evill*." [1] The only standard we can use for what is good, Hobbes says, is what we ourselves want. The world turns only by appealing to people's self-interest, and we should expect nothing else. Indeed, egoists argue, we are all better off in a world where everyone acts out their

---

[1] Thomas Hobbes, *Leviathan* (Cambridge: Cambridge University Press, 1991), p. 39. Egoism is often mistakenly associated with the views of Adam Smith, who does argue that a healthy dose of self-interest is useful for a capitalist economy, but who also thinks it can lead to gross injustices. See Adam Smith, *An Inquiry into the Nature and Causes of the Wealth of Nations* (Oxford: Oxford University Press, 1976), I.ii.2 and V.i.f.50, and *The Theory of Moral Sentiments* (Oxford: Oxford University Press, 1976).

own self-interest than in a world where everyone is constantly interfering with others.

While we may be tempted to think otherwise, egoism is not an incoherent view. The interests of the Ewoks may be to enjoy the natural beauty of the forest and to live in harmony with the other living things there, and those of the Empire may be to level the trees to create a base that will better protect the construction of the second Death Star. But the conflict that results isn't a *logical* contradiction. Each can still maintain that what they are doing is morally correct. It is, however, a *practical* contradiction since they can't both do what they want. Dedicated egoists argue we each have an interest in living in an ordered society where conflicts about trees do not lead to either violence or to ongoing hostility, and so we need to think about the interests of others to some degree if we want to promote our own interests in the long run. Indeed, an enlightened egoism that takes seriously what is needed to make society work will make a place for loyalty, dedication, and even charity. Egoists can also recognize that people's interests are directed not only towards themselves, but also towards their loved ones, their country, and even towards the environment. An enlightened egoism can, then, include much of what is usually considered moral.

Han, unlike Jango, shows the necessary dispositions for this better form of egoism: he shows, for example, genuine loyalty from the very beginning. His affection for Chewbacca is obvious from our first encounter with him, and he quickly develops an older brother's affection for Luke. Even more importantly, Han shows a capacity for something more. When Leia rebukes him, "If money is all that you love, then that's what you'll receive" and then turns to Luke to add, "I wonder if he really cares about anything or anyone," Han is clearly hurt. When Luke chides him for refusing to join the Rebel attack on the Death Star, Han looks obviously guilty, and Chewie reproaches him as only he can. So while Han claims that he rescues Luke from Darth Vader in the Death Star trench because "I wasn't going to let you [Luke] get all the credit and take all the reward," we know that he does it for Luke. Han demonstrates that loyalty once again on the ice planet Hoth. When no one is able to find Luke in the base, Han sets off to find him over the objections of the other rebels. By the time he rescues Luke against the odds (725 to 1 against, Artoo calculates), we have little doubt where his affections lie.

Later, he delays his own escape from the planet to ensure that Leia can get off too, and when he's captured by Darth Vader on Bespin, he tells Chewie not to resist the Imperial forces because he needs him to take care of Leia. Unlike the narrowly-egoistic Jango, Han is capable of true and deep friendships. He is willing to risk all for both Luke and Leia.

Yet even on Hoth and Bespin, his own affairs still take precedence: despite the Rebellion's need for his skills and his leadership, he tries to leave the rebels so that he can pay off Jabba. To think a bounty hunter will be able to capture him in the Rebellion's secret hideout surrounded by loyal troops is simply implausible. When Leia argues truthfully (albeit to hide her own feelings, even from herself) that "We need you," Han's only interested in whether *she* needs him. And when they finally escape to Bespin, he's still set on abandoning the Alliance. Despite the overwhelming needs of others, Han still feels that he has to look after his own affairs, no matter what the cost to others. He still has no loyalty to the Rebellion or to the greater good, and he's still quick to look after himself and his own affairs rather than the interests of others.

At this point, then, Han is still an egoist, albeit an enlightened one. He cares for others, and so their welfare counts as part of Han's own self-interest. What they need is part of what he considers when he thinks about what he wants, and so he can then sometimes act for the sake of others. Moreover, Han's egoism has its limits; we could never imagine Han taking money to assassinate a political leader. With a broadened self-interest, Han is certainly better morally than he seemed when we first met him, but more is needed before he can acknowledge the moral value of something greater than himself.

Yet his friendships with Leia and Luke allow him to see the importance of the cause that they so easily embrace. His love for them eventually leads him to commit himself to a greater good and to express a moral regard for oppressed people everywhere. Following their moral examples, he becomes a full member of the Rebel Alliance and one of its most important leaders. By committing himself to a genuinely moral cause, he escapes his egoism. Or perhaps, he does not so much escape his egoism as much as his self-interest becomes so broad that it encompasses all of morality. In any case, Han has been transformed from an arrogant and self-centered smuggler into a moral leader.

"This Deal Is Getting Worse All the Time"

At first glance, Lando Calrissian seems to be just like Han. Indeed, he and Han ran in the same circles earlier in their lives, and he lost the Millennium Falcon to Han in a card game. Like Han, Lando was a scoundrel. For that reason, we may be tempted to see his decisions as egoistic as well. Yet, when we meet Lando in *The Empire Strikes Back*, he is the administrator of Bespin, an independent mining colony. He has become, as Han puts it, "a businessman, a responsible leader." Dealing with supply problems, labor difficulties, and the complexities of running a large enterprise, Lando understands, is "the price you pay for being successful." Yet even before we actually meet him, he has been confronted with a nasty moral dilemma: he can either betray his old friend Han and turn him over to Darth Vader, or he can allow Bespin to be overrun by Imperial stormtroopers. We might view Lando's decision as egoistic: he betrays Han to save his own neck. But Lando's decision is not so self-serving. The lives of everyone on Bespin will be made substantially worse if the Empire controls it, so Lando make a fairly straightforward *utilitarian* decision.

Utilitarianism is the view that, as the nineteenth-century philosopher John Stuart Mill puts it, "actions are right in proportion as they tend to promote happiness; wrong as they tend to produce the reverse of happiness."[2] While the egoist promotes only her own happiness, the utilitarian promotes the happiness of everyone. The correct moral action is the one that creates the most happiness for the world: "*the greatest happiness of the greatest number*," to use the Jeremy Bentham's famous phrase.[3] To determine the right act, we look at each of the options that are available to us and calculate the likely consequences of choosing that option. We then add up the happiness that would be created for every person affected if we choose that option and subtract the unhappiness. We then compare this result with those of the other options, and then pick the one with the highest total. Every person's happiness or unhappiness

social morality

---

[2] John Stuart Mill, *Utilitarianism*. Second edition, edited by George Sher (Indianapolis: Hackett, 2001), p. 7.
[3] Jeremy Bentham, *A Fragment on Government*, edited by J.H. Burns and H.L.A. Hart (Cambridge: Cambridge University Press, 1977), p. 3.

is weighed equally in the calculation, so from a utilitarian point of view, the increased happiness of a large number of people usually outweighs the pain suffered by one. So when Lando gives up Han to prevent the great harms that his people would suffer if the Empire commands his colony, he is simply weighing the good of the many against the harm to one.

In the context of *The Empire Strikes Back*, this decision looks like moral cowardice. We want Lando to stand up to the Empire, to try to save his friends, no matter what the cost. With E.M. Forster, we think that "if I had to choose between betraying my country and betraying my friend, I hope I should have the guts to betray my country."[4] We empathize so much with Han and Leia that we simply ignore the thousands of other people who are affected by Lando's decision. But to put it in these terms shows how narrow-minded such a judgment is. In fact, we expect the government to look after the welfare of the whole society rather than the needs of a single individual. Within some limits (which can often be justified on utilitarian grounds),[5] we expect government officials to act as utilitarians, maximizing the good for the whole community. Officials should think of the nation and only incidentally of individuals, even if the individuals in question are personal friends of the leader—indeed, *especially* if the individuals are personal friends. We expect governmental officers to go out of their way to avoid charges that they are acting out of their own interests or those of their friends rather than out of those of the nation as a whole. Imagine how we would judge the President of the United States if he were willing to give in to terrorist demands to save the life of an old hunting buddy from Mexico. Lando's actions would be exactly the same: he would be turning over the colony to the tyranny of the Empire just to save a gambling buddy who does not even belong to the colony. Seen in this light, Lando's decision is not only reasonable, it's also what we would expect from someone in his position.

---

[4] E.M. Forster, "What I Believe," in *Two Cheers for Democracy* (New York: Harcourt, Brace, 1951), p. 68.

[5] These restrictions usually take the form of individual rights, which utilitarians think can be grounded in what creates the greatest happiness in the long run. See John Stuart Mill, *On Liberty*, edited by Elizabeth Rapaport (Indianapolis: Hackett, 1978), especially Chapter II.

Moreover, whatever Han thinks, Lando's choice is not between giving up Han and saving his colony. No matter what Lando does, Han will be captured by Darth Vader: either Lando will surrender Han to Vader or the stormtroopers will capture him in their assault on the planet. So Lando's real choice is only whether he's going to try to save the mining colony or not. The choice he actually faces is much like one discussed by the moral philosopher Bernard Williams: an evil commandant offers to save nineteen of his twenty innocent captives slated for execution if you personally will shoot one of them, despite your own pacifist convictions. The captive you kill will die no matter what you do, so the question is whether you should act to save the other nineteen.[6] Williams argues that a utilitarian morality—indeed, any abstract morality—requires too much if it expects you to give up your own convictions to kill the one. Such a moral demand would violate your personal integrity, he claims. While Williams's position is appealing, it is ultimately based on a kind of moral selfishness: *I* will never get *my* hands dirty, though the heavens may fall. Undoubtedly, both you and Lando give up something important if you act as morality requires: you each give up a sense of moral purity. But ultimately, that sense is a kind of moral vanity: it is the view that *my* moral sensibilities are worth more than the *lives* of the others. Even if Lando and you don't entirely trust either Darth Vader or the commandant to keep his word, the decision to try to help the many is not one of moral cowardice. Indeed, valuing the actual lives of others over your own moral scruples is an act of moral courage. Yet even if we think that this reasoning is faulty and that in the final analysis Lando is wrong, we shouldn't judge him a coward. He's not acting in a clearly unreasonable or selfish manner. He simply weighs the moral options differently.

In fact, Lando never really has any choice whatsoever. No matter what he does, the Empire is going to take over his colony and Han is going to be captured. So his plaintive refrain, "I had no choice," is really true. But Lando doesn't act immorally for trying to produce a different outcome. To his credit, when he realizes that his goals are hopeless, he does what he can both to evacuate

---

[6] Bernard Williams, "A Critique of Utilitarianism," in J.J.C. Smart and Bernard Williams, *Utilitarianism: For and Against* (Cambridge: Cambridge University Press, 1973), pp. 98–100.

as much of the colony as possible and to save Leia, Chewie, and
Threepio from Vader. After losing his colony, he doesn't think of
himself at all. He immediately joins Luke and Leia's plans to rescue Han, and we see him at the end of *The Empire Strikes Back*
setting off to find Han on Tatooine. He thus immediately tries to
make right the harm that was done to Han through his actions,
even if that harm was caused by no fault of his own. And, once
he has rescued Han, he doesn't hesitate to join the Rebel forces
in what looks like a suicide mission to attack the second Death
Star. Far from being a narrow egoist, Lando is in fact one of the
most morally courageous figures in the *Star Wars* saga.

"Together . . . We Can Destroy the Sith"

Count Dooku is first introduced in *Attack of the Clones* as a
"political idealist, not a murderer." Dooku is a former Jedi who
leads a separatist rebellion against the Republic. The case for
rebellion that Dooku presents to Obi-Wan is compelling: "What
if I told you that the Republic was now under the control of the
Dark Lord of the Sith? . . . Hundreds of senators are now under
the influence of a Sith Lord called Darth Sidious." Dooku's argument is that the Republic is under the control of a senate that
has been hopelessly corrupted by an agent of evil. The only
chance to destroy the Sith, he argues, is to break with the
Republic completely and to undermine the power of the Senate.
In other words, the only choice is to join him. Obi-Wan, of
course, refuses to believe that the Jedi Council could be so thoroughly deceived about the power that the Sith Lord wields, and
so he sees Dooku only as a "traitor."

Here's an interestingly ambiguous scenario. We have two
characters, each of whom is acting on what he thinks is best for
everyone. We know Obi-Wan better, so we're more likely to
trust his judgment, but we also know that the information provided by Dooku is accurate. Dooku sees a corrupt government,
controlled by pure evil; rebellion, he thinks, is the only possibility of keeping the galaxy from falling under the complete
sway of those hidden forces. Although Obi-Wan objects to this
possibility, we can easily imagine that Dooku would be joined
by an independently-minded Jedi like Qui-Gon Jinn, who was
only too-eager to ignore the advice of the Jedi Council with
respect to Anakin Skywalker.

On the other hand, because Obi-Wan completely trusts the capacity of the Jedi Council to detect the Sith, he sees only a rebel, looking after his own interests and those of his cronies. The only evil he sees is that of the separatist rebellion itself. However much Obi-Wan's intentions are good, he fails to see the greater danger. His arrogance in his own knowledge and in that of his leaders leaves unquestioned his misguided assumptions. Dooku understands that the "Dark Side of the Force has clouded their [the Jedi Council's] vision," and he knows that drastic action is needed to avert catastrophe, so he's willing to take enormous risks for the good of all.

We have, then, a conflict between people with different views of what is needed to advance the good, neither of whom is in a position to convince the other of his point of view. The dispute is a conflict of visions, based partially on a conflict in knowledge. Each man acts reasonably given the information he has, relying most on those whom he trusts. Each is thus acting out of good intentions, yet one must have unwittingly become a tool of evil. Without further information, such conflicts can't be resolved, and so one of them must be horribly mistaken. In such scenarios lie great moral tragedies.

To be a great tragedy, however, each side must be acting out of good will, but one unwittingly aids evil. Unfortunately, such an interestingly ambiguous scenario is not the one we actually find in *Attack of the Clones*. By the time we see him with Obi-Wan, we already know that Dooku is no idealist and that he does not have any good intentions. The Trade Federation will join the separatists only if Padmé Amidala has been eliminated, and Dooku has assured Nute Gunray that his hired assassin, Jango Fett, will not fail. His participation shortly thereafter in the attempt to execute Obi-Wan, Padmé, and Anakin leaves us no room to think that he was ever acting for good. The later revelation that Dooku is actually the Sith apprentice Darth Tyrannus is thus hardly surprising. It is merely an irony that Dooku exercises his deception by telling an important truth, while Obi-Wan later conveys a deeper truth by lying to Luke about the death of his father.[7] Dooku, as it turns out, is not morally ambiguous at all: he's simply a subtle instrument of evil. The movies thus miss

---

[7] For more on the Sith's and Jedi's use of deception and truth, see Chapter 16 in this volume.

the opportunity to teach an important moral lesson: sincere people can honestly disagree about the correct moral course.

"I'm a Jedi . . . I Know I'm Better Than This"

On the face of it, the most morally ambiguous character in the *Star Wars* saga must be Anakin Skywalker. He changes from an innocent and good-hearted young boy into a servant of the Emperor, the embodiment of darkness itself. But I think that Anakin is not in fact so ambiguous.

As a child, Anakin is clearly on the side of good. He reaches out to Padmé and Qui-Gon on Tatooine, offering them shelter from a sandstorm. Hearing their troubles, he immediately seeks to help them, risking his own life in the Boonta Eve Podrace to win the prize money that Qui-Gon needs to buy the spare parts for their damaged starship. In *The Phantom Menace*, Anakin is nothing but innocence and goodness. No moral ambiguities here. As a young man, however, Anakin becomes Darth Vader; by *A New Hope*, he is, as Obi-Wan puts it, "more machine now than man, twisted and evil." No moral ambiguities there either.

We might then expect to see some signs of ambiguity in the interim. But in *Attack of the Clones*, we never see the kind boy we met on Tatooine. Not once during the entire movie does he show basic compassion. He's rude, arrogant, and ungrateful. While he talks about the respect he has for Obi-Wan's wisdom, he never acts as if he believes that Obi-Wan has anything to teach him. He ignores Obi-Wan's explicit instructions at every opportunity, he picks a fight with Obi-Wan in front of Padmé to prove his loyalty to her over his teacher, he refuses to listen to Obi-Wan while chasing Zam Wesell, and he abandons his mission to Naboo to look after his own personal affairs. His smarmy resistance to Obi-Wan's teachings turns his otherwise patient and kind master into a hectoring nag. His pursuit of his love for Padmé, while understandable, jeopardizes not only their careers, but also their lives—not to mention the lives of those who find themselves in the path of their recklessness.

The only step he takes that seems selfless is his attempt to save Obi-Wan on Geonosis, but his actions are ill-conceived and rash, an ill-advised attempt to make up for abandoning his post earlier. His duty was clearly to protect his charge, yet he allows Padmé to convince him to do what he himself wants to do.

Once there, he has to be reminded to keep to his mission when Padmé falls out of their gunship, and he rushes into combat with Count Dooku so carelessly that he ends up causing unnecessary injuries both to Obi-Wan and to himself. Most of these actions are thoughtless rather than intentionally immoral, so we may be inclined to see them as well-intentioned, if mistaken. Even so, their sheer stupidity makes them morally defective.

The problem is not that he acts on his emotions. Emotions play an important role in our moral evaluations. The eighteenth-century Scottish philosopher David Hume even argues, "Morality . . . is more properly felt than judg'd of."[8] Yet even Hume thinks that reason plays an important role in morality. We need to use our reason to assess the facts properly and to keep our priorities straight. To act coherently, much less morally, we can't lose our heads; we have to be able to reflect on what we are doing. When people disregard the moral judgments that emerge from reflection, we rightly view them as morally flawed. And when they willfully refuse to engage in reflection at all, when they rush to action without any use of their reason, we should judge them similarly. So when Anakin tells Padmé, "You are asking me to be rational. That is something I know I cannot do," he is admitting to a great moral failing. If we willfully ignore what reason tells us, we become controlled by every whim of our emotions, and we lose our capacity to make moral decisions. Anakin's recklessness is, then, a vice.

Yet all Anakin's reckless actions pale in comparison to what he does to the Sand People who've captured his mother. Even from Naboo, Anakin feels his mother's pain, and he rushes to Tattooine to help her. But when she dies in his arms, he destroys an entire village, the innocent and the guilty alike, out of revenge. It's an act of unspeakable cruelty.

Oddly, the horror of this act is downplayed in the movie. Padmé only seems to feel sorry for Anakin, reacting little to the depths of the horror. She consoles him and rather lamely insists that "to be angry is to be human." Anakin himself *seems* to feel sorry for what he has done, but even this apparent regret seems to be more about failing his ideal of a Jedi than about the act itself. Indeed, he seems much more upset that he couldn't save

---

[8] David Hume, *A Treatise of Human Nature*, edited by David Fate Norton and Mary J. Norton (Oxford: Oxford University Press, 2000), III.1.ii.1.

his mother, and so vows to be "all-powerful" so that he can "learn to stop people from dying."

We could try to argue that the killings, though horrendous, are at least somewhat morally ambiguous. We can distinguish between dispositions and character traits that lie behind an action and the consequences of the action itself. As Mill puts it, "the motive has nothing to do with the morality of the action, though much to do with the worth of the agent."[9] We can then argue that Anakin, by acting out of love for his mother, is acting from a good disposition. A world in which people love their parents and their children so much that they are willing to go to great lengths to save them is a morally better world than one in which people lack such feelings. People are more likely to develop a strong moral character, and to have richer lives in general, when they are capable of such great and unconditional love for others. The development of such attachments is thus a great moral good. The hatred Anakin feels towards the Sand People, we could then argue, is a natural outcome of having such a great love. They have slowly and painfully tortured Shmi, and Anakin reacts passionately and violently to their brutality.[10] So, although destroying the Sand People was wrong, we could argue that Anakin's reaction is a byproduct of a character trait that is generally virtuous. We could then still think of Anakin as a good person.

What Anakin does, however, can bear no such justification. First, to massacre many for the sake of one is egregiously disproportionate. Indeed, to kill *any* innocent person just to save a family member is morally dubious. We should always "act so that we treat humanity . . . always as an end in itself and never as a means only," as the great Prussian philosopher Immanuel Kant puts it.[11] By sacrificing innocent people to save our loved one, we are using them merely as tools for our own purposes. We do not respect them as full human beings with their own goals and values, but as something expendable whenever they get in our way. Moreover, to do so when those actions will not

---

[9] Mill, *Utilitarianism*, p. 18.

[10] For further discussion of the value of love and attachment from a Hegelian philosophical perspective, see Chapter 12 in this volume

[11] Immanuel Kant, *Foundations of the Metaphysics of Morals*, translated by Lewis White Beck (Indianapolis: Bobbs-Merrill, 1959), p. 47, Ak. 429.

even help our loved one treats the Sand People in just the way Anakin thinks of them: "They're like animals and I slaughtered them like animals." Anakin's capacity to treat people as mere beasts is such a fundamental moral flaw that his capacity for love can't redeem his character.

Second, and more importantly, for all the good it creates, the love of family is not always a good moral motive. Certainly, love is a powerful motive, and it can be difficult to control. In addition, the capacity to love is itself intrinsically good, and it thereby creates a great good in people's lives. Besides being good in its own right, it can also help to generate other goods. It teaches us to look at the world from the point of view of others and to take into account the interests of those outside us.

Yet despite its great potential, love can also be morally selfish. Han, remember, is a better person because he loves, but his moral perspective is still limited. When we focus our attention exclusively on those we love, we can become blind to the anguish of others. They can cease to exist for us morally. Indeed, too often, we fail to think of outsiders as human at all. The exclusive love of our own families and our own groups is the root cause of the intolerance that leads to too many of the great crimes committed by humanity. So Anakin's love makes his anger understandable, but what he does with that anger is no less horrible because love lies behind it.

Anakin's murder of the Sand People is, then, in no way morally ambiguous. It's simply the first of Anakin's many future acts of barbarity. We are supposed to see Anakin's actions as a result of his all-too-human love for his mother and hatred for those who harm her, a flaw that will eventually lead him down the path to the Dark Side of the Force. In fact, however, he is far along that path the second he kills those innocent villagers. Only our (and Padmé's) sympathy for Anakin as a character prevents us from seeing that he's already an "agent of evil."

If Anakin as a young man is not morally ambiguous, we could argue, with some justice, that once he becomes Darth Vader he's more ambiguous than we might think. First, Vader's motivations are not entirely bad. He asks Luke to join him so that they can destroy the Emperor and rule the galaxy together as father and son: "With our combined strength, we can end this destructive conflict and bring order to the galaxy." Vader seeks peace and order for the galaxy, ruled by the wise leadership of a single man or perhaps a single family. Here Vader expresses Anakin's earlier sentiment that "we need a system where the politicians sit down and discuss the problem, agree what's in the best interest of all the people, and then do it." And if people don't agree, he continues, "then they should be made to." Even then, it doesn't bother Anakin that such a system sounds like a dictatorship: "Well, if it works . . ." Anakin can be seduced by the Dark Side because although he wants the world to be a better place, he refuses to absorb the lessons of his wiser, if less talented, teacher. As a result, he doesn't appreciate how naïve his view of the world is, and he can't control himself when he confronts the traps—like the one on Tatooine—that Darth Sidious sets for him. His good motives are thus put to evil use.

Second, we could argue that Vader is morally ambiguous, because Luke does, after all, feel the good in him. Faced with the torture and the destruction of his own son, he destroys the Emperor instead. What goodness remains allows him to resist the absolute evil of the Emperor, but only when his own son is involved. His motivations in killing the Emperor are not that different from his earlier motivations in killing the Sand People: he acts out of love for a member of his family. But, as we have already seen, killing others for the sake of a family member is not always—or even usually—morally praiseworthy. So his motivations don't make his action here better. What does make it better is that this time at least, he kills only the guilty, and he does so when it's the only way to save the innocent person who happens to be his son. The fact that in saving his son, he also kills the Emperor and helps to destroy the Empire that has tyrannized the galaxy is an important added bonus. It is, then, a morally good act—even if the motivations behind it are not entirely praiseworthy. So oddly, at the end of *Return of the Jedi*, Anakin finally does become a morally ambiguous figure. He does great good, even if the motivations are not entirely good, and even if they do not begin to atone for the great evils he has done in his life.

"You Know . . . What They're Up Against"

Moral ambiguity can appear in a number of surprising places. It emerges when characters are basically good, but have to learn to get outside their egoistic tendencies, like Han. It can be found where evil characters pretend to be good to use the goodness of others against them, like Dooku. It appears not when people with whom we empathize, like Anakin, do horrific evil, but when good manages to eke its way out of an evil character, like Vader. Most importantly, it can appear when seemingly easy decisions, like Lando's, are given their full due.

Most moral decisions we make in our lives are relatively easy. We help a friend with a project; we give up a concert to see our daughter's recital; we give directions to a stranger. Few decisions require us to consider anyone outside a small circle of acquaintances or the strangers who present themselves to us. These decisions are so ordinary that we hardly think of them as moral decisions at all. But the ease with which we handle most moral situations can leave us ill-prepared to think about the difficult moral decisions which may confront us and which could prove to be the crucible of our moral characters.

A rare few of us may be blessed with a strong moral compass that invariably leads us to the right path, no matter how confusing the signs might be. The rest of us can only prepare ourselves by thinking about our possible reactions to many different situations so that we can know how we should handle ourselves when the time comes. Thinking about it is not enough, of course, but it's a necessary first step to facing any challenge. In thinking about the moral ambiguity of the seemingly black-and-white universe of *Star Wars*, we can see how morally complex a simple world can be, and we can begin to prepare for the moral complexities of our own less-than-simple world.[12]

[12] I would like to thank Jason Eberl, Kevin Decker, and Jennifer Kwon for their comments on earlier drafts of this chapter.

Part II

"Try Not—Do or Do Not"

Ethics in a Galaxy, Far, Far Away

5

The Aspiring Jedi's
Handbook of Virtue

JUDITH BARAD

So, you'd like to be a Jedi Knight? Surely a good part of the appeal is the adventure, the excitement, the glory of this undertaking. But wait a minute! When Obi-Wan Kenobi attempts to persuade Yoda to train Luke, the diminutive Jedi Master objects that Luke isn't a good candidate for training because all his life he has craved adventure and excitement. In Yoda's words, "A Jedi craves not these things." The path to becoming a Jedi lies within.

Suppose you're not deterred. You still want to be a Jedi Knight just as much as you wanted to the first time you saw *Star Wars*. As a would-be Jedi student, you'll need to have a teacher. Yoda is probably your best bet, given his experience. For over eight hundred years, the small, green Master has trained Jedi Knights. But having identified a teacher doesn't mean that the teacher will accept you as a student. Being someone's student is a privilege, not an entitlement. Yoda will most likely examine your mental attitudes before he accepts or rejects you for training. He will insist that you must have "the deepest commitment, the most serious mind." If you're committed and serious, there is one more prerequisite that must be met before training can commence. You must have the patience to finish what you begin. The process of becoming a Jedi Knight is definitely not quick and easy.

The Old Republic and the Older Republic

If you find these prerequisites within you, it's important to keep the underlying purpose of being a Jedi firmly in mind. The ultimate aims of the Jedi are peace and justice. When Obi-Wan first presents Luke Skywalker with a lightsaber, he explains that the Jedi Knights "were the guardians of peace and justice in the Old Republic." If we really want to know about the "Old Republic" we should turn to Plato's seminal work entitled, oddly enough, *The Republic*. Plato suggests that an ideal society should train a group of virtuous warriors to preserve peace and justice in the commonwealth. It's true that Plato's *Republic* doesn't have the galactic proportions we see depicted in *Star Wars*; but much of Plato's teachings *are* reflected in the *Star Wars* galaxy. By comparing Plato's notion of a warrior class to the Jedi Knights and his *Republic's* Guardians to the Jedi Masters, we can acquire a richer understanding of the Jedi. With this understanding, we will be more successful in living our life to the full, just as a Jedi should.

Plato prescribes a long and rigorous period of training, which he thinks will yield knowledge of goodness and justice. Those who complete this training successfully, he insists, are fit to guard society for they will have developed the virtues associated with goodness and justice. A central feature of *virtue ethics* is the claim that an action is right if and only if it's what a person with a virtuous character would do in the circumstances. Plato thus emphasizes the development of virtues. An initial step in the testing that Plato requires is hard physical training for the future Guardians. However, the purpose of this training is not simply muscular strength. Rather, it is undertaken to improve the soul, that is, the mind. Unless you train your body to obey your mental commands, Plato teaches, you won't be able to have within yourself the necessary power to drive you forward on the road to even greater mental control over other things. Proper physical training produces the virtues of courage and endurance. But training to the exclusion of intellectual development may make a person may become hard and savage. Just glance at the wrestling shows on television, like WWE Smackdown!

Just as Plato requires a training program that combines physical and mental skills, so does Yoda. The training you'll receive will probably be similar to the training young Luke Skywalker receives from Yoda, since you're probably nearer his age than younger padawans. Throughout his training, Luke questions Yoda about good and evil, the Force, and other concepts important to a Jedi. Likewise, Plato's *Republic* features a question-and- ~~Q & A~~ answer interplay between teacher and students as Socrates's "padawans" question him about justice and injustice, the nature of the Good, and the ideal government.

The first step in the Jedi training Yoda imposes on Luke is intensely physical. Its point is not only to increase his endurance but to provide a crash course in Jedi virtues of discipline and persistence. By developing endurance, a Jedi padawan has the capacity to work his way through difficulties despite the frustration inherent in the task. One will learn to continue striving in the face of seemingly insurmountable obstacles and defeat. Endurance, requiring self-control, provides a padawan with the ability to struggle over an extended time to achieve their goals. On Dagobah, the Jedi Master pushes his young student to the limit. Racing in and out of the heavy ground fog with Yoda on his back, Luke is winded as he climbs, flips through the air, and leaps over roots. Yet, he endures and continues striving.

A Balancing Act

The next step in Luke's training is to learn physical *balance*. He stands on his head while Yoda perches on the soles of his feet. Like the other physical exercises, this one also has a predominantly mental objective. It requires such great concentration that nothing can distract him. By maintaining his balance, Luke is in control of himself and the circumstances around him.

Perhaps Plato's padawan, Aristotle, can help us understand the importance of balance. To avoid being overcome by strong emotions, Aristotle recommends that we have the right balance *not bipolar* of virtue—the "Golden Mean." Here, all actions can be evaluated on a scale of excess to deficiency. Virtue is "the mean" or the intermediate between excess and deficiency. It's a *balanced* action responding to a particular situation at the *right* time, in relation to the *right* people, with the *right* motive, and in the *right* way. For instance, you can fear something either too much or too little. Fearing too much may lead to cowardice, as when Chewie ran from the Dianoga in *A New Hope*. Fearing too little, as was the case when Anakin rushed headlong to confront

Count Dooku in *Attack of the Clones,* may lead to rashness, both undesirable traits. The balanced trait, that is, the virtue between fearing too much or too little, is virtue.

Suppose you face an ethical dilemma and fear making a decision because you have only incomplete information regarding the circumstances. You want to make the best decision possible and so try to collect as much information as you can. But, in reality, that's often not possible. Saddled with incomplete information, you may fear making a decision that might end up being wrong. But perhaps it's worse not to attempt to find a solution to the dilemma than to risk making a mistake, and so you rationally conclude that you shouldn't fear making such a mistake. Reason can help remove excess fear about being wrong, as well as inspire a proper respect for the gravity of the situation. By balancing too much fear against too little fear, you can attain the virtue of courage.

We see this illustrated near the end of Luke's training period. Sensing that his friends are in pain and suffering, he asks Yoda, "Will they die?" But Yoda can't see their fate. Luke is in anguish. Both of his teachers, Yoda and Obi-Wan, counsel him to wait before going to their aid. If he decides to help them, he risks possible danger to himself. Yet if he decides not to help them, they may die. Even though Luke has incomplete information and is aware that he may be mistaken, he arrives at a decision, one that he has not reached lightly. He courageously decides to help his friends.

So suppose you fear skydiving, but you learn to overcome your fear. If you decide to go ahead and skydive because you are essentially a thrill-seeker, would this count as a courageous act? While Aristotle would applaud Luke's decision to help his friends as a courageous act, he would probably label your decision to satisfy your thrill-seeking desire as a rash act rather than a courageous one. What's the difference? Well, for Aristotle, the act of confronting danger or risk becomes courageous *if and only if* both decision and *just cause* enter the picture. The skydiving decision lacks just cause, which is essential to a courageous act. In contrast, Luke's decision, reached after serious consideration, involves a just cause—the lives of his friends.

Yet the very notion of fear seems to oppose the Jedi teaching at its core. Yoda tells Anakin that he's not fit to begin training because of the great fear the young boy feels. The Jedi

Master warns, "Fear is the path to the Dark Side. Fear leads to anger, anger leads to hate, hate leads to suffering." Yoda also warns Luke about anger, fear, and aggression. Does Yoda mean a Jedi should *never* experience fear and anger? His words *could* be interpreted in this way. But if we think about it, although the virtue of courage and the emotion of fear may *seem* to be mutually exclusive, they're actually quite compatible. The truly courageous person not only fears what she should when there's a reasonable basis for fear, but she can also stand up to fear and confront risk or danger. This is also true of anger, provided that anger is guided by reason. When Luke battles his father for the last time, as the Emperor goads Luke to "use your aggressive feelings" and to "let the hate flow through you," he controls his anger when he realizes it will lead him to the Dark Side. He reasons that the only way to destroy the Dark Side is to renounce it. Yet his anger, controlled by reason, is what gives him the courage to stand up to the evil, powerful Emperor. Throwing his lightsaber aside, he says with resolve, "I'll never turn to the Dark Side. You've failed, your highness. I am a Jedi, like my father before me."

Not only is "righteous" anger compatible with courage, but it can also result in acting *justly*—another virtue. Feeling angry about someone's unfair treatment could lead you to take positive action to correct this treatment. For the Jedi, it's important to stop violent and abusive behavior, and to defend the innocent against assault. Yet, if possible, a Jedi should use nonviolent means to accomplish this. It is true, now, that your emotions enable you to act more promptly and easily than merely reasoning about a situation. So if controlled by reason, emotions can actually fuel the kind of virtuous action a Jedi should engage in.

It's thus unlikely that Yoda's admonitions about fear and anger should be interpreted as meaning that a Jedi *never* feels those emotions. Rather, he probably means that a Jedi never *acts* from fear and anger. A Jedi acts when reason is in control, when he's "calm, at peace, passive." In fact, as Yoda tells Luke, only a calm mind can distinguish the good side from the bad. In contrast, acting from an agitated condition clouds one's mind from knowing right from wrong. Anakin acts from uncontrolled anger when he sees his mother die at the hands of the Sand People. He confesses to Padmé that, in retaliation, he killed them all: "They're dead, every single one of them. And not just the men . . . But the women and the children, too. They're like animals, and I slaughtered them like animals . . . *I hate them*." Padmé attempts to console Anakin by reminding him that "to be angry is to be human," to which Anakin responds sharply, "I'm a *Jedi*, I know I'm better than this."

Entering the Deep, Dark Cave

In order to succeed as a Jedi Knight, one must identify one's deepest fears and learn to overcome them. As part of his Jedi training, Yoda makes Luke enter the recesses of a dark cave where he will come face to face with himself as he confronts the fearsome apparition of Darth Vader. When Luke enters the cave, he's ignorant of the nature of these fears; he doesn't know himself as well as he should. Clearly, this lack of self-knowledge can interfere with his self-control. It's difficult to control what you don't understand. Self-knowledge entails an understanding of our fears and other emotions, habits, and personal relationships. It implies an understanding of the possibilities that are open to us, as well as a realistic sense of our limitations. And it implies an understanding of our strengths, weaknesses, and faults. So when Luke enters the cave, as frightening as it is, he's given an opportunity for self-knowledge, a release from his ignorance of the hidden aspects of his nature.

Similarly, Plato has a famous story about a cave of ignorance, the condition he thinks most people live in. Here chained prisoners, unable to see one another, see only the wall of the cave in front of them upon which appear shadows cast by small statuettes of animals and objects that are passed before a burning fire by people behind a low wall. The prisoners believe that the shadows they see are all there is in the world. By this imagery, Plato wants to show us that most people are ignorant of their true selves and reality. Although they're deeply ignorant, the cave dwellers are content with the "knowledge" they think they have. Then someone releases one of the prisoners. Standing up and looking around him, the former prisoner now has a clearer perception of the cave he inhabits. Yet the light from the fire, which he has never seen before, hurts his eyes. In other words, he is quite uncomfortable with his new knowledge. It even pains him and he desires to return to his chained position. Aside from the literal experience of suddenly looking at a bright light, why would he experience discomfort and pain from learning something new? Well, looking at himself in this new light would force him to revise the familiar image he had of himself and of the world he's been living in. He may then have to change his former beliefs, values, and ways of doing things. Few people welcome this kind of change in their lives. Yet his rescuer encourages him to search further until he's finally freed from the cave's confines and attains a vision of the Good, Plato's highest principle.

Yoda, of course, corresponds to the rescuer. When he sends Luke into the cave, Luke first sees shadows of the truth, for the youth mistakenly believes that his deepest fear is Darth Vader. However, after decapitating Vader's image, he sees the severed head more clearly. The experience provides him with an alternative shadow to help him discover his true nature. Gazing in horror, he recognizes that the face looking up at him isn't Vader's, but his own! Corresponding to the freed prisoner's first sight of the fire, Luke first recognizes his real fears. He realizes that he's afraid of becoming evil, fears that his weaknesses of unrestrained anger and impatience would prevent him from becoming the Jedi he yearns to be. These fears are based on his failure to fully trust himself to resist temptation. By realizing and confronting the implications of his fears about himself, Luke is liberated from the chains of ignorance.

When Luke meets his father for the second time in a real battle, he succeeds in overcoming his anger and hatred by seeing the good in his father. His vision of this good results in forgiveness and compassion, such that he refuses to kill Vader. At this moment, Luke experiences the ultimate triumph of a Jedi Knight. The Jedi Knight resists evil, but does so motivated by a compassion that remains open to forgiveness and reconciliation.

Both Luke's experience and Plato's story urge us to look beyond the familiar image each of us has of ourselves, so that we can be aware of our weaknesses. Being aware of our weaknesses, we are able to rectify them. Once our weaknesses are rectified, we will have the stability of character that is desirable both in a Guardian and in a Jedi since it enables them to remain unchangeable in the face of dangerous internal and external forces. If someone displays the character traits of justice, courage, and compassion to the extent that it has become a habit for them to act in these ways, they can be counted on to

behave in these ways. They will rarely be influenced by con-
flicting self-interests or swayed by temptations, as Obi-Wan was-
n't at all tempted to join Dooku to obtain release from captivity.
When Obi-Wan refuses to join the Dark Side, he displays the
virtue of *integrity*. Having integrity, he can discern what is right
from wrong and act on what he discerns, even at personal cost.

Just as the former prisoner in Plato's Cave Allegory at last
sees the Good, the successful Jedi must see the good in others,
a recognition which motivates forgiveness and compassion.
These two virtues drive out uncontrolled anger and hatred so
that the Dark Side is no longer a threat. Forgiveness frees a Jedi
to overlook transgressions made against him so that he no
longer needs to carry around the burdens of resentment and
hostility. Even without saying the words "I forgive you" to his
father, Luke's forgiveness of his father is clear as Vader lies dying
in his son's arms.

The Right Kind of Love

The other virtue that's generated by seeing the Good is *compassion*. Anakin, in an intimate moment with Padmé, defines
compassion as "unconditional love" which is "central to a Jedi's
life." There's a huge difference between unconditional love and
erotic or romantic love. In the scene where Anakin defines compassion for Padmé, she's beginning to fall in love with him.
Aware that he's very attracted to her, she asks Anakin, "Are you
allowed to love? I thought that was forbidden for a Jedi." The
young Jedi responds with his definition of compassion, distinguishing it from attachment and possession, which are both forbidden to a Jedi. The Jedi approve of compassion, a higher and
more universal form of love, while attachment to a particular
individual is frowned upon. Personal attachment to someone or
something is an intense emotion, which can lead to fear of losing what one is attracted to, and we know already where fear
leads; compassion is a virtue. More precisely, compassion is a
selfless love, involving a deep, cherishing concern for each individual as having *intrinsic* value. That is, individuals are valued
for their own sake, regardless of their capacity to achieve anything else.[1]

---

[1] For further discussion of love and attachment, see Chapter 12 in this volume.

Plato also seeks to prevent the Guardians from having private attachments and possessions, which might conflict with wholehearted devotion to the public welfare. Since the Guardians are servants of the Republic, they should have no temptations to neglect the public interest; they should have no land, houses, or money of their own. This approach avoids the corruption and conflicts that can happen when it's possible for authorities to place their own good above the public good.

Plato maintains that the virtuous life is much more satisfying than personal relationships. It is so much more real than romantic attachments that those who live it will lose a great deal of the ordinary person's interest in sexual satisfaction. The very intensity of a guardian's universal love or compassion will make him less dependent upon particular attachments. The Guardians devote as much of themselves as they can to public service. By forbidding romantic attachments, Plato hopes to free the Guardians from the competition and jealousy of these exclusive relationships. More importantly, without romantic attachments, the Guardians won't be tempted to prefer such private interests to those of the entire community. We see how Anakin almost puts his love for Padmé above the safety of the entire galaxy when she falls out of a gunship chasing Count Dooku. Aware that he may be expelled from the Jedi Order, Anakin wants to rescue her, even if it means that Dooku might escape and the Clone Wars expand beyond Geonosis. Only when Obi-Wan reminds him that in such circumstances Padmé would fulfill her duty does Anakin agree to fulfill his.

But does compassion for others necessarily require people to sacrifice personal attachments to concern for the larger society? Compassion is at the root of virtuous conduct; it is the notion that everyone counts. But to say that is to say that *you* count as well. And an individual may feel more fulfilled when allowed to love particular others and to be loved by them in return. At the end of Luke's training on Dagobah, he experiences an internal conflict between his commitment to becoming a Jedi and his loyalty to his friends, whom he senses are suffering. *Loyalty* is a Jedi virtue for clearly the Jedi should be loyal to one another, to their ideals, and to the Republic. Yet loyalty also entails an unwavering commitment to the people you value. It involves the subordination of your private interests in favor of their more pressing needs. Not only would

Luke have been disloyal if he had ignored his closest friends in their distress, but he would also have lacked compassion. And it is the virtue of compassion that enables him to see through Vader to the good within him and to bring that goodness out. There's nothing inherently unethical about living in a way that enhances one's personal relationships. But neither does the advancement of personal relationships allow one to disregard the well-being of others or ignore duties. So perhaps the Jedi Order should allow family life, but prevent it from interfering with public duty. *Catholic priests*

Is Brainwashing Ethically Sanitary?

One more problem about Jedi training requires some reflection. Part of Luke's training is to learn to control objects with his mind. First, he levitates a small rock, and then his sunken X-wing fighter. Now if this exercise is meant simply to learn concentration, there would be nothing wrong with it. Concentration, in itself, is a valuable skill and a necessary one for a Jedi Knight. But, eventually a Jedi progresses from mentally controlling inanimate objects to being able to mentally control "weak-minded" individuals. The Jedi can use mind control to plant suggestions in weak minds, making them do things they wouldn't ordinarily do. For instance, at Mos Eisley Spaceport a trooper demands Obi-Wan's and Luke's identification, but speaking in a very controlled voice and with a slight wave of his hand, Obi-Wan makes the trooper think that he doesn't need to see their identification. A much younger Obi-Wan used mind control to convince a young drug pusher that he doesn't need to sell "death sticks" (which look suspiciously like cigarettes) any more and that he should go home and rethink his life. Now using mind control over others is a kind of brainwashing, a practice most people think of as horrible. But is the practice justifiable if it's used for a good purpose? The problem is that anyone who brainwashes or controls the mind of another believes they are doing so for a good purpose. Can Plato help us out here?

Plato sympathizes with the desire to influence weak-minded people. However, rather than directly controlling the minds of such people by the power of his own will, he uses the power of his thought to construct a myth designed to control the beliefs of the weak-minded by appealing to their imagination. The myth is this: the earth gives birth to people, so that all citizens are born of the same soil and must protect the land that is their mother. Additionally, some people have gold in their souls (the Guardians), some have silver (the warriors), and some have iron on bronze (everyone else). The type of metal that courses through each person will determine the role they will play in the Republic. Plato suggests this influential myth in the interest of a higher purpose, namely, the unity of society. Unity is achieved when people prove that they can bear responsibility and give up self-interest in order to fulfill the common good. Most people won't understand that it's important for each individual to subordinate their self-interests to the common good. But patriotism is easily inculcated by careful control of information, and it serves the same purpose of producing unity in society. Plato thinks that using a myth to mentally manipulate the weak-minded will encourage the kind of allegiance to the Republic that people usually feel toward their family members. So, when the Jedi use their more direct mental manipulation for the good of the Republic, whether to fulfill a mission or reform a drug pusher, Plato would certainly validate this.

Also, in Plato's Cave Allegory, the people who carry the objects that project the shadows on the cave wall are manipulating the minds of the chained prisoners. The weak-minded are always being mentally manipulated by other people. Since they dislike thinking for themselves or are unable to do so, they turn to others to figure things out for them: family members, authority figures, the media, the rich and the powerful—you know, the Watto or Jabba the Hutt types who, interestingly, are immune to Jedi "mind tricks." The weak-minded uncritically accept what such people want them to believe. They're being mentally manipulated, although they're unaware of it. Now it's reasonable to believe that the overwhelming majority of mind-controllers have their own selfish interests at heart, rather than the common good, when they put thoughts in the minds of others. Since weak-minded people desire others to figure things out for them, and since there will always be people willing to do so, isn't it better that the controllers be people who authentically care about the common good rather than people who seek to advance their own vested interests?

The Jedi Model

Despite the problem of controlling others' thoughts, the virtues the Jedi possess make them great models to aspire to. As we've seen, in the eyes of an ancient Greek master and his padawan, the Jedi would likely appear courageous, loyal, compassionate, just, and forgiving. They have endurance (otherwise referred to as perseverance), are mentally focused, and have a healthy humility. Also, the Jedi have *honor*: they live by a code or a set of principles, and find such value in so doing that they count it as a basis of self-worth. For a Jedi, honor is closely connected to one's role as a Jedi Knight as defined by the Jedi Code. Further, the Jedi regularly manifest *nobility*, a desire for moral excellence that permits them to overcome personal interests in favor or some purpose larger than themselves. They show great stature of character by holding to the virtues that define them. Nobility involves admiration of the virtues of others and a desire to realize one's potential or, as the Army used to say, "Be all that you can be." Such admiration for the virtues of others and desire to bring out what is best in oneself are part and parcel of Jedi training. Due to their desire to perfect their own virtue, noble persons serve as good role models for others. Having the tendency to influence others, the noble person provides a persuasive example of what can be done in the service of goodness, peace and justice, which are, after all, the ultimate aims of being a Jedi Knight.

Being a Jedi certainly involves a lot of hard work. Fortunately, the various *Star Wars* movies have showed you how to awaken your "inner" Jedi. Just as fortunately, a couple of ancient Greek philosophers shed even more light on the process. Developing the kind of character a Jedi possesses may be far more rewarding to you in the long run than learning how to wield a lightsaber. So if you're still serious and have the commitment to be a Jedi, it would be wise to follow the examples of virtuous character illustrated in *Star Wars* and explicated by Plato and Aristotle.

6

"A Wretched Hive of Scum and Villainy": *Star Wars* and the Problem of Evil

CHRISTOPHER M. BROWN

Why do bad things happen to good people? This perennial question has been especially troubling for philosophically inclined men and women who believe that some all-powerful, perfectly good being rules the universe. Why? Because a perfectly good being that has control of all things would presumably have created a world where good people are rewarded for their virtue and evil people are punished for their crimes. Yet good people often go unrewarded for their good deeds, and some even suffer terribly in this life. Meanwhile, bad people prosper. They even manage to attain the most prominent places of power. If goodness is more powerful than evil, why is there so much evil in the world? Could it be that evil is actually stronger?

In *The Empire Strikes Back*, Luke Skywalker raises this very question while listening to one of Master Yoda's early lessons on the Force. Yoda warns Luke about the Dark Side, the path that Darth Vader has followed. Luke asks Yoda, "Is the Dark Side stronger?" Yoda responds: "No . . . No [*softer*] . . . No [*even softer yet*]. Quicker, easier, more seductive." Although Yoda answers Luke's question in the negative, his delivery suggests that Yoda is not certain, but at most only wistfully hopeful, that good will overcome evil in the end.

Intelligent attempts to make sense of the apparent power that evil has over goodness in this life are bound to lead to more basic questions about evil. Why do bad things happen at all? What is the ultimate origin of evil? And what is evil, anyway?

Something Wicked This Way Comes. But From Whence Does It Come?

There is genuine evil in the universe. This is obvious to most of us. Philosophers of religion—those who try to make sense of, support, or refute the claims of world religions—traditionally have distinguished two varieties of evil: natural evil and moral evil. A *natural* evil is an event that occurs in the universe that is painful, unpleasant, or destructive and does not occur as a direct result of someone's choosing to do what is harmful. Examples of natural evils are Luke's being attacked by a wampa on Hoth and bigger fish eating smaller fish on Naboo. Although it is *good* for a wampa to eat, Luke isn't too happy about the prospect of being on the menu that particular day! And though it isn't morally wrong for one fish to eat another fish, because the destruction of a living organism is something bad—at least for the fish that's eaten—philosophers call it a "natural" evil. In contrast to natural evil, *moral* evil results from someone's *choosing* to do what's harmful to either one's self or another. Grand Moff Tarkin's ordering the destruction of Alderaan and Darth Maul's murdering Qui-Gon Jinn are prime examples of moral evils.

But why do we live in a universe full of natural and moral evils? Maybe any serious talk of goodness in the world implies that there is evil in the world too. Perhaps the relation between good and evil is analogous to the relation between light and darkness. Darkness is the absence of light and light is the absence of darkness. In a world of perpetual light—where one would have no conception at all of darkness—the word 'light' would have a meaning totally different from what it has for us who dwell in alternating periods of light and darkness. Indeed, we might think that the words 'light' and 'dark' would have no meaning for us at all in such a context. If good and evil are opposites in the same way as light and darkness, then in order for us to have any real experience that we might label 'good,' we must also have genuine experience of evil.

As Qui-Gon Jinn reminds Masters Yoda and Windu, the ancient Jedi prophecies speak of "one who will bring balance to the Force." Harmony in the universe will not be brought about by destroying evil. Indeed, if good and evil are opposites, it may be impossible to destroy evil in the universe without also destroying the possibility of real goodness. The best state of affairs for the universe would then involve keeping the Dark *linguistic* Side in check, or "balanced" against the Light Side of the Force. There would be no need for Luke's courageous and selfless actions to save his friend Han Solo if it weren't for Jabba the Hutt's greed and inordinate desire for revenge. Nor would Luke have displayed the kind of compassion implicit in his refusal to kill his own father if Darth Vader hadn't been seduced by the Dark Side of the Force. There would be no cause for the kind of heroism displayed by the likes of Princess Leia, Han Solo, and Lando Calrissian if there were no evil Empires to rebel against. It may be that the Dark Side serves a good and necessary purpose: there would be no *genuine* goodness in the universe without the Dark Side as an impetus for noble action. A universe without villainy—and therefore without heroism—would be morally lifeless, inert. *so who need to fight? ego?*

We know evil existed a long time ago, in a galaxy far, far away. But has evil always existed? If evil came into existence at some point in history, what was its cause? It couldn't come from what's truly good, for if goodness gives rise to evil then it *tautology* wouldn't really be good in the first place. It makes more sense to say that, like goodness, evil is simply a basic feature of the universe and has no cause—it has always existed along with goodness. Western philosophy offers this kind of *dualistic* account of good and evil in both non-religious and religious forms.

The ancient Greek philosopher Plato articulates perhaps the most influential non-religious expression of a dualism of good and evil. He argues that the existence of a world such as ours— a world that on the whole is quite harmonious and orderly— must have a maker, a divine craftsman, and a plan that's followed in constructing the universe.[1] However, any construction project requires more than simply a design and a builder. It also requires raw materials. For Plato, *matter* is the ultimate raw material of the divine craftsman's building project that is our universe, much as life forms the basis for the existence of the Force in the *Star Wars* galaxy.

Yoda didn't create the raw materials from which his hut on Dagobah was constructed; the tree, sticks, and mud that he used to build his home pre-existed the finished product. Plato thinks

---

[1] See Plato, *Timaeus*, 28b–29; *Republic*, Book X, 596b–597d.

the divine craftsman, as powerful and perfect as he is, works under the same basic restrictions. Although there hasn't always been a visible universe with planets, living things, and machines in existence, *matter*, the "stuff" out of which all of these particular things are made, has always been around.

The fact that matter is uncreated also explains why the world can't be perfectly harmonious and orderly according to Plato. Even if the divine craftsman necessarily creates the best world he can, this doesn't mean that such a world is an absolutely *perfect* world, since the divine craftsman must create the visible world out of matter, and the matter out of which the world is fashioned isn't perfect but is by its nature impure, disordered, and discordant. Let's assume that when Yoda did anything— even something as mundane as building a home out of sticks and mud—he did a great job. But even a home built by a Jedi Master is not completely impervious to decay at the hands of the forces of nature over time. Similarly, the visible world as a whole—with all of its evils—is the best that the divine craftsman could manage, given the limitations inherent in the raw material he's got to work with.

The Platonic tradition in Western philosophy has often considered matter to be not just limiting, but positively evil. Since matter is inherently evil, so are the individual bodies composed of it. Platonists look with suspicion on activities associated with the body, such as eating and drinking for pleasure, as well as sexual activity. Our bodies distract us from the more worthy pursuits of thinking and doing morally virtuous deeds. As Plato, in the voice of Socrates, remarks, "So long as we have the body accompanying our reason in its inquiries, so long as our souls are befouled by this evil admixture, we shall assuredly never fully possess that which we desire, to wit truth."[2] In addition, we often identify ourselves with our bodies, when in fact, we're really spirits trapped in bodies. As Yoda teaches Luke: "Luminous beings are we . . . [*Yoda pinches Luke's shoulder*] . . . not this crude matter."

In the Platonic tradition evil has its ultimate source in matter, and this goes for moral evil as well as natural evil, since all moral evil originates in excessive attachment to the body. The

---

[2] Plato, *Phaedo*, 66–67, translated by R. Hackforth, in R.E. Allen, ed., *Greek Philosophy: Thales to Aristotle* (New York: The Free Press, 1991), p. 164.

good person isn't a slave to the body and its passions, and so she isn't excessively afraid of death. Obi-Wan's last lesson for Luke comes when he allows himself to be killed by Darth Vader—thereby freeing himself from the confines of the body— rather than have Luke watch him attack in order to kill. Obi-Wan warns Vader, "You can't win, Darth. If you strike me down, I shall become more powerful than you can possibly imagine." Obi-Wan's death allows him to be released from the limitations of bodily existence. In addition, Obi-Wan will have a power that Vader *can't* imagine—since Vader thinks, like his master the Emperor, that real power comes with the ability to manipulate one's physical surroundings, particularly through the threat of death. For Yoda, Obi-Wan, and Plato, true power is spiritual power—having control of one's own self. The Emperor, by contrast, teaches his disciples to use the Force and channel bodily passions such as fear, anger, and hate in order to acquire power over nature and bodily death. As Anakin confesses to Padmé after taking his first steps toward the Dark Side, "I *should* be [all-powerful]. Someday I *will* be . . . I will even learn to stop people from dying." By contrast, Yoda teaches that "a Jedi uses the Force for knowledge and defense, never for attack" and he accepts the reality of bodily death: "Twilight is upon me, and soon night must fall. That is the way of things . . . the way of the Force."

"One All-Powerful Force Controlling Everything"

Many people don't accept the Platonic view that God couldn't have made a physical universe without evil because it conflicts with their belief that God is the omnipotent (all-powerful) creator of the universe. On the other hand, the presence of evil in the world is often cited as evidence that there is no God, at least not a perfectly good *and* all-powerful one. As Han Solo says to Luke in *A New Hope*, "Kid, I've flown from one side of this galaxy to the other. I've seen a lot of strange stuff, but I've never seen anything to make me believe that there's one all-powerful Force controlling everything."

One of the most important religious philosophers to have grappled with the question of the origin of evil is the fourth-century Christian philosopher, St. Augustine. Although Augustine was raised as a "traditional" Christian, he did not fully accept the traditional form of the Christian faith until around thirty years of age. In fact, Augustine spent much of his earlier life as a member of a gnostic Christian sect known as the Manichees.

The Manichees accept two Platonic ideas about evil: evil finds its primary locus in bodily existence and evil is a necessary feature of the universe. Thus, like Plato, the Manichees are dualists about the existence of good and evil: both good and evil have always existed in the universe—goodness doesn't come from evil and evil doesn't originate from something good. However, whereas Plato traces the origin of evil to the universe's being material, the Manichees locate it in the will of a single person.

The Manichees see the whole history of the universe as one long, cosmic struggle between the forces of good and evil. Each of these forces has a kind of divinity associated with it: a good God of light and spirit, and an evil God of darkness and flesh. Personifying evil is one way of explaining why there is moral evil in the universe. *Star Wars* is replete with examples of such personifications: Darth Vader, the Emperor, Darth Maul, the Emperor's Royal Guards, and so on. The Manichees think "the evil that men do" can ultimately be traced back to the evil God, a mastermind of all evil who is evil by his very nature; we might say that such a person is "evil incarnate."

One of the skeptical questions that the Manichees raise against traditional Christianity is this: If God is all-powerful and perfectly good, then why or how is there any evil in the world? A perfectly good God would not want to create evil in the first place and an all-powerful God could prevent evil from coming into existence. But there is evil in the universe. So God is not *both* perfectly good *and* all-powerful as traditional Christians suppose. This argument against the existence of God—at least the existence of a perfectly good and all-powerful divinity—is known as "the problem of evil." Since the Manichees, like Plato, deny that the good God of the universe is all-powerful, they don't have to worry about the problem of evil.

The Manichees, however, are left with a problem (or two) of their own. If one lets go of the idea that God is *all-powerful*, what reason is there to believe that God is *more powerful* than the forces of darkness? Might it not be that evil is stronger than goodness, as often appears to be the case in our universe and to the characters in *Star Wars*? Recall Luke's question to Yoda,

"Is the Dark Side stronger?" and Yoda's negative (yet tentative) reply: "No . . . No [*softer*] . . . No [*even softer yet*]. Quicker, easier, more seductive." There's also Vader's constant assertion of "the *power* of the Dark Side." Even if the Dark Side of the Force isn't stronger than the Light Side as Yoda supposes, it might be that the Light Side has no real advantage over the Dark Side either. Bad things happen to good people and many of these bad things will *never* eventually lead to anything good. One reason that religious believers defend God's omnipotence is that an all-powerful God can redeem the evil that occurs in this life by drawing from it more valuable goods. For example, a good person becomes even better as a result of suffering pain, whether psychological or physical. Why? She learns to better empathize with others who suffer. She more clearly realizes what's really important in life: not the pursuit of pleasure, but serving others.

But this brings us back to the problem of evil. Why is there evil in the first place if God is omnipotent? Augustine argues that evil's presence in the universe is directly caused by the free choices of God's creatures and not by God's direct choice. Human beings are created with free will, and (unfortunately) many of us have willingly chosen to do evil instead of remaining steadfast in choosing to do good. Although God could have prevented evil's actual presence in the universe by choosing not to create a universe at all (or by choosing to create a universe without creatures who have the ability to choose between good and evil), a universe with free creatures (even free creatures that do evil) is "better" than a universe that contains only mindless automatons programmed to always do good.[3] This is why God created the universe, even a universe that carries with it the real possibility of becoming tainted with evil. But Augustine recognizes that simply saying that creatures have free choice doesn't fully solve the problem of evil:

> Where then does evil come from since the good God made everything good? Certainly the greatest and supreme Good made lesser goods; yet the Creator and all he created are good. What then is the origin of evil? Is it that the matter from which he made things was somehow evil? He gave it form and order, but did he leave in it an element which he could not transform into good? If so, why?

---

[3] For more on the issue of freedom, see Chapter 1 in this volume.

Was he powerless to turn and transform all matter so that no evil remained, even though God is omnipotent?[4]

Augustine believes the answer to the last question is "no." Unlike Plato's divine craftsman, Augustine's God created the whole universe out of nothing. This means for him there was no pre-existing stuff out of which the physical universe was formed. Evil in this world can't be traced back to defective matter for Augustine, for matter isn't inherently evil but good, since it too has its source in the perfectly good Creator of the universe.

"If Once You Start Down the Dark Path . . ."

Why did Anakin turn to the Dark Side? It's not as easy as it first appears to make sense of such a transformation. Did Anakin *choose* to turn to the Dark Side, so that he is ultimately responsible for his "fall from grace"? Or did the devil (the Emperor) make him do it? If the Emperor is ultimately responsible for Anakin's turning to the Dark Side, then we may have found answers to such questions. But we're still left with the question of the Emperor's own allegiance to the Dark Side. Does the Emperor represent an incarnation of evil? Is he really just a personification of the Dark Side of the Force itself? Maybe the Emperor never *turned* to the Dark Side but rather is inherently evil. The Emperor would then be "evil incarnate": he isn't only evil himself but provides the ultimate explanation for why there are other (less-powerful) evil persons in that galaxy far, far away. This would be evil in true Manichean fashion.

On the other hand, if the Emperor was himself once turned by another—imagine that he too was once some venerable Sith Lord's apprentice—we might want to know who turned the Emperor's master. Surely not *every* evil person could have been turned by another. There must be an end to the chain of evil persons that culminates in at least one first seducer, some servant of the Dark Side who either is evil by his very nature (as the Manichees think of the evil God) or else was once good but *turned himself* to evil.

---

[4] Augustine, *Confessions*, Book VII, paragraph 7, translated by Henry Chadwick (Oxford: Oxford University Press, 1998), p. 116.

Augustine rejects the Manichean explanation of evil because he believes that the supremely good God creates all beings in the universe and so no creature is inherently evil. Instead, since rational creatures such as the Emperor, Darth Maul, and Darth Vader have free will, each one of them is ultimately responsible for their own turn to the Dark Side. Obi-Wan hints at this when he says: "Vader was *seduced* by the Dark Side of the Force." For we typically think that every seduction requires two willing participants: the seducer and the one seduced.

Let's assume that Anakin Skywalker is responsible in this way for his turn to the Dark Side. Factors external to Anakin may still have an influence on his choice: the Emperor's temptations, Anakin's desires for Padmé, his mother's death at the hands of the Sand People, and his conflicted relationship with Obi-Wan certainly all go some distance towards making sense of his fall. But Anakin did not *have* to turn to the Dark Side as a result of these events. Anakin made choices in all of these contexts that he knew were evil; he didn't have to make such choices. As Anakin confesses to Padmé after slaughtering a tribe of Sand People, "I'm a *Jedi*. I know I'm better than this."

But why do otherwise good people do bad things in the first place? Augustine is particularly perplexed by this question. If God is the perfectly good and all-powerful creator of the universe, how could one of God's good creatures turn to evil? According to Christian tradition, the original sin is *pride*: wanting to find oneself in a place of honor higher than one deserves. Indeed, pride appears to be Anakin's original sin too. He thinks he doesn't need Obi-Wan as a master, when it's obvious that Obi-Wan has much to teach the young padawan. Anakin chooses to begin thinking of himself as better than Obi-Wan, even though in some way he knows he isn't. In a moment of unguarded anger, Anakin says to Padmé: "It's all Obi-Wan's fault. He's jealous. He's holding me back!"

The question of the origin of evil is no problem for the Manichees since for them evil has always existed in the form of the evil God. But this Manichean view—as Augustine began to see as a young man—has the problematic consequence that people aren't really responsible for their actions. Why does Anakin turn to the Dark Side? The Manichean answer: "The Emperor made him do it!" But Augustine wants to maintain that we're free and morally responsible for our actions. Anakin is ultimately responsible for his turn to the Dark Side. The origin of moral evil in Anakin is Anakin himself and *his own* pride. Much the same could be said of the Emperor, Darth Maul, and Jabba the Hutt. A creature that freely wills to do evil is the first cause of moral evil in that creature. Therefore, there are as many causes of moral evil in the universe as there are persons who have freely willed to do evil.

The Fate of Evil after the Overthrow of the Empire

Does the following plot-line for a Hollywood movie sound familiar? Hero emerges. Hero shows promise in battling evil, but suffers some temporary setback because of a lack of knowledge and experience. Finally, hero blossoms in a way that surpasses all hopes, and everyone—except the villain, of course—lives happily ever after. And at least for a while, we as movie-goers are lost in the possibility that we too might one day live happily ever after. That evil can be roundly defeated is an assumption driving almost every Hollywood movie (not to mention some great works of literature).

The *Star Wars* saga has its Hollywood ending too. We're left with the distinct impression at the end of *Return of the Jedi* that the Dark Side has been vanquished by the Jedi once and for all. Not only is the Emperor overthrown, but Luke has refused to do what his father and so many others had done before him: give in to the temptation to use the Force to serve the darker side of our nature. He's done what others could (or would) not do. The film ends with nothing less than Anakin Skywalker's own redemption, largely inspired by Luke's filial love and devotion. Although three of the six *Star Wars* films end with a victory celebration, there's something different about the party on Endor. After all, consider who shows up: Obi-Wan, Yoda, and Anakin, complete in their other-worldly, luminescent attire.[5] Without explicitly saying so, *Return of the Jedi* leaves the viewer with the distinct impression that "everyone lived happily ever after."

---

[5] In the recent DVD release of *Return of the Jedi*, Hayden Christensen (the young Anakin) appears as Anakin at the victory celebration instead of Sebastian Shaw (the old Anakin), further underscoring the theme of triumphant redemption.

Perhaps films that intend to entertain must have their Hollywood endings. An epic like *Star Wars* would seem incomplete without it. But maybe there is some deeper significance in the universal human desire—codified in the stories we choose to tell ourselves—that everything will turn out alright in the end. Although the young and selfish Han Solo can't quite believe it, perhaps there is some "all-powerful Force controlling everything."

Will we always be at the mercy of evil and its effects? If evil is a necessary part of reality—the "flipside" of goodness, so to speak—then the answer to this question must be "yes." Evil will always be with us, at least as a very real possibility. The Emperor may be dead and all may seem well, but somewhere out there another Emperor-like figure is already scheming and angling for power. And there will always be plenty of Anakin Skywalkers in the world—persons of great talent and potential who could, at any moment, fall from grace and give in to the Dark Side's temptation to believe that power is more important than moral purity. If evil has the nature envisioned by Plato and the Manichees, then the most that we can reasonably hope for are longer periods of time when the Dark Side lies dormant.

Imagine that the fall of good and the rise of evil is something inevitable—that evil is really a necessary feature of the universe. If this is the case, one might well wonder, what's the point of fighting evil at all, if it can't be completely defeated? Can we really be expected to fight evil without any hope of victory in the end? What's so good (for me) about being good? Providing satisfactory answers to these questions is at least one reason philosophers such as Augustine think it's important to defend the notion that God exists and is omnipotent. Human beings have a need to believe that everything will turn out alright in the end. Augustine's defense of the existence of a perfectly good and all-powerful Creator is one important and influential philosophical attempt to show that the human desire for closure in the saga that is our universe is a well-founded one.

7

"Be Mindful of the *Living* Force": Environmental Ethics in *Star Wars*

ELIZABETH F. COOKE

A long time ago, in a galaxy far, far away, good and evil looked remarkably similar to the good and evil we see in our world today. Of course, most of the species, planetary systems, and technological gadgets are foreign to us living in the twenty-first century, but the basic values of democracy, equality, and justice are the same. And the epic hero, the Jedi Knight, shares the same characteristics of the warrior hero in Western culture since the Homeric Age. He's a brave and skilled fighter devoted to a just cause, and, above all, a master over his mind and body. These common values at play in *Star Wars* allow the story to speak to us, despite such an unfamiliar backdrop.

But something else comes to light when the backdrop involves intergalactic travel, the power of the Force, Death Stars, the Dagobah System, Wookiees, Ewoks, and Gungans. We find that the *Star Wars* galaxy reveals a rich approach to environmental ethics—one quite relevant for issues in our own world. Environmental ethics is a branch of philosophy which uses ethical theories to solve very practical matters concerning animals, plants, and the environment as a whole. Now the environmental ethic at work in *Star Wars* is probably not readily apparent. After all, the Rebel Alliance concerns itself with only the *humanist* values of democracy and freedom. And the Jedi Knights, guardians of peace and justice, exemplars of all that is good, don't seem all that concerned for animals or the environment. What set of values then can account for restoring balance to the Force which somehow includes all the different creatures, cultures, and planets? This issue requires our attention to the fact that the Force is indeed a *living* Force. And here, as Yoda would say, the answer to our question, we will find.

Wookiees and Mynocks and Hutts, *Oh My!*

Environmental ethics is concerned with the proper relationship between humans and their environment. Generally it asks what our responsibilities are beyond the human community and whether we owe ethical treatment to nonhuman animals, plants, and ecosystems. A central issue then is just what *kind* of value animals, plants, and ecosystems have: intrinsic value (as goods in themselves) or mere instrumental value (insofar as they're useful for something else). Some environmental ethicists argue that the environment has instrumental value only. While humans may have intrinsic value, we *give* value to other nonhuman things by virtue of our valuing them. So everything from cell phones to lightsabers to the *Mona Lisa* has value only because humans deem it to. These environmental ethicists urge us to see that the environment offers us tremendous goods (food, oxygen, aesthetic enjoyment, and more) which are instrumental in pursuing our goals, but *not in infinite supply*. Thus, to protect our long-term interests and those of future generations, we should work to preserve the environment.

Other philosophers argue that this "resource management" approach misses the point of an environmental ethic. It's criticized for being yet another "anthropocentric ethic," which unjustly places humans at the center of what is to be valued.[1] One such critic is the contemporary philosopher Peter Singer, who agrees with the view that value depends on a conscious being (a *valuer*), who gives value to things, but disagrees that humans are the only beings who count as conscious valuers. For Singer, ethics is concerned with protecting the interests of others, which essentially requires working to increase others' pleasure and alleviate their suffering. And he holds that "consciousness, or the capacity for subjective experience, is both a

---

[1] See Richard Routley and Val Routley, "Against the Inevitability of Human Chauvinism," in K.E. Goodpaster and K. M. Sayre, eds., *Ethics and Problems of the Twenty-First Century* (Notre Dame: University of Notre Dame Press, 1979).

necessary and a sufficient condition for having an interest."[2] This means that to have an interest, one must be capable of feeling (being consciously aware of) pleasure and pain. But of course many nonhuman animals have this ability. Animals too are conscious valuers and have interests—at the very least the interest to seek pleasure and avoid pain. Humans thus owe animals decent and humane treatment, just as we do other humans.[3] Singer argues that we have no good reason to extend ethical treatment *solely* to humans—a bias he calls "speciesism." Speciesism parallels the injustice of racism by arbitrarily giving special status to the interests of individual humans (over and above the interests of other animals) just because they're members of our same species. Singer's point is that consciousness is what's morally relevant, not membership in a certain species. And while there may not be an absolutely clear line of demarcation between animals which have consciousness and animals which don't, according to Singer, all mammals and birds should clearly be included because they can feel pain. But then what are we to think of Luke Skywalker, who shoots womprats in his T-16 and even brags about it to his friend Wedge? Presumably womprats can feel pain, yet this is of no concern to our otherwise moral young hero.

The question of the ethical treatment of animals in *Star Wars* proves difficult, since the distinction between human and animal simply doesn't hold—or at least not in the same way. After all, Yoda clearly isn't human, but we couldn't call him a "mere" animal either. And other nonhuman creatures like Watto the Toydarian junk dealer and Jabba the Hutt raise similar problems. At the same time, some creatures certainly behave like animals—for example, mynocks and wampas. So perhaps our question should be rephrased: Are "animal-like" creatures treated ethically by the "human-like" creatures?

We do see some humane relationships between human-like and animal-like creatures. Han Solo and Chewbacca have a kind of friendship, albeit not one of equals—a point parodied in the film *Spaceballs*. Chewie is like a pet dog—loyal, dependable,

---

[2] Peter Singer, "Not for Humans Only: The Place of Nonhumans in Environmental Issues," in *Ethics and Problems of the Twenty-First Century, op. cit.*, p. 194.
[3] Peter Singer, *Animal Liberation* (St. Albinos: Paladin, 1975).

and even well-trained, but not completely so (apparently Wookiees just aren't good losers, or so Han warns C-3PO while R2-D2 plots to defeat Chewie at a board game). But overall, Chewbacca is treated *almost* like one of us. And on the other side, ethical corruption in *Star Wars* is often illustrated through the *inhumane* treatment of animals by characters such as Jabba the Hutt and Count Dooku. Creatures like the reek, the nexu, and the acklay are unleashed on Obi-Wan, Padmé, and Anakin in the Geonosian arena as a spectator sport (like the lions of the ancient Roman coliseum). And Jabba casts a slave-dancer down to a dungeon pit to be eaten by the wild rancor. In addition to the potential harm to the human-like characters in these cases, there's the questionable presence of exotic animals, far from their natural habitats, in circus-like roles serving humans (or the human-like) for entertainment as well as other purposes. These animals are "owned" and their natural functions (like eating meat) are put on display. As we'll see, this is completely out-of-sync with the Jedi way.

Although there's no mention of "rights" for animal-like creatures by the "good guys" in *Star Wars*, they can't be guilty of simple speciesism. Surely something like *inter-species rights* is at work in the Galactic Senate. Members of different species work together, co-operatively for the most part, toward the same political and ethical goals. Their different appearances are so irrelevant for the purposes of democratic participation that different species intermingle as if they're merely different cultures or ethnic groups. We see inter-species co-operation in the Jedi Order and the Rebel Alliance as well. What brings these creatures together is capability, rather than species. In particular, self-consciousness is important here. The abilities to self-reflect and rationally deliberate are the very conditions for participation in democracy, which has at its center equality, rights, and justice based on the intrinsic value of every human being or human-like creature. Here we see the very strong *humanist* element in *Star Wars*—with a reminder that "human" need not apply only to Luke, Han, and the like.

But many environmental ethicists would argue that the inter-species relations we see in *Star Wars* fall short of an animal ethic, since equal treatment and respect extends only to those creatures who are "human-like," while there's no mention of ethical treatment for the animal-like creatures. *Star Wars* seems to employ an anthropocentric ethic in that only human-like traits are valued—and only *because* they're human-like. In the end, critics argue that an ethic which excludes nonhuman animals allows for their use or destruction in the name of human interests.

Value in Nature

Beyond animal ethics, the philosopher Holmes Rolston, III argues for the intrinsic value of both animal and non-animal life. If something is said to have intrinsic value, it usually implies that it should be respected and not used or destroyed. For example, the intrinsic value of each human being means that we owe respect to every individual, and are not permitted under any circumstances to practice slavery or use humans as test subjects without their knowledge and consent. In the same sense, Rolston argues that we're obligated to respect nature due to its intrinsic value, rather than its instrumental value for humans. Humans don't put value in the environment; it's already there. All of nature is a productive and creative process and "there is value wherever there is positive creativity."[4] Rolston reminds us that when we're walking in the woods, far from other humans, something "tells us" that although no other human may walk this path again to see the beautiful flowers, we still ought not to pick them. Each flower struggles to survive, to defend its life, and we should not interrupt this process needlessly. The organism seeks its own good or *telos*, the natural goal of an organism, which requires different actions depending on its species—a plant photosynthesizes, while a wampa seeks and eats meat. And this process is itself intrinsically creative. If a plant's stem is cut off, it will repair itself; it will work to recover in a way that a blaster or an AT-AT Walker won't. Although plants and (some) animals are not conscious of this process, it's the creative process, not the awareness of it, that has value.

By itself, this view would appear to be an environmental *individualism,* the view that we have ethical obligations to distinct individuals (in this case, each living organism) and not necessarily to species or the environment as a whole. But Rolston

---

[4] Holmes Rolston, III, *Environmental Ethics: Duties to and Values in the Natural World* (Philadelphia: Temple University Press, 1988), p. 199.

argues that ultimately each individual organism shouldn't be seen apart from its relationships with other organisms, or from those processes which produced it—in other words, their *ecosystem*. The sea monsters in the waters of Naboo, for example, must be seen as part of their larger ecosystem, including the water, the caves, and the other organisms in the food chain to which they've had to adapt. An ecosystem isn't simply a collection of interacting individuals, but a system of processes and relationships between different organisms; this system creates and sustains life.[5] Natural processes don't just create organisms; they create diversity *within* species. And this ends up being good for the overall ecosystem. In this sense, ecosystems seek their own good and for this reason the ecosystem should be valued as well. So, while intrinsic value is typically considered independent of all else, Rolston insists that it be considered within a whole system. In other words, each organism has intrinsic value, but intrinsic value isn't *absolute* value (as is normally believed).[6] He says:

> The dialectic of instrumental and intrinsic values, embedded in systemic value, is communitarian without subtracting anything organismic because it integrates organic parts in a community whole. Earthworms are of value because they aerate the soil for grasses and supply food for catbirds, but also because they have an inherent good of their own. Neither their instrumental value to grasses and catbirds or to the system, nor their intrinsic value in themselves—no single thing alone but the fusion of all contributes to integrity, stability, and beauty in the community.[7]

This position, called environmental *holism*, maintains that the good of the whole biotic community requires recognizing the interdependence of organisms, and that the individual health and integrity of each organism depends on the health and integrity of the entire natural world.

So while the intrinsic value of living individuals militates against their arbitrary destruction or use, the fact that intrinsic value doesn't imply absolute value means that sometimes our

---

[5] Holmes Rolston, III, *Conserving Natural Value* (New York: Columbia University Press, 1994), p. 81.

[6] *Ibid.*, p. 174.

[7] Rolston, *Environmental Ethics*, p. 228.

ethical obligations to organisms may be trumped by other obligations. Choices can be made as to the importance of competing
values. For Rolston, there's a hierarchy of value in nature, such
that some values can be overridden by others. Respecting
"nature" because it has value doesn't mean respecting "equality"
among all living things. A self-conscious animal, say a Wookiee,
can be said to have more value than a less conscious animal like
a mynock. And yet a mynock, insofar as it has an ability to feel
pleasure and pain, will have more value than a non-conscious
rock.

But while there's hierarchy of value in Rolston's philosophy
such that more sophisticated organisms have more value, this
doesn't always mean "humans first." As he says, "Humans count
enough to have the right to flourish here on Earth, but not so
much that we have the right to degrade or shut down ecosystems, not at least without a burden of proof that there is an over-
riding cultural gain."[8] But although human interests will lose
sometimes (when it comes to deforestation, for example), what
we lose is also a *good* thing to lose, namely, the exploitative attitude toward nature. And what we stand to gain is a more harmonious relationship with nature.[9] Our obligation is to become
responsible members of a human and biotic community. Rolston
holds that many things need to be taken into account when making moral choices between individual animal, environmental,
and human interests. For example, in our efforts to preserve the
environment while pursuing human interests, special priority
should be given to rare species, to species which play particularly vital roles in ecosystems, to biodiversity in the ecosystem,
and to the process (rather than just the products) of nature.

Now when it comes to the *Star Wars* galaxy, environmental
concerns aren't exactly the first priority. Yet there is evidence of
a respect for nature and life evident in the Jedi worldview.

"May The Force Be with You": Lessons from the Jedi

On the face of it, the Jedi way has much in common with a kind
of mind-body dualism, whereby one must *overcome* his biolog-

---

[8] Rolston, *Conserving Natural Value*, p. 177.
[9] *Ibid.*, pp. 143–44.

ical nature rather than become unified with it.[10] After all, Yoda affirms to Luke that "luminous beings are we . . . not this crude matter." Yoda further insists that we not judge him by his physical size and proves why in *Attack of the Clones* and *Revenge of the Sith*. After death, a Jedi's body may disappear, and indeed Obi-Wan Kenobi becomes even *more powerful* after he dies and loses his physical being. This seems to suggest that the Jedi are more like "minds" who temporarily learn to work within their bodies, as one might learn to move around in a car. At the very least, this means that consciousness, the mental life of the Jedi, is more than just biological matter.

But this isn't the whole picture. After all, *life* creates the Force. "It's an energy field created by all living things," Obi-Wan tells Luke. The point is echoed by Yoda: "For my ally is the Force. And a powerful ally it is. Life creates it, makes it grow. Its energy surrounds us and binds us . . . You must feel the Force around you. Here, between you . . . me . . . the tree . . . the rock . . . everywhere!" This isn't so much the "mind-over-matter" picture as one of mind and matter interacting as two parts of a whole. A Jedi padawan's task is to become more in touch with the physical world by being more at one with the Force—a task achieved through both physical and mental training. A Jedi must learn to *feel* the Force, rather than just think about it. This allows him to move physical objects without touching them, influence other minds, and "see" without looking.

There's an important biological basis here. The Force speaks *through* living creatures and only *to* other living creatures. This may be explained by what Qui-Gon Jinn says to young Anakin Skywalker, that "midi-chlorians" are a microscopic life form residing in all living cells. We have a symbiotic relationship with them—"living together for mutual advantage." As Qui-Gon puts it "Without the midi-chlorians life could not exist. They continually speak to us, telling us the will of the Force." This implies that we already exist in a symbiotic relationship with these messengers of the Force, and when a young padawan learns to quiet the mind he can learn the will of the Force by feeling it through the midi-chlorians in his cells. Control of one's mind then is also control of, and a kind of listening to, one's body so

---

[10] For more on this Platonic view of the Force, see Chapter 6 in this volume.

that mind and body can be *one*. So when a Jedi says, "May the Force be with you," he really means, "May *you* be with the Force—and may you quiet your mind to listen to it, to be aware of it."

Learning to listen to the Force also connects the Jedi with other living things, creating a kind of harmony with them. And in this sense, Jedi training *is* training in respecting nature—after all, it is a respect for the *living* Force. The Jedi learns to recognize symbiotic relationships of the natural world.[11] Once he learns this, he grows in wisdom by understanding the entire natural world and his proper place within it.

"Mudhole? Slimy? My *Home* This Is": Jedi Living in the Natural World

The natural world confers powers of wisdom and balance, and it's natural environments in which Jedi feel most at home. During the "dark times" of the Empire, the surviving Jedi retreat from the city-planet Coruscant to hide among the natural caves of the Tatooine desert or the swampy marshes of Dagobah. They live with nature, rather than against it, in sparse, simple dwellings.

And when a Jedi gets into trouble, he consistently finds an ally in the natives of some very natural environments. The "eco-communities" of the Gungans and the Ewoks are very much at one with their environments. The Gungans are less technologically advanced than most other nearby cultures, while the Ewoks have virtually no technology. Ewoks live within the trees and their homes, clothes, and weapons are made out of simple materials directly from their environment. Right away Leia and Wicket the Ewok are natural allies against the stormtroopers. There seems to be no genuine evil found on Endor. Never mind that the Ewoks originally captured and planned to eat Han, Luke, and Chewie—it was nothing personal! In *Star Wars* there's a big ethical difference between violence done out of duty or necessity (the Jedi and the Ewoks, respectively) and violence

---

[11] Symbiotic relationships regularly occur in the natural world; for example, think of all the good that bacteria do to clean environments. Rolston describes an ecosystem as "a community, where parts fit together in symbiosis" (Rolston, *Environmental Ethics*, p. 311).

done out of anger or greed (Anakin slaughtering the Sand People in revenge and the bounty hunters, respectively).

Strangely enough, the Jedi are fighting to establish what these "natural" communities already have—a unity and harmony with the world. For if we asked ourselves what the galaxy would look like after balance is restored to the Force, we might guess that it's a galaxy where democracy reigns, but an intergalactic democracy that lets eco-communities like the Ewoks and the Gungans live harmoniously and maintain their distinct identities as "peoples." In other words, it would be a galaxy where harmony and diversity are supreme, which are the very ideals of environmental ethics.

Only biological creatures are in touch with the Force in this way. Here we learn of a key distinction between "artifacts" and "organisms" in *Star Wars*. And Rolston makes this same point, first made by Aristotle: A machine doesn't have its own natural goal, but instead receives its purpose from humans.[12] A machine has no self-generating or self-defending tendencies. In our world, as of yet, only biological creatures have this. Robots can't reprogram themselves the way that even earthworms or algae can in order to adapt creatively to a change in the environment.

And time and again we see that for all the threat and intimidation of the technologically advanced stormtroopers, battle droids, AT-AT walkers, and the Death Star, ultimately they can't outdo biological creatures working in harmony. When battle droids collide with the Gungans, and stormtroopers with the Ewoks, the biological creatures always have the surprising advantage: They work with nature to defend nature, and nature is one with the Force. By doing this, they can respond to new and challenging environments. Jedi know this and while they use technology, it's always in the service of the Force of nature. So, while the Dark Side moves closer and closer to overcoming the natural world, it fails in the end. When push comes to shove, the natural processes in the biological world can always overcome human creations of technology, even if it's the "ultimate power in the universe"—the Death Star. As Darth Vader admonishes one Imperial officer: "Don't be too proud at this

---

[12] Rolston, *Environmental Ethics*, p. 105. See Aristotle, *Physics*, Book II, Chapter 1, 192b10–35, in *The Basic Works of Aristotle*, edited by Richard McKeon (New York: Random House, 1941), p. 236.

technological terror you've constructed. The ability to destroy a planet is insignificant next to the power of the Force."[13]

Culture versus Nature

Environmental philosophers differ when it comes to whether human culture is part of the natural world or is significantly distinct because it's a product of deliberate behavior and not the spontaneous processes of nature. This is also left unclear in *Star Wars*. On the one hand, the Jedi are cosmopolitan. They find the city-planet Coruscant comfortable enough to base their Temple where they reside, meet, and educate young Jedi. On the other hand, many cities in *Star Wars* are full of corruption and decay. Obi-Wan warns Luke as they enter the urban world of Mos Eisely, "You will never find a more wretched hive of scum and villainy." The upside of cities is that they allow different people to meet, live, and come together for intergalactic deliberations. The downside is that they offer anonymity which shelters and disguises dark characters, like shape-shifting bounty hunters and Dark Lords of the Sith. Consequently, in cities, people try to mind their own business—no one is bothered in the slightest by Han killing Greedo in the Mos Eisley cantina. And as Qui-Gon says of Mos Espa, "Spaceports like this one are havens for those who *don't* wish to be found."

Of course, for all the dangers of living in one of the major cities, the dangers of not living in them can be just as great—if not greater. The humanist values of the Republic, manifest in its anti-slavery laws, are simply ignored on Tatooine. The remote world, apart from civilization, can become its own breeding ground for evil. To reconcile the values in the natural world with the humanist values of the Republic, we might look to Obi-Wan's explanation to Boss Nass, the ruler of the Gungans. In order to convince him that he should be concerned for the Naboo during their time of crisis, Obi-Wan reminds him that the Gungans have a symbiotic relationship with the Naboo: "What happens to one affects the other, you must realize this." Later this natural alliance between the two peoples proves vital for saving both from the Trade Federation. Indeed, the Force's fun-

---

[13] For further discussion of a philosophical view of technology, see Chapter 9 in this volume.

damentally symbiotic relations exist not only at the microscopic level of the midi-chlorians, but among different cultures and forms of beings. As Padmé is quite aware, once this point is conceded, an even stronger organic relation is possible—one capable of fighting an entire droid army.

For an environmental philosopher like Rolston, natural communities are held together by causal relations, whereas human communities are held together by additional meaningful relations.[14] Perhaps Obi-Wan's description of the relationship between the Gungans and the Naboo is only a metaphor, since there's a similar split between the natural world and the cultural world of the democratic Republic. After all, when traveling through the planet core on Naboo, Qui-Gon doesn't make such a big deal when his little sea craft nearly gets eaten by a fish, which in turn gets eaten. "There's always a bigger fish," he says calmly. Yet, he wouldn't so casually describe the Trade Federation's pressure on the Naboo in this way. Despite his respect for the natural world, he sees that it's governed by very different principles. By contrast, human-like relationships should be governed by democratic principles, which the Jedi regularly defend.

Restoring Balance to the Force

Rolston reminds us that even in a humanist ethic there's still a sense that individual welfare is inseparable from the good of the whole, "recognizing on a moral level in human affairs the symbiosis in biology."[15] But ultimately, the goal in environmental ethics is to balance the goods of human culture and the goods of the natural world. Achieving balance for humans is actually *restoring* balance, since it's out of an intricately balanced natural world that we have evolved. Although distinct human communities and natural communities have developed, they're not so different that they can't live in harmony. Restoring balance to the Force, for the Jedi, must mean restoring balance within the *entire* living community—including cultural and natural worlds. Whether there exists a real or only a metaphorical symbiotic relationship between human communities may be left some-

---

[14] Rolston, *Conserving Natural Value*, p. 81.
[15] *Ibid.*, p. 311.

what unclear in *Star Wars*. But in either case, restoring the natural symbiotic-like relationship is what the Jedi consistently work toward. It's evident in all they do: deliberations among the Jedi and between other peoples, diplomatic missions, and sometimes "aggressive negotiations . . . negotiations with a lightsaber." The Jedi see themselves as part of a greater whole with other living things. When Anakin begins to see himself as more important than the whole, he begins his break with the Jedi way. Conversely, the redemption of both Han Solo and Lando Calrissian comes about when they each begin to see their role in the larger cause of the Rebellion.

The Jedi worldview brings us toward an ethic which includes all living things. But unlike environmental ethics, here the interconnections are not just within ecosystems, but to the one living system of the Force. Ultimately, all living things are unified by the living Force, regardless of place. But an important general view of Jedi philosophy is shared with an environmental ethic, namely, that we should extend our ethical worldview to include all living things. The point of environmental ethics is just this idea of inclusion. Such a view reminds conscious beings of their dependence on the natural world and of the interdependence of all living things. Each individual, as precious as he is, is part of a greater whole. And as it happens, the reward is internal too. For if we're all part of the living Force, then restoring its balance is also restoring the balance within each of us.[16]

---

[16] This chapter has benefited from helpful comments and suggestions from Jerold J. Abrams, Jason Eberl, Kevin Decker, and Bill Irwin. May the Force be with them.

8

Send In the Clones:
The Ethics of Future Wars

RICHARD HANLEY

Clones can think creatively. You'll find they are immensely superior to droids . . . They are totally obedient, taking any order, without question. We modified their genetic structure to make them less independent than the original host."

—LAMA SU, Prime Minister of Kamino

It's called *Star Wars,* and warfare is definitely a *very bad* thing, with loss of life, injury, and myriad other kinds of suffering. The toughest kind of ethical question is: *When is it okay to do very bad things?* When you're the good guys? Maybe that's true, but it's rather unhelpful. When God is on your side? Again, maybe true, but unhelpful. And anyway, isn't the Force with the bad guys as well, in a big way?

Two critical questions arise for the moral justification of warfare: when is it okay to engage in warfare, and how should you conduct yourself in warfare? It also matters, of course, how you conduct yourself after warfare. But overlooked in the standard approaches to the ethics of warfare is the question of how to recruit and treat your own combatants.

In *Attack of the Clones*, the Republic faces the prospect of war within its own ranks, as a separatist movement led by Count Dooku assembles a massive droid army. Supreme Chancellor Palpatine engineers a vote to counter the threat with an army of clones which happens to be ready and waiting on Kamino. A battle ensues, and Yoda grimly notes, "Begun, the Clone War has."

This story raises another important contemporary moral issue besides warfare: cloning. Can it be permissible to produce clones of whole organisms? (That's what I'll mean by "cloning" in what follows.) What if the organism is a person, like Jango Fett? Can it be permissible to manipulate the process to engineer clones' characteristics, the way the clone army is engineered on Kamino? And in warfare, can it be permissible to use a clone army, rather than typical human beings? In what follows, I'll answer, "Yes" to all the above.

Cloning Gets a Bum Rap

The defender of warfare takes for granted that something can be inherently bad *and* permissible. It's also true that something can be wrong and not inherently bad. Public opposition to cloning is visceral, but I'll argue that much of it is misplaced. I don't think cloning is inherently bad. It can be wrong, but we have to answer ethical questions about the wrongness of actions that are not inherently bad by using a cost-benefit analysis. Cloning might be dangerous (like not letting a Wookiee win), or consume valuable resources needed elsewhere (like pod racing), or expensive (like renting the Millennium Falcon), or unreliable (like Han Solo's word), or liable to corruption and abuse (like the Force). It might have little application to human social and medical problems. It might in practice require the wholesale loss of valuable human lives (as those who object to the destruction of human embryos might claim). But if cloning is not inherently bad, and harms no one (or does relatively little harm), it's not wrong. Moreover, the burden of proof would be on the opponent of cloning—in the absence of clear evidence that the harms outweigh the benefits, we ought to permit things that are not inherently bad.

So why think cloning is not inherently bad? Because there's no good reason to think it is. First, set aside the "yuck" factor. That the idea of something is disgusting or creepy—giving Jabba the Hutt a sponge bath, say—has no tendency to show that it is inherently bad. Second, set aside the popular rhetoric. People are apt to use impressive language in condemning cloning—claiming that it's contrary to human dignity, for instance—but what's really needed is cogent argument that it's *inherently* so.

Yet there doesn't seem anything inherently bad about having a clone or being a clone. Unless you have very strange ideas about identity, having a clone is no threat to your numerical uniqueness. Boba Fett is genetically identical to Jango Fett, but that makes him a cross between a son and a very late identical twin.

Sometimes people claim that it's a bad thing to have another individual around that is too much like them. But this is hard to take seriously. We do not regard the lives of genetically identical twins as significantly inferior to those of fraternal twins, or non-twins. When Luke discovers he has a long-lost twin, is it a happy occasion if Leia is fraternal, and not if (as can happen, but very rarely), she is a differently gendered identical? Even outside of family, we actively seek out those who have a lot in common with ourselves, and we think that the more commonality, the better. Maybe we don't want another person to be *exactly* like us, but there's no danger of that from cloning, given the enormous contribution of *nurture* in shaping our characteristics.

Looking at it from the other side, from the clone's point of view, if all else is equal, what difference does it make that you're a clone? (Sadly, I doubt that all else would ever be equal. But if we treat clones as less deserving of respect than the rest of us, that is our own moral failing, not theirs).

Finally, there's a general worry about the employment of artificial or "unnatural" reproductive procedures. If you still think there's something inherently bad about cloning, compare it with ordinary human reproduction (OHR), and with reproduction by in vitro fertilization (IVF). I submit that if OHR is not inherently bad, then neither is IVF. (Remember, I'm not thereby claiming that either is always permissible—if it helps, imagine an IVF case where no embryo is lost or discarded.) The point is that we can imagine cases of cloning that parallel a typical IVF case in all the messy details. If *the only difference* is that we use one hundred percent of one person's genetic material to produce the embryo, instead of fifty percent each of two persons, then surely the cloning is not inherently wrong if the IVF isn't. *not logical*

Curiously, for a good deal of our recent history it was believed that in OHR, all the essential character of the embryo came exclusively from the man, and that the woman was little more than an incubator. Cloning might be viewed as the equal opportunity realization of this!

Assuming I'm right, then cloning has gotten a bum rap. And if cloning is permissibly used to solve social problems, the case for cloning is bolstered (even if it has other costs). So it's good news for cloning if we discover that clone *warfare* is possible and acceptable. And it's not necessarily bad news for cloning if clone warfare is not a benefit of the process, as long as it's not a significant harm.

Getting into Your Genes

The possibility of a clone army scares a lot of people. Perhaps it's because they think that clones will be more easily manipulated: to control one is to control them all. This danger looms most clearly in the case of genetically determined traits. In a blooper that somehow survived the editing process, an Imperial stormtrooper bumps his head in *A New Hope*. According to George Lucas, this incident receives a genetic explanation when we see Jango Fett similarly bump his head entering his ship on Kamino, and realize that the trooper is his cloned descendant. Jango Fett is not generally a klutz, of course, otherwise it would make little sense to clone him for an army.

But "nature" isn't the end of the story: clones of the same host can still vary greatly in their characteristics. If an army consists of genetic duplicates of the original—an army of Bobas, say—then their similarities will ultimately depend on "nurture," on environmental factors such as diet and education. Raise and socialize them all the same way, and they'll presumably be very similar. But that has little if anything to do with cloning. Surely the same thing can be achieved with non-clones, with about the same rate of success. Clones can be bent to an iron will, but so can we. And it doesn't follow that the army will be superior by being raised in a uniform environment. Perhaps it's better to use a variety of environments, and see which produces the best soldiers—a survival of the *Fett*est!

Indeed, part of the point of the clone army is that it's superior to the droid army because the clones are more flexible, more "creative." It's the droids that are supposed to lack autonomy—the capacity to direct their own lives—so there's no need to *bend* them at all. And they can all be stood down in an instant, as happened when Anakin destroyed the Droid Control Ship in *The Phantom Menace*.

The other clones are *not* like Boba, however. They are genetically manipulated to reduce their autonomy, to make them a bit more like droids than you and I are. Genetic manipulation scares people, too, with or without cloning. But genetic manipulation does not seem inherently bad, either. It's playing God, but so what? Genetic manipulation doesn't necessarily harm anyone, as we can see from the following example. Suppose that in the story, Luke Skywalker's parents, other things being equal, would have conceived a genetically deficient child, because of an abnormality in the egg. (Leia can be safely ignored, since she almost certainly came from a different egg, but if it helps, feel free to suppose there never was a twin). The genetic deficiency is this: the child that would have been born in the absence of treatment would have been missing an arm (a fate that befalls Luke anyway, but from environmental causes). However, the genetic deficiency is corrected prior to conception.

There are two ways of describing the outcome. First, we might say that one and the same child, Luke, benefits from the procedure by having two arms rather than one, so the treatment is not inherently bad. (I assume that having both arms is a lot better than having just one.) But if we intuitively tie identity to genetics, and given that the genetic difference is significant, a better description is that the two-armed Luke is *not the same child* as the one-armed would have been. You cannot harm a non-existent child, and the existing one—Luke—is certainly not harmed by the treatment, so the genetic manipulation is not inherently bad. *plush*

Now consider the opposite sort of treatment. It clearly harms a normal child to surgically remove its arm, presumably even in the world of *Star Wars* with its impressive prosthetics. But suppose the "treatment" had been to alter the genetics of the egg prior to conception, resulting in an armless child, when otherwise a normal child—Luke—would have resulted. Given that genetics is essential to identity, as long as the armless child's life is on balance worth living, it cannot be said that *that child* has been harmed by the procedure, since without the procedure it wouldn't have existed at all. This is not to claim that it isn't *wrong*. But if the procedure is wrong, it's not because some child is a victim of it. Such cases can be puzzling, and it's not clear exactly what form the cost-benefit analysis ought to take, but the fact that they involve genetic manipulation settles nothing.

Note the application of this line of reasoning to the production of the clone army. Grant me for the sake of the argument that more autonomy is a lot better than less. Then if the genetic manipulation occurs early enough, it will be reasonable to maintain that no clone is harmed by the process—not the diminished one, and not the "normal" one that would have resulted in the absence of manipulation—as long as the diminished clone's life is on balance worthwhile.

I'm inclined to grant that such a life can be worthwhile. First, there are human beings with diminished autonomy who still have happy lives. And second, any worries about the life of a clone soldier being not worth living have more to do with their being *soldiers* than with their being clones. If it's bad to bring cloned soldiers into existence because they will have miserable lives, they arguably are victims whether or not there is genetic manipulation. And if it does not harm the clones, it still may be wrong on other grounds, but the fact that the procedure involves genetic manipulation settles nothing.

Different Strokes for Different Folks

There's an alternative to genetic manipulation that has nothing especially to do with cloning: environmental engineering of the clones as they develop. "Hot-housed," the Fett clones develop at a faster rate biologically, and are indoctrinated with intensive military training. Is such environmental manipulation inherently bad? It clearly can have victims, but also can have beneficiaries, since in many cases environmental engineering (education, for instance) improves the lives of those educated.

Two possible features of environmental manipulation are of particular moral concern: *deception* and *coercion*, bending another person's will to your own ends by threats. Some popular ethical theories hold that deception and coercion are inherently bad, and so manipulation involving one or both is inherently bad. According to the philosopher Immanuel Kant, for instance, deception and coercion are wrong because it is always wrong to treat another person merely as a means to your ends.

Take *brainwashing*. This is likely involves both deception and coercion, and so is a candidate for inherently bad environmental manipulation. One of the objectionable things about some forms of terrorism is that suicidal terrorists seem to have been brainwashed into unreasonable actions. But even here, we should not jump to the conclusion that manipulating a person's will by coercion or deception is always wrong. When Obi-Wan uses his Jedi powers on the "death-stick" dealer in a Coruscant sports bar, that individual changes his desires drastically. He repeats mechanically, "I don't want to sell you death-sticks . . . I want to go home and rethink my life," and leaves. The implication is that Obi-Wan has done him a big favor.

So when is it okay to manipulate someone's will? One reasonable answer is: when that person already has diminished ⁇ autonomy. In the attempt to protect children, for instance, we often cultivate attitudes in a manner analogous to brainwashing (we also may deceive them in the process). Perhaps this applies to the death-stick dealer, perhaps not. He is apparently young, and has made some bad choices, and so may warrant <u>protection from himself.</u> Another reasonable answer is: environmental manipulation of another's will is okay when it is necessary to protect others from the person to be manipulated. This is the thinking behind ordering someone into therapy as part of their sentence for criminal behavior, and certainly could apply to the death-stick dealer.[1]

The manipulation of a person's will, genetically or environmentally, is not the only way to get them to do what you want. Another way is to use the desires they already have, by making them an offer "too *bad* to refuse"—this is a clear case of coercion. When Lando Calrissian betrays Han Solo and his companions, he admits that he does it under threat from Darth Vader. Extraction of information under threat of torture—as Vader does to Han shortly thereafter—is another example. Such coercion seems to be always wrong.

Yet another way to get someone to do what you want is to use the desires they already have, by giving them an offer too *good* to refuse—call this *inducement*. It seems we are more comfortable morally with inducement than with brainwashing. Indeed, I think that our intuitions tend to go in opposite directions in the two cases: we find inducement more morally

---

[1] For further discussion of the ethics of Jedi "mind tricks," see Chapter 5 in this volume.

problematic the *less* autonomous the induced individual is. The rather childlike Jar-Jar Binks is induced into supporting Chancellor Palpatine's grab for power by his overweening desire to play an important role in the Senate.

This leaves us with an interesting question. Given that there's nothing inherently bad about producing the clones in the first place, even with genetic manipulation, might the clones be victims of brainwashing or inducement? And if so, are they any worse off than other combatants in warfare? Are they perhaps better off? Can such treatment be justified, in virtue of its role in warfare? To answer, we need to examine the ethics of warfare in general.

War: What Is It Good For?

Warfare involves death, injury, and myriad other kinds of suffering. The battles spectacularly depicted in *Star Wars* are entirely typical in this regard. Warfare is inherently bad. But this doesn't mean warfare is always wrong. Sometimes it's permissible to do inherently bad things, such as killing a human being in genuine self-defense.

It is sometimes claimed that morality doesn't apply in warfare, a view with the strange name of "realism." If true, realism would of course have the consequence that in warfare you can do no wrong, no matter how much harm you do, or to whom. In this respect, "realism" is hopelessly unrealistic.

Equally implausible is *absolute pacifism*: the view that all violence, and especially killing, is wrong. We are shocked that Obi-Wan allows Vader to kill him. We do seem to allow that a person may lay down their own life for a noble cause, if they so choose. Notice, however, that if absolute pacifism is correct, then you are *obligated* to let an evil attacker kill you, and moreover to let them kill anyone else. It is hard to reconcile this judgment with the claim that lives are of equal value. If your life is as valuable as your attacker's, then it's permissible to choose yours over theirs by killing in self-defense.

It will come as no surprise, then, that the standard approach to the ethics of warfare is in fact modeled on permissible violence between individuals. In order for violence against another to count as genuine self-defense, it must satisfy the following conditions: *reasonable belief*—it must be reasonable for you to believe you are under significant threat, and that must be the reason you use violence; *last resort*—if you could simply run away from your attacker, and not put anyone else in danger, you ought to run away rather than kill them; and *reasonable force*—the response must be proportional to the threat, and not significantly threaten others in turn. This also applies to the use of violence to protect others.

There are circumstances in which it is permissible to engage in violence to protect your nation or others. The traditional account of these circumstances is called "Just War theory." There must be: *just cause*—a credible threat; *right intention*—the reason for fighting is to respond to the threat, with the ultimate aim of a just peace; *competent authority*—the decision to fight is made by true representatives of the nation or group; *last resort*—peaceful means have been exhausted; *reasonable prospect of success*—it is credible that a just peace will result. In addition, a nation or group engaged in warfare must satisfy the conditions of *discrimination*—only combatants are to be targeted, and *proportionality*—the force used must be proportionate to the threat faced.

These conditions are not easily satisfied, and all must be satisfied for warfare to be permissible. Only the very best of reasons will do. By analogy, consider Anakin's wholesale slaughter of the Sand People. He certainly had something like just cause, since they were responsible for the undeserved suffering and death of his mother. But he acted out of anger and a desire for revenge, and so failed to satisfy the condition of right intention. His response was out of proportion to any threat they presented to him. It certainly wasn't a last resort, and he failed to discriminate by killing the women and children. It is also highly problematic that he acted unilaterally, in vigilante fashion.

To Be All You Can Be, or Not?—That Is the Question

Whatever its success, Just War theory has had very little to say about the recruitment, training, and deployment of one's own troops. The same is true of international agreements governing warfare, such as the Geneva Convention.

Take recruitment. Plato apparently thought that homosexual men make better soldiers, at least in couples, dubiously claiming each will fight more ardently to prove himself a worthy lover. Historically, financial reward has probably delivered more recruits than the promise of glory: mercenaries like Jango Fett have formed a substantial complement of most armies (an interesting feature of the Iraq campaign is the relatively high—by modern standards—number of mercenaries employed by the United States). Financial rewards can be less direct, too. Free college tuition is a tempting reason to join the military, as is the prospect of gainful employment.

Recruitment practices can be morally problematic in a variety of ways. They might be unfairly exclusionary (for instance, the U.S. military's attitude to homosexuals is rather different from Plato's). The institution of a draft might violate autonomy, forcing individuals to fight against their will. Even volunteer armies are constituted to a disproportionately large extent by underprivileged social groups, especially when it comes to fighting, raising concerns of social justice—the poor used as cannon fodder by the wealthy, to put it polemically. Or a volunteer army might attract mostly thugs, who will use membership in the military as a pretext to commit moral violations.

Next, consider training of a specifically military sort: to fight and kill. How do you get people to fight at all? The prevailing strategy is to *condition* military personnel, so that they will respond appropriately to situations and orders without having to think about them. They need to be physically fit, and the physical training is employed in a disciplinary fashion, to discourage individuality and develop a team mentality. To appropriately react to situations, it's desirable to have ingrained responses—to make them a part of "muscle memory"—so that trained individuals will just execute as desired, when required. The "education and combat training" programs on Kamino that Lama Su is so proud of seem to accomplish this very efficiently.

Take the case of Anakin Skywalker. His Jedi training came relatively late. We see other Jedi being inducted into Jedi ways as small children by Yoda, away from the influence of their families and others, rather like being raised in a monastery. The clear implication is that part of Anakin's problem is that he was not sufficiently inculcated—not brainwashed enough—to cope fully with his ability to use the Force, and the responsibility that goes with it. Presumably, it would have been better either that he had undergone the full training, or else not have been trained at all.

Typical military training can be morally problematic. The more autonomy soldiers have to begin with, the more problematic it is to employ brainwashing techniques to get them to do what we want—to fight, kill and die for the rest of us.

With humans, it doesn't seem as problematic to provide positive inducements to fight, at least for mercenaries. But inducements such as a free college education are directed more towards the young, who may not be properly assessing the very real risk that they will actually be called on to fight. Even where autonomy is diminished, the justification of brainwashing is usually that it is for the individual's own good: to protect them from themselves until they are better able to choose. This argument cannot be generally deployed in the case of military training. Granted, if a man is going to fight anyway, he might be better off with full military training. But other things being equal, he is surely better off not to be in the military at all, or if he is in the military, not in a fighting capacity.

That military training is morally problematic does not altogether prohibit it. But it does seem that, if it were to be justified, it would have to promise and deliver much good. When we add these considerations to the already strong presumption against warfare, it may be that very few actual campaigns have sufficient merit.

Send in the Clones!

Clones with relatively diminished autonomy may provide the most morally satisfying solution. They are not offered inducements to fight, removing one area of concern about those with diminished autonomy. Moreover, since they will never acquire full autonomy, the argument that they need protection from themselves until they know better is undercut.

There are still moral problems with an army of diminished clones. We tend to find the training and deployment of fighting dogs to be more distasteful than the training and deployment of human soldiers, in part because the dogs are relatively lacking in autonomy. So we should likewise be concerned about raising fighting men and women who really don't know any better. But given the alternatives, all in all it may be best to send in the clones.

Part III

"Don't Call Me a Mindless Philosopher!"

Alien Technologies and the Metaphysics of The Force

9

A Technological Galaxy: Heidegger and the Philosophy of Technology in *Star Wars*

JEROLD J. ABRAMS

In the Dark Age of the Empire the light of the Force has all but gone out of the world, and the few remaining Jedi look to misty ages of an ancient past for guidance in their struggle against the forces of evil. Obi-Wan refers to the lightsaber as "an elegant weapon for a more civilized age" and describes the Jedi Knights as "guardians of peace and justice in the old Republic. Before the dark times, before the Empire."

The same view of history is echoed in the writings of the twentieth-century German philosopher Martin Heidegger (1889–1976): rather than making progress, our greatest days are, in fact, behind us; and history is actually getting *worse*.[1] A corruption has set in, like the Fall in the Garden of Eden; only *here*, in Heidegger and *Star Wars*, our sin is technology, or, more specifically, what Heidegger calls "enframing."[2] This is the process of reorganizing all the various elements of nature, trees and rocks, rivers and animals, carving them up and placing them into so many artificial "frames," all to be used up as "resources."

---

[1] See Martin Heidegger, *Being and Time*, translated by Joan Staumbaugh (New York: SUNY Press, 1996).

[2] For an excellent study of Heidegger's philosophy of technology, see George Pattison, *The Later Heidegger* (New York: Routledge, 2000). For an analysis of Heidegger's general philosophy, see Magda King, *A Guide to Heidegger's* Being and Time (Albany: State University of New York Press, 2001); and George Steiner, *Martin Heidegger* (Chicago: University of Chicago Press, 1978, 1989).

Ultimately, at the end of our present age, all that will remain of the earth is a synthetic ball of parts and wires, glass and steel—all uniform and very unnatural—like a Death Star residing in the cold dark reaches of space. Indeed, this is precisely the problem of technology we find in *Star Wars*. True, it may at first glance *appear* that progress is defined by the ascent of technology—a view advanced, for example, by Han Solo—but on closer analysis, the path of technological enframing is precisely what distorts our vision of the Force.

Heidegger on Technology

In philosophizing about the present age, Heidegger wants to understand what exactly went wrong with our culture, how we ended up with all these atom bombs and world wars and nuclear waste. So, acting as a kind of philosophical detective, he traces the modern crisis back to the earliest stages of thought, when "thinking" just began. And it began, he claims, in ancient Greece, particularly with the Presocratic philosophers, like Parmenides and Heraclitus, who started asking about the nature of the universe. Their basic question can be put a number of different ways: "What is being?" or "What does 'being' mean?" or "Why is there something rather than nothing?" Similarly, we can imagine ancient Jedi first philosophizing about the nature of the Force, which eventually leads to the discovery and use of its Dark Side.

The Presocratics' response to being was pure "astonishment," which was appropriate. Indeed, we too should be blown away by the sheer being of being, and in our astonishment we should not attempt to divide up reality into scientific parts, but to marvel at being—to marvel that there is a universe at all—through poetry, just as the Presocratics did, and just as the Jedi marvel at the Force. This was a noble beginning to thought; but today, according to Heidegger, the question of being doesn't really even come up on the screen anymore. As Heidegger puts it in *Being and Time*, "The question has today been forgotten."[3] Moreover, Heidegger doesn't mean a little "memory-loss," but a much *deeper* sense of forgetfulness. We actually forget about our

---

[3] Heidegger, *Being and Time*, p. 1.

presume our scanner

own existence—a kind of ontological amnesia.[4] And if the question of being (or the Force) does happen to arise, we are always quick to dismiss it as a meaningless garble. Consider, for example, the many non-Jedi, like Han Solo and Admiral Motti, who simply don't recognize the power of the Force. What the Jedi call the Force, Han refers to as "a lot of simple tricks and nonsense." And Motti condescendingly mocks Vader's "sad devotion to that ancient religion."

So why exactly did we forget the question of being? The answer, in a word, is technology, and especially, for Heidegger, *modern* technology. Historically speaking, technology was at its best in the age of the ancient Greeks, who conceived it as art and as craft. But gradually technology was corrupted. In order to explain this historical transition, Heidegger distinguishes between two kinds of technological experience: the "ready-to-hand" and the "present-at-hand." The ready-to-hand is our primitive tool-use relation: we experience tools and the external environment as natural extensions of our bodies. In Heidegger's terminology we are "attuned" to our world through our basic "equipment"—we are "at home" in the world. As we'll see, the Jedi use technology—such as the lightsaber—in just this way. This is "authentic" existence, our authentic "being-in-the-world," being at one with the world. As such, we "care" for nature in this mode. We care for our homes, for each other, and above all for the earth, and thereby allow nature to reveal its own internal natural forms on its own terms. We care for being, in general, just as a nerfherder cares for his nerfs. As Heidegger puts it, "Man is not the lord of beings. Man is the shepherd of Being."[5]

---

[4] True thinking for Heidegger has been lost today—lost really ever since the fifth century B.C. It was Plato and Aristotle who started to lose sight of the question of being. They effectively shifted the problem to a new set of questions: "How can we know beings?" and "How are beings related to one another?" The medieval philosophers, such as Augustine and Thomas Aquinas, were not much better, following closely in the footsteps of Plato and Aristotle. But it was really Descartes who achieved the modern shift in knowledge, putting the human knower over and above the material world, separate from nature and matter as the set of objects to be known and controlled.

[5] Martin Heidegger, "Letter on Humanism," in Heidegger, *Basic Writings*, edited by David Farrell Krell (New York: Harper and Row, Publishers, 1977), p. 221.

objectification

The "present-at-hand," by contrast, is the opposite: we experience ourselves as the "lords of beings," who are detached from the environment by way of high-tech tools. Not so much in our various machine products (like AT-AT walkers, X-wing fighters, and hologram generators)—but more in our basic *attitude* toward the universe. The *"essence* of technology," according to Heidegger, is really a new way of seeing. In the present-at-hand we experience nature as a set of detached objects, as though we've put on some new and super-powerful goggles that allow us to see far deeper into the hidden layers of nature. And, of course, the more we can *see*, the more we can *control*. In fact, nowadays we can grind up or reprogram just about anything: with hydroelectric dams and deforestation, unlimited surveillance and nanotechnology. But in so doing, we are, in fact, "challenging" nature to reveal itself to us as something "for us," something which serves our instrumental needs, and not as being in itself. Rather than caring for being and allowing it to reveal itself on its *own* terms, we challenge it to reveal itself on *our* terms.

So, in effect, while we're forcing nature to reveal a side to us, simultaneously, with regard to being *as being*, it's "covered up," as Heidegger puts it, and it "shows itself only in a distorted way,"[6] just as the Emperor appears distorted in *Return of the Jedi* and *Revenge of the Sith*. Heidegger calls this process of distortion "enframing." Here everything natural, everything good, is pounded into an artificial frame, everything is *looked at* with a cold hard gaze, objectified and detached—all material for the sterile stare of white-jacketed lab men or gray-suited Imperial officers. Each part of nature is sliced clean from the whole and examined under a thousand microscopes, prodded with lasers and high-tech pitchforks—all to squeeze out maximal output, maximal efficiency, and total control. This is "The Age of the World Picture," as Heidegger puts it, when nature is placed inside a frame for us to objectify as a mere representation of our own instrumental will. Think of how the lush planet of Alderaan is "enframed" within the Death Star's main viewscreen just prior to its destruction.

Once we have set upon this path of enframing, all that will be left of the earth are masses of "standing reserve." This means

---

[6] Heidegger, *Being and Time*, p. 31.

reality converted by technology into mere stuff, always standing by, always ready to be used up. Forests become "lumber," and rivers become "hydro-electric power." Nature thus appears only as a set of lifeless objects always ready for quick use. But a further problem arises: in boxing-up the earth, we gradually lose sight of the natural order of things. Out of *sight*, out of *mind*— our new technological vision clouds our old understanding of the world. And slowly but surely, we begin to forget the question of being.

In his later years, Heidegger reflected on these phenomena of progressive enframing and increasing forgetfulness, but with an apparent sense of despair. There's nothing we can do to stop the massive machine of enframing; it's completely out of our hands. Perhaps we once could, but now it's impossible. We simply cannot save ourselves. As Heidegger says, "Only a god can save us."[7] *from ourselves*

"An Elegant Weapon": The Lightsaber as Ready-To-Hand

We find the same Heideggerian saga of technology in *Star Wars*. Here the natural ready-to-hand is corrupted by the present-at-hand relation and the will to enframe all things. Moreover, in the wake of the path of enframing by the Empire, masses of standing reserve are generated. And as a consequence of this enframing and standing reserve, a certain forgetting occurs, particularly evident in Vader's own forgetfulness of himself. Ultimately, this forgetting is so deep, the standing reserve so massive, and the path of enframing so aggressive, that in the end only a god can save us . . . or, in this case, only the Jedi Knight Luke Skywalker.

Luke's adventure begins on Tatooine. Following his runaway droid R2-D2, Luke encounters Obi-Wan Kenobi, who has, in fact, been waiting a long time to give Luke something very special: "Your father's lightsaber. This is the weapon of a Jedi Knight. Not as clumsy or random as a blaster . . . An elegant weapon for a more civilized age." On board the *Millennium*

---

[7] Heidegger made this remark in an interview with *Der Spiegel*, entitled "Only a God Can Save Us," translated by Maria P. Alter and John D. Caputo in *Philosophy Today* 20 (4th April, 1976), pp. 267–285.

Falcon, Luke starts his (very Heideggerian) training. He must learn to think of his lightsaber not as some external and value-neutral object that's *present to him*, but as a natural part of his body, an extension of his very being. In other words, he must make the transition from the "present-at-hand" to the "ready-to-hand." And, more importantly, he must conceive both himself *and* his lightsaber as dynamic and fluid extensions of the Force itself. Luke practices his swordsmanship with a training remote (a small floating sphere), which hovers around him, stinging him with laser beams. Failing at first to defend himself, Obi-Wan suggests Luke wear a helmet with the blast-shield down so he cannot see at all, which Luke can hardly understand. But Obi-Wan instructs him: "Your eyes can deceive you. Don't trust them." Effectively, Luke is warned *not* to use the present-at-hand, but to *feel* the moment: "Remember, a Jedi can *feel* the Force flowing through him." Luke re-engages the training remote and immediately succeeds. "You know, I did feel something," Luke tells Obi-Wan. He has begun to learn that the Force is not at all a *visual* experience, but one of *feeling*, as though an energy field were flowing through him, connecting him to all things.

In the words of Yoda, Luke is beginning to "unlearn what he has learned"—and indeed, a lesson that will prove valuable later on, when Luke must battle a much greater artificial sphere: the Death Star. "Use the Force, Luke," he hears Obi-Wan's voice speaking through the Force—"Let go, Luke." Quickly approaching his final target, and remembering his early training with the remote, Luke turns off his computer-controlled targeting system (much to the worry of his team), effectively blinding himself again. Aiming *only through the Force*, he fires a perfect shot into the Death Star's core, blowing it to pieces.

Yoda as Being-in-the-Dagobah System

As great as this accomplishment is, however, Luke is not yet a Jedi Knight. He must continue his training under a new Jedi master, Yoda, who lives in the Dagobah system. Yoda appears as an organic extension of his natural environment, perhaps the best example of Heideggerian "attunement" in *Star Wars*. Yoda's "being-in-the-world" is one entirely based in the "ready-to-hand." With no technology to speak of, Yoda has only some basic equipment for cooking and living in his natural environment—and his dwelling is made of earth and mud. As a "being-in-the-world" (a being connected with his environment), Yoda lives as one with his surroundings, in perfect harmony with nature. Emerald green like the lush marshes all around him, he's similarly filled with the natural light of the Force. He's "at home" in the world, and nothing on Dagobah is "covered over"; his existence here is authentic.

Indeed, the contrast with the hard lines and right angles of the Galactic Republic is made quite explicit when Luke descends on Dagobah, covered in technology: his X-wing fighter, his high-tech uniform, his companion R2-D2, and even his food all appear very synthetic. Amused at the absurdity, Yoda asks Luke directly, "How you get so big, eating food of this kind?" None of this sort of thing is essential to Yoda—and still less is it essential for Luke's own Jedi training in the swamp. Although Yoda apparently cannot help himself from stealing Luke's little light pen: "Mine! Or I will help you not"—probably because it reminds him of the old days of the Republic and of his own lightsaber, an essential piece of Jedi technology that Yoda no longer wears on his person.

Only a few feet tall, long-eared and green, hobbling along on tridactyl feet with the aid of his Gimer stick,[8] Yoda seems harmless . . . even ridiculous. And Luke cannot, for the life of him, imagine that this pesky little creature is a great Jedi warrior (not that wars make one great, as Yoda later notes). From Luke's *still-clouded* perspective of things, Yoda is simply *too small* to be a Jedi, just as Luke's X-wing fighter is simply *too large* to retrieve from the swamp. Luke is still very young, though, and not yet well-trained in the ways of the Force—"Too much of his father in him," as Luke's perceptive Aunt Beru foresees. But before he leaves Dagobah, Luke will learn a great many things—and beginning precisely here, with his own inverted view of the world. Yoda tells Luke:

> Size matters not. Look at me. Judge me by my size, do you? Mm? Mmmm . . . And well you should not. For my ally is the Force. And a powerful ally it is. Life creates it, makes it grow. Its energy sur-

---

[8] David West Reynolds, *Star Wars: The Visual Dictionary* (New York: DK Publishing), p. 25.

rounds us and binds us . . . You must feel the Force around you. Here, between you . . . me . . . the tree . . . the rock . . . everywhere! Yes, even between the land and the ship!

This description of the Force also closely resembles Heidegger's conception of being. Like the Force, being is everywhere, all around us. It binds all the elements of the universe together: it's that which undergirds the rocks just as surely as starfighters. Yet, in being everywhere, the Force, or being, is equally nowhere. For being everywhere at once, it isn't easily locatable, which makes it so easy to forget. But we must learn to experience it through the art of the ready-to-hand and above all through meditation, as Yoda advises Luke on Dagobah. Similarly, Qui-Gon tells young Anakin that when he learns to quiet his mind and meditate, the Force will speak to him. For Heidegger, too, we must meditate on being in order for it to speak to us. For just as there is a voice of the Force, so too is there a voice of being. As Heidegger puts it, "For, strictly, it is language that speaks. Man first speaks when, and only when, he responds to language by listening to its appeal."[9] And language, according to Heidegger, is speaking as being: "Language is the house of Being. In its home man dwells."[10]

Enframing and the Eye of the Empire

Powerful as the Light Side of the Force may be, however, the Dark Side is also very strong. And those who follow its path are the Dark Lords of the Sith. Rather than emphasizing the importance of a passive and quiet, contemplative mind, the Sith are trained in aggression and technical thinking, control and domination. In a word, they're trained in the mode of the *present*-at-hand, rather than the illumined *ready*-to-hand. Instead of feeling the Force, the Sith are trained visually to control nature as a set of external objects. All of reality, on this view, is ready to be subordinated and controlled, and all for the sole purpose of increasing their power over nature. Filled with anger, filled with fear, the Dark Side of the Force—taken

---

[9] Martin Heidegger, *Poetry, Language, Thought*, translated by Albert Hofstadter (New York: Harper and Row, 1971), p. 214.
[10] See Heidegger, "Letter on Humanism," in *Basic Writings*, p. 193.

to its logical limit—is precisely what gives rise to the darkest phenomenon of reality: *enframing*.[11]

Perhaps nowhere in *Star Wars* is this combination of the present-at-hand and enframing more evident than in the Death Star. Resembling a "small moon," the Death Star is, in fact, a space station. But on even closer inspection, it actually resembles a massive artificial eyeball (much like the gigantic eye in Tolkien's *The Lord of the Rings*). It has a windowed iris and a distinct pupil, out of which Darth Vader and the Emperor watch—and the entire structure rotates to observe its territory within a massive solar socket of space. Moreover, under this present-at-hand gaze, the Empire steadily builds masses of standing reserve, most evident in the droid army and the clone factory on the ocean planet Kamino. These clones are enframed "internally" through genetic engineering, to *decrease* their autonomy and *increase* their collective thought. While later they are enframed "externally" as they are sheathed in the hard white armor and helmets of the Imperial stormtroopers. One should note here, however, that the standing reserve is not all on the Empire's side. Both sides use masses of droids and spacecraft. And the Republic (before it becomes the Empire) uses the clone army to fight the Separatists in *Attack of the Clones*.

On the other hand, the massive rise of enframing and standing reserve is hardly being directed by Yoda and Mace Windu, or even through the Light Side of the Force. Rather the Dark Side has stealthily gained control of the process of enframing without the Jedi knowing it. As Count Dooku confidently informs Obi-Wan, "The Dark Side of the Force has clouded their [the Jedis'] vision, my friend." The void of darkness is slowly but surely spreading, and extinguishing the Jedis' power to use the Force. And this applies equally to young Anakin Skywalker, the soon-to-be Darth Vader. With not a little concern about Anakin's fear of losing his mother, Yoda warns, "Clouded this boy's future is." In Heidegger's terms, this clouding of the Force by the Dark Side is precisely the covering up of being by enframing. Heidegger says, "[Being] can be covered up to such a degree that it is forgotten and the question about it and its meaning

---

[11] Martin Heidegger, "The Question Concerning Technology," in *Basic Writings*, p. 301.

altogether omitted."[12] In Anakin's case, at the very height of his own enframing, this clouding will indeed become "forgetting," as Luke rightly points out.

The Enframing of Anakin Skywalker

Anakin and his mother Shmi are slaves, both owned by Watto, a Toydarian junk dealer. And Anakin knows it's wrong. Even as a little boy, he's well aware that Watto subordinates his person-hood—evident in his first meeting with Padmé. "You're a slave?" she asks him. "I'm a *person*, and my name is Anakin!" he responds. As a slave, Anakin works on all manner of machines and is actually quite gifted in his work. He even brags to Qui-Gon that he can help fix their ship's hyperdrive, and also takes considerable pride in showing Padmé his newest creation, a protocol droid for his mother—C-3PO. But despite all his tal-ents, Anakin's powers have already been wrongly honed in the service of control. He lives in a world of high-tech tools and so many enframed things which themselves require tools. Indeed, at a very basic level, Anakin himself is Watto's own living tool, which is precisely how Aristotle defines a "slave" in the *Politics*.[13]

These distortions of slavery and the immersion in technology are the initial steps of a descent that will later spiral downward and out of control with the death of Anakin's mother at the hands of the vulgar and nomadic Sand People. Infuriated at his powerlessness to keep Shmi alive, as her poor tortured body goes limp in his arms, Anakin, aflame with rage, proceeds to slaughter the entire community of Sand People (including the women and children). Trying to console him, Padmé clumsily explains that Shmi's death was not his fault: "You're not all-pow-erful." But furious, Anakin insists, "Well I *should* be. Someday I will be. I will be the most powerful Jedi ever." At this point, Anakin's early technological skills and interests become obses-sions for control and manipulation. Perhaps once he wanted to

---

[12] Heidegger, *Being and Time*, p. 31.

[13] See Aristotle, *Politics*, Book I, Chapter 4, 1253b20–35, in *The Basic Works of Aristotle*, translated by Richard McKeon (New York: Random House, 1941), p. 1131. For more of Aristotle's theory of technology, see his *Physics*, Book II, Chapter 1, 192b10–193b20, in *Basic Works*, pp. 236–38.

free the slaves (as he told Qui-Gon he had dreamed) and be the "shepherd of being"—as Heidegger means "shepherd" in the sense not only of "caring for," but also "setting free." But *now* he is on the path to becoming the "lord of beings" in the form of Lord Vader.

His rage has permanently unbalanced him, and this is nowhere more evident than in his futile charging attack on Count Dooku against Obi-Wan's desperate warning. Ultimately, Yoda rescues Anakin and Obi-Wan from the powerful Sith Lord, but Anakin has lost his arm to Dooku's lightsaber. Severed from his natural ready-to-hand relation, his natural being-in-the-world is now robotically mediated through an artificial hand attached to a cyborg arm. As a result of his thoughtless fury, Anakin has now shifted from the ready-to-hand (a *natural* hand-link to the Force and humanity) to the present-at-hand (the *artificial* hand-link to the Dark Side).

And this is only the beginning. His next step toward becoming fully enframed is brought about by Obi-Wan himself, Anakin's teacher. Following a violent battle of lightsabers between the two, Anakin is left severely maimed and his biological body is no longer capable of sustaining itself on its own. After an extensive robotic rebuilding of his body, Anakin now wears a full suit of black armor and a helmet with a mask covering his entire face. His senses are now all artificially mediated through technology, while he is fed through an internal tube in his helmet. Virtually everything vital has been replaced: his spine, his internal organs—his entire experience of the world is completely mediated by artifice. Even his voice is translated through a computer; while his breathing is controlled by an internal ventilator: "He's more machine now than man. Twisted and evil." And this new machine of a man is a terribly imposing figure, to say the least. Only later are we given a rare voyeuristic look into the layers of Vader's enframing. In *The Empire Strikes Back* an Imperial officer accidentally witnesses Vader privately "dressing." We even see his pale human skin (kept private from the light) and his awful mutilated skull—but only for a second as a quick robotic arm plunges down his helmet. Freshly closed to the world, Vader now commands the officer, only to turn away as the top of his demonic black nest closes down all around him.

Ultimately, this same process of descent into enframing happens to Luke as well, whose hand is severed by Vader and replaced with a robotic hand. And even later, Vader loses his hand *again* to Luke's lightsaber. But upon cutting off Vader's robotic hand, Luke notices his own robotic hand (covered by a black glove similar to Vader's). Luke now understands Yoda's earlier concern—he may yet follow the same path:

> YODA: A Jedi's strength flows from the Force. But beware of the Dark Side. Anger . . . fear . . . aggression. The Dark Side of the Force are they. Easily they flow, quick to join you in a fight. If once you start down the dark path, forever will it dominate your destiny, consume you it will, as it did Obi-Wan's apprentice.
> LUKE: Vader. Is the Dark Side stronger?
> YODA: No . . . no . . . no. Quicker, easier, more seductive.

We hear the same worry from Obi-Wan: "Vader was seduced by the Dark Side of the Force." Indeed, the Dark Side's powers are incredibly intense, as Vader tries to explain to Luke: "You don't know the *power* of the Dark Side." In the end, however, Luke does not succumb. And his own artificial enframing remains relatively minimal compared to Vader's.

Only a Jedi Can Save Us: Forgetting and Recollecting

Vader's enframing is, to be sure, all but complete. His being-in-the-world is so artificially mediated, so incredibly distorted, that he no longer fully *understands* what it is he's doing—or *why*. No longer human, he has entirely lost touch with himself. It's true that Vader may not have forgotten the question of being in general, as Heidegger conceives it. But clearly he has forgotten *something*. He has, at the very least, forgotten the man he used to be. And beyond that, in a very Heideggerian sense, he has equally forgotten his own original being-in-the-world—indeed he has even forgotten his own name. Luke makes exactly this point to Vader, when he calls him by his original name, "Anakin Skywalker." Vader (irritated) scolds Luke: "That name no longer has any meaning for me." But Luke persists: "It is the name of your true self. You've only forgotten." And he has forgotten precisely because of his detachment from the being of the Force and his horrible descent into the darkness of enframing.

And now, at the end of the saga, it would indeed appear, with Vader's almost complete forgetfulness, that only a god can save him.[14] Only there is conspicuous absence of God or gods in the *Star Wars* galaxy—although "angels" apparently reside in deep space and the Ewoks mistake Threepio for a god. Nevertheless, Vader is ultimately saved by the semi-divine power of the Force and through the actions of Luke. Inspired by Luke's dedication to him, Vader begins to remember. He returns to himself and becomes Anakin Skywalker once again. Now with his "own eyes" he vanquishes the Emperor and turns his back on the Dark Side of the Force. But while his soul is saved, his body/machine is badly broken and he succumbs to death— although not before asking Luke to take off his horrible mask and "uncover" his true being from the shroud of artifice. The layers of enframing are at last peeled back to reveal the man. His spirits recharged, Luke has not come this far to watch his father die in the Death Star (only moments from destruction). "I've got to save you," he declares. But Anakin knows all too well, "You already have, Luke."[15]

---

[14] Heidegger writes: "Saving does not only snatch something from a danger. To save really means to set something free into its own essence. To save the earth is more than to exploit it or even wear it out. Saving the earth does not master the earth and does not subjugate it, which is merely one step from boundless spoliation" ("Building Dwelling Thinking," in *Basic Writings*, p. 328).

[15] I would like to thank Bill Irwin, Jason Eberl, Kevin Decker, and Elizabeth Cooke for reading and commenting on an earlier draft of this chapter, and Chris Pliatska for many discussions of *Star Wars*.

10

"If Droids Could Think . . .": Droids as Slaves and Persons

ROBERT ARP

Years ago, I watched *A New Hope* with a blind person named Mary. She asked if I could describe to her what was going on throughout the movie. After the Twentieth Century Fox fanfare ended and the wonderful John Williams soundtrack began, I read the opening paragraphs to her. What happened after the next few scenes was fascinating. She listened to C-3PO's opening dialogue where he says somewhat frantically, "Did you hear that? They shut down the main reactor. We'll be destroyed for sure! This is madness! We're doomed ..." However, before I could describe the scene to her, Mary asked me, "What does that *man* look like?" I told her it was not a man, but a *droid*—a gold-plated robot who looks like a man. She paused a moment and continued, "Oh . . . It sounded just like a man." Being naturally inquisitive, I asked Mary what made her think that C-3PO was a man. Her response was that C-3PO used language, and had expressed the emotions of fear and concern.

My exchange with Mary was fascinating for two reasons. First, if I were blind, and a robot approached me on the street and started talking to me the way C-3PO does—with all of his over-dramatizing of events, expressions of reluctance, and name-calling—most likely I would think a human being was talking to me. Second, my exchange with Mary made me re-think Threepio's role as a protocol droid built to serve other human beings in a slavish capacity. If C-3PO looks and acts like a person—if he uses language, has certain advanced cognitive skills, is aware of his surroundings, and can feel emotions and express concerns—then what really separates him from actually being a person, other than his silicon and metallic innards and appearance? Furthermore, if he could qualify as a person, then shouldn't such a robot be granted the same kinds of rights and privileges as any other human being who qualifies as a person? If droids meet the conditions for personhood, I question whether they should be granted at least *limited* rights and privileges, including the ability to choose to work in the *Star Wars* galaxy, as opposed to being slavishly "made to suffer, it's our lot in life" (to use Threepio's words) at the hands of biological persons.

"He's Quite Clever, You Know . . . For a Human Being"

The first thing we need to do is get at the fundamental nature or essence of what it means to be a person. So, what is the definition of a person? A person is a being who has the capacity for (1) reason or rationality; (2) mental states like beliefs, intentions, desires, and emotions; (3) language; (4) entering into social relationships with other persons; and (5) being considered a responsible moral agent.[1]

Before asking whether droids meet these criteria—and if so, which droids—we should consider the matter of whether a body is absolutely necessary in order to be considered a person. Among the criteria for personhood just given, there is no mention of a physical body. Important implications can be drawn from this omission. First, what it means to be a person is not tied directly to having an intact bodily existence. Take someone like the famous physicist Stephen Hawking. Here is a man whose body is ravaged by disease, is confined to a wheelchair, and needs machines in order to communicate. Yet, we would still consider him a person because, despite his bodily limitations, he fulfills criteria (1)–(5). He does this because his *brain* is still

---

[1] See John Locke, *An Essay Concerning Human Understanding* (Oxford: Clarendon, 1975 [1694]), Book 2, Chapter 27; John Barresi, "On Becoming a Person," *Philosophical Psychology* 12 (1999), pp. 79–98; Daniel Dennett, *Brainstorms* (Montgomery: Bradford, 1978); Derek Parfit, *Reasons and Persons* (New York: Oxford University Press, 1984); Scott Glynn, *Identity, Intersubjectivity, and Communicative Action* (Athens: Paideia Project, 2000).

functioning properly and his cognitive capacities remain intact. He reasons, feels, communicates (albeit, with the help of machines), and has been able to form strong social bonds in the scientific community, as well as in his personal life. So, on the face of it, it appears that *cognitive capacities* are what to look for when trying to discern whether a being qualifies as a person, and the brain, or something that functions like the brain, is the seat of this cognitive capacity.[2]

If bodily existence is downplayed and cognitive capacities are what really count when defining a person, then droids like C-3PO and R2-D2 could be considered persons, provided their cognitive capacities are the same as other persons. We naturally think that persons will be biological entities with brains who breathe air, metabolize carbohydrates, and take in water for nourishment. Right now, however, it's possible to simulate various biological parts of bodies artificially; there are artificial hearts, artificial kidneys, and even artificial eyes.

Suppose that a scientist develops an artificial occipital lobe (the back part of the brain) out of silicon and metal, and implants it into the brain of an adult female human being. The artificial lobe performs the same functions that a natural occipital lobe performs: it processes visual information from the environment. So, with her artificial lobe she can do the same thing that she could do with her natural lobe—she can see the world around her. Say that the scientist develops artificial silicon and metallic parts of the brain responsible for memory, and implants these into our subject's brain. She now can store and recall memories with the artificial parts of the brain in the same way she could with her natural parts. Now, say the scientist develops an artificial silicon and metal *brain in its entirety*, and implants it into our subject. With this artificial brain, she can do all of the

---

[2] Most thinkers doing work in psychology, philosophy of mind, and the neurosciences subscribe to the idea that "the mind is what the brain does." Those doing work in artificial intelligence alter this by saying that "the mind is what *something that functions like* the brain does." Since personhood is an extension of one's mind, it is safe to say that for these folks *personhood* is what the brain (or something that functions like it) does as well. See Daniel Dennett, *Consciousness Explained* (Boston: Little, Brown, 1991); Hans Hermans *et al.*, "The Dialogical Self: Beyond Individualism and Rationalism," *American Psychologist* 47 (1992), pp. 23–33; Eric Kandel *et al.*, eds., *Principles of Neural Science* (New York: McGraw-Hill, 2000).

same things she did before her transplant; she lives, loves, lies, and meets all of the criteria for personhood. Would she actually *be* a person, however, given that her brain is *robotic?* Say the scientist can simulate all parts of her body with silicon and metal, and thus replaces her biological body with a robotic body. She now is fully a robotic being with all of the same hopes, fears, responsibilities, loyalties, and so on, as any other human being. Would she (or should we say *it?*) actually be a person?

It seems possible to simulate the mental capacities necessary for personhood through physical things other than the brain. Why would one *need* to have a brain in order to think, believe, feel, experience, and the like, if such cognitive capacities can be simulated by other means? Think of an android like Data in *Star Trek: The Next Generation*, or the replicants in the movie *Blade Runner*, or the synthetics like Bishop (as Bishop says they prefer to be called) in the *Alien* movies. These are examples of beings that act like persons, yet the internal workings of their "brains" consist of a series of silicon and metallic connections, or other artificial systems, that are very different from the gray matter of the brain. So it seems that a functioning brain, or something that *functions like* a brain, with all of the cognitive capacities associated with such functioning, is the most important thing to consider when determining whether something qualifies as a person.[3]

"If Droids Could Think, There'd Be None of Us Here, Would There?"

Now we can address the question as to whether droids qualify as persons. The first qualification has to do with the capacity for reason or rationality. In one sense, reasoning is the same thing as *intelligence*, and involves a variety of capacities, including (a) calculating; (b) making associations between present stimuli and stored memories; (c) problem solving; and (d) drawing new

---

[3] See Dennett, *Consciousness Explained*; Ned Block, "Troubles with Functionalism," in Ned Block, ed., *Readings in the Philosophy of Psychology*, Volume 1 (Cambridge, Massachusetts: Harvard University Press, 1980), pp. 268–305; Philip Johnson-Laird, *Mental Models* (Cambridge: Cambridge University Press, 1983); and Paul Churchland, *Matter and Consciousness: A Contemporary Introduction to the Philosophy of Mind* (Cambridge, Massachusetts: MIT Press, 1984).

conclusions or inferences from old information.[4] Do droids qualify as rational or intelligent in these senses?

Droids obviously make calculations. In *The Empire Strikes Back*, C-3PO lets Han Solo know that the odds of successfully navigating an asteroid field are approximately 3,720 to one against. Also, in *The Phantom Menace* Droidekas judge distances while rolling up to, and firing their lasers at, Qui-Gon and Obi-Wan aboard the Trade Federation ship. Droids also have memory storage capabilities, and can recall memories based upon present stimuli. When Jabba's droid manager, EV-9D9, notes that R2-D2 will make a fine addition to Jabba's sail barge crew, he can do so only because he has a memory of the barge, the crew, the work detail, as well as a capacity to associate Artoo's actions with the barge, crew, and work detail. C-3PO knows "six million forms of communication," has been on many adventures with Artoo, and is able to recount his past experiences to Luke—he even recounts the story of the previous *Star Wars* films to the Ewoks in *Return of the Jedi*. Furthermore, droids can solve problems. In *Return of the Jedi*, Artoo takes the initiative to open the door to the command center on Endor while he, Leia, and Han are under attack by stormtroopers. Artoo performs similar mechanical problem-solving when he gets the Millennium Falcon's hyperdrive to work in *The Empire Strikes Back* and the Naboo Royal Starship's shields up to escape the Trade Federation blockade in *The Phantom Menace*.

Finally, droids seem to be able to reason by deductively drawing conclusions and making inferences. Think of the holographic chess game played between Artoo and Chewbacca on board the Millennium Falcon in *A New Hope*, and Han's comment that "droids don't pull people's arms out of their sockets when they lose. Wookiees are known to do that." C-3PO comes to the conclusion that Artoo should choose "a new strategy. Let the Wookiee win." This conclusion is arrived at by a process of reasoning that goes something like this:

[4] See George Boolos and Robert Jeffrey, *Computability and Logic* (Cambridge: Cambridge University Press, 1989), and James Robert Brown, *The Laboratory of the Mind: Thought Experiments in the Natural Sciences* (London: Routledge, 1991).

1) Premise 1: If Artoo wins, my arms will be pulled out of their sockets.
2) Premise 2: I don't want my arms pulled out of their sockets.
3) Conclusion: Thus, Artoo should let the Wookiee win.

Artoo also displays some clever deductive reasoning in his first conversation with Luke. He deceives Luke into removing his restraining bolt by falsely claiming that its removal will enable the image of Princess Leia to return, knowing how much Luke would want to see the entire message. The little manipulator appears to have reasoned his actions through quite well.

"I Am Fluent in Over Six Million Forms of Communication"

Just because something can reason does not mean that it is a person. A computer can be trained to reason in the same way that C-3PO does with Chewbacca, or Artoo does with Luke—making step-by-step calculations—yet, we would not consider a computer a person because of this capacity alone.[5] Persons have the capacity for mental states and language. Mental states are a part of a human being's psychological life and include such things as holding a belief, having a desire, feeling a pain, or experiencing some event.[6]

Probably the best way to understand what a mental state consists of is to close your eyes and think about experiences where you felt some pain, jumped for joy, or regretted a decision you made. First, think about the pain you experienced. Maybe it had to do with touching something that was very hot. Recall how that pain was all-consuming for its duration, how it lingered in your body, and how you thought, "Ow! That *hurt!*" (and maybe expressed some other choice intergalactic expletives). That was *your* pain, and no one else's; only *you* could know what that pain was like. Only Han knows what his pain is like when the hydrospanners fall on his head in *The Empire*

---

[5] See Hubert Dreyfus, *What Computers Can't Do* (New York: Harper and Row, 1979).
[6] See David Chalmers, *The Conscious Mind: In Search of a Fundamental Theory* (New York: Oxford University Press), pp. 6–11.

Strikes Back. All we can know is that he experienced pain based on his vocal expression: "Ow! . . . Chewie!"

Now, recall a time when you felt joy and elation over some accomplishment of your own or of someone else's, like winning an award, or your favorite team scoring the winning goal in the last seconds of the game. Recall the experience: how you smiled, relished the moment, and wished that every moment could be like this one. Only Luke and Han know the joy of receiving a medal for heroism from the beautiful Princess Leia at the end of *A New Hope*—poor Chewie doesn't get to have that experience himself.

Finally, think of a decision you made that you have come to regret. You believe now that you could have made a different, better decision back then. And now, having thought about it, it may cause you pain. Surely many such regrets passed through the dying Anakin Skywalker's mind after his redemption at the end of *Return of the Jedi*.

These three experiences seem to get at the idea of a mental state because they entail beliefs, emotions, desires, and intentions. It would seem that only members of the human race experience such mental states. We don't have any evidence of other animals realizing that their pain is *their* pain, relishing moments, thinking back to past events with regret, or looking forward to future events with joy and anticipation.[7]

The capacity for language is another qualification for being considered a person. Language is a tricky thing to understand, and many people think that each kind of animal has its own language, including bees, ants, apes, dolphins, and even Tauntauns (just to name a few). We must distinguish, though, between *communicating some information* and *speaking a language*. Whereas communicating some information does not require having mental states, speaking a language does entail mental states. When speaking a language, it seems that more than mere information is communicated; beliefs, desires, intentions, hopes, dreams, fears, and the like are relayed from one person to another.

Many beings can communicate information by relaying some useful data back and forth to one another. All animals do this to

---

[7] See George Roth and Michael Wullimann, *Brain, Evolution, and Cognition* (Cambridge: Cambridge University Press, 2001).

some extent. A bee is not *speaking* to another bee when doing his little bee dance in order to communicate information about where pollen is located outside of the hive. I know this is going to sound controversial, but even apes who have been taught sign-language are not speaking (using a language) to their trainers; they merely are associating stimuli with stored memories. As far as we know, no bees or apes have experiences of joy, hope, or anticipation to communicate.

Do droids have capacities for mental states and language? There are plenty of examples of droids *apparently* engaged in behaviors expressive of mental states and language. One glaring example is the torturing of a droid at Jabba the Hutt's palace in *Return of the Jedi*. When the droid's "feet" are burned, the little guy appears to know what is going on, anticipates the pain he's going to experience, and screams in pain and terror when the hot iron is lowered. (Interestingly enough, one also gets the sense that the droid administering the torture is enjoying what he's doing.)

C-3PO expresses emotions himself on numerous occasions. Before getting into an escape pod with Artoo he claims, "I'm going to regret this." On Tatooine he despairs, "How did we get into this mess ... We seem to be made to suffer; it's our lot in life." After reuniting with Artoo in the Jawa sandcrawler, Threepio exclaims, "R2-D2! It *is* you! It *is* you!" When Luke comes back to discover Artoo has gone off to look for Obi-Wan Kenobi, he finds Threepio hiding (expressive of shame) and begging not to be deactivated (expressive of fear). When Luke returns to Yavin Four after destroying the Death Star, and Threepio realizes that Artoo has been damaged, he offers his own body parts in order to save his little friend. In *The Empire Strikes Back*, C-3PO expresses sorrow and reverence when Luke cannot be located before the main doors of the Hoth outpost are shut for the night (because Luke likely will freeze to death), frustration at having Han's hand placed over his mouth in order to shut him up, as well as fear before being shot by stormtroopers on Cloud City.

C-3PO exhibits many more examples of anticipation, fear, anger, joy, as well as put-downs ("you near-sighted scrap-pile" and "overweight glob of grease," directed toward Artoo) and passive aggression ("fine, go that way, you'll be malfunctioning in a day," again directed toward Artoo). Threepio and Artoo

share a very human-like, *person*able relationship wrought with
the same kinds of normal, as well as abnormal, communication
that any person may have in relationships. This is probably why
we find them so appealing as characters—sometimes more so
than the actual human characters in the films. Think of the brief
exchange between Threepio and Artoo in *A New Hope* after
Luke leaves for dinner with his aunt and uncle, Artoo asks C-
3PO if Luke "likes him" and C-3PO responds, "No, I don't think
he likes you at all. (Plaintive whistle from Artoo). No! I don't like
you either." It's an adorable scene to the viewer precisely
because the communication is tongue-in-cheek and somewhat
dysfunctional. It would seem that this kind of communication
takes place only between beings having true mental states.

Besides having and expressing emotions, droids also seem to
have beliefs about themselves, others, and the world around
them. And they act on those beliefs whether it is to save themselves, aid others, or engage in other kinds of actions. Put
another way, they appear to be *free* in their actions precisely
because they form beliefs and can act on those beliefs. In *A New
Hope*, while stormtroopers are searching Mos Eisley, C-3PO
holds the belief that if Artoo locks the door to the room in which
they are hiding, then the stormtroopers will check the door, note
that it is locked, and move on. Sure enough, that's exactly what
happens and Threepio's belief is ratified. When Artoo is roam-
ing by himself on Tatooine near caves where Jawas are hiding,
he holds the belief that danger is near, adjusts his direction, and
rotates his head back and forth to keep an eye out for the sus-
pected danger. He engages in these actions precisely because he
holds the *belief* that danger is near.

Finally, droids have the capacity for language. When Artoo
beeps a series of electronic sounds into Luke's computer on
board his X-wing fighter, or to Threepio for translation, this isn't
merely an expression of data communication. Language is
dependent upon and expressive of true mental states. It would
appear that droids have mental states, and so when they communicate it would appear that what's being communicated constitutes linguistic expression, and not simply data transference.
Droids want other droids and other beings to *understand* what
they are communicating. I want you to understand what I'm
experiencing, feeling, thinking, and the like, when I speak to
you. So too, when Threepio tries to reassure Luke that Artoo is

a reliable droid (while the two are being sold by the Jawas), he wants Luke to *understand* where he's coming from in terms of his beliefs about Artoo being a "real bargain."

"You've Been a Great Pal . . . I'll Make Sure Mom Doesn't Sell You"

Do droids have the capacity to enter into social relationships with other persons? Social relationships can be divided into: (a) family relationships, such as Luke's relationship with his Uncle Owen and Aunt Beru; (b) economic relationships, such as Han Solo or Boba Fett's relationship with Jabba the Hutt; (c) allegiance relationships, such as those among the multi-species members of the Rebel Alliance; and (d) civil relationships, such as the relationship among the citizens of Naboo, and between them and their elected queen.[8] In each one of these relationships, one finds duties, rights, laws, and obligations that would be appropriate to each relationship. For example, in a family a parent has a duty to take care of a child, and one of the fundamental "laws" in such a relationship is unconditional love. In economic transactions, the fundamental obligation is to the "bottom line" of staying in the black, and the law may include something like "let the buyer beware" or "don't drop your spice shipment at the first sign of an Imperial cruiser." In civil relationships, rights and laws are utilized in the most commonly understood way so as to protect citizens from harm, and ensure the prospering of societies as a whole.

On the face of it, it would seem that droids don't have the capacity to enter into any one of these relationships. After all, they don't have families, they seem to be barred from economic transactions ("We don't serve their kind here," declares the bartender at the Mos Eisley cantina), they aren't a part of any "droid" interest groups, and they definitely aren't citizens who bear any rights in either the Republic or the Rebel Alliance. However, two scenes in *The Empire Strikes Back* make it possible to believe that a kind of familial relationship can be fostered between a droid and a non-droid. First, we note the care and

---

[8] See Mark Hollis, *The Philosophy of the Social Sciences* (Cambridge: Cambridge University Press, 1994), and Ronald Lipsey, *Introduction to Positive Economics* (New York: Harper and Row, 1972).

concern Chewie takes when he tries to put C-3PO back together in the cell on Cloud City, and later when he straps C-3PO to his back so as not to abandon him while he and Leia try to free Han and flee from Vader. There is also Luke's reaction to Artoo's falling into the swamp after they land on Dagobah. Luke expresses shock, concern, and is even willing to fight to save Artoo from being eaten by whatever monster sucked him up (and subsequently spit him out). The care expressed in both of these cases is analogous to the care a father might have for his son, or an older brother might have for a younger brother. These characters form a kind of family.

Droids also seem to care for their "masters," as in *The Empire Strikes Back* when Artoo sits at the foot of the door probing for Luke who is lost out in the cold on Hoth, or in *Attack of the Clones* when C-3PO's head realizes (to his shock!) that his battle droid body is shooting at friendly Jedi in the arena on Geonosis: "I'm terribly sorry about all of this!" This indicates, at the very least, a rudimentary reciprocal social relationship.

Yet, droids are exploited. They are treated as little more than pieces of machinery—slaves whose purpose is to serve non-droids. Threepio and Artoo are hunted down, fitted with restraining bolts, and sold by Jawas into slavery. And Threepio refers to his previous "master" when giving his work history to Luke in their initial conversation. Droids lack the rights and responsibilities afforded to other beings such as humans and Wookiees, as well as fish-headed and hammerheaded creatures in the *Star Wars* galaxy.

Given what we know about droids such as Artoo and Threepio, it is unfortunate that they are treated as slaves. Droids communicate, have the capacity for reason, and can be involved in complex social relationships. More importantly, they express feelings of disillusion, contempt, pain, and suffering, as well as joy, satisfaction, and contentment. A being that has these traits appears to have mental states, and such a being is arguably a person, regardless of having been created by persons.

Maybe it's time for droid liberation in the *Star Wars* galaxy, in much the same way that other groups of people who have been unjustly enslaved throughout human history have been liberated. Of course, if droids were liberated, then they would need to establish their own social relationships, ways to propagate, moral laws, and the like, for themselves. At the same time, there would need to be adjustments made in the existing social spheres of the *Star Wars* galaxy to accommodate droid needs and wants, and to mainstream them into existing social spheres, in much the same way Wookiees, Gungans, and other creatures have been incorporated.

It's *Not* Our Lot in Life!

I have a proposal to make. Droids appear to meet the qualifications for personhood, so droids should be granted *limited* rights and privileges. The practical specifics of what that means would need to be worked out by the Galactic Senate. However, such limited rights and privileges minimally would include the *choice* to work for human beings, as opposed to being slavishly "made to suffer, it's our lot in life" (to use Threepio's words in *A New Hope*) at the hands of humans. I realize, however, that giving them the choice to work for humans probably means that we would be granting them a person-like status, in which case we are well on our way to recognizing droids as deserving of the same kinds of rights and privileges afforded to any other person.

The case can be made that droids are an oppressed group in the *Star Wars* galaxy. Perhaps we ought to cheer for a *droid* rebellion against an *organic* empire? The issue of treating droids as persons may seem silly to talk about because, after all, *it's just a make-believe story!* As history has proven, though, science *fiction* has a way of becoming science *fact*. The famous robotics engineer and theorist, Hans Moravec, claims that by 2050 robots actually will surpass humans in intellectual capacity.[9] The way in which advances in computer and robotic technology are being made at an astronomical rate gives us cause to pause and consider that, in the not-so-distant future, there most likely will be advanced forms of machinery that behave much like C-3PO and R2-D2. How then, will the organic community react? How should such non-organic persons who seem to behave like organic persons be treated?

---

[9] Hans Moravec, *Robot: Mere Machine to Transcendent Mind* (New York: Oxford University Press, 1999), pp. 58–61.

11

"Size Matters Not": The Force as the Causal Power of the Jedi

JAN-ERIK JONES

Before Luke meets Obi-Wan Kenobi, his life is relatively uneventful. The only thing he wants is to leave Tatooine and enroll at the Academy. While living on his Uncle Owen's farm he has no idea of the kind of power he has at his disposal. As fate would have it, Luke and Obi-Wan meet and his odyssey to help restore balance to the Force begins.

The Force, Obi-Wan tells us "is what gives the Jedi his power. It's an energy field created by all living things. It surrounds us and penetrates us. It binds the galaxy together." The appeal of the Force to viewers of *Star Wars* is that it gives the Jedi power over the physical world in ways that defy the natural order of events with which we are familiar. In our world, lifting an X-wing fighter from a swamp would require more than mental focus and control over our emotions. And as Qui-Gon, Obi-Wan, and Yoda teach Anakin and Luke about the Force and how to use it, we can't help but wish we had that kind of power over our environment.

The reason why the Force in *Star Wars* has such a grip on the viewer's imagination is because it makes us ask the fundamental metaphysical questions that have driven science and philosophy from the beginning; questions about cause and effect, the laws of nature, the possibility of foreknowledge, and the relationship between the mind and the physical world.

The Source of the Jedi's Power

The Force is described in two very different ways in *Star Wars*. First, Obi-Wan describes it as an omnipresent energy field created by all living things that binds the galaxy together. Obi-Wan thus makes it sound as if the Force *depends* on living things for its existence, while *causing* the galaxy itself to cohere. Indeed, this latter feature of it makes it sounds like one of the fundamental causal laws of the universe, akin to gravity or electromagnetism.

Qui-Gon Jinn, on the other hand, tells us that there are some symbionts, called "midi-chlorians," that live in large concentrations in potential Jedi and convey the *will* of the Force to their host. If Qui-Gon is right, the Force has some sort of *awareness* and a will or preference about how things go in the universe. The Force also provides the Jedi with (among other powers) occasional glimpses into the future and gives them their unique psychokinetic power—the ability to move things with their minds.

While these two accounts are not irreconcilable, the Force, as described by both, plays at least two roles: it explains the Jedi's special knowledge and it's a causal power. While both of these issues have a long and interesting philosophical history, I'll limit myself to discussing the latter: "What is the nature of causation?" And, perhaps, the answer to this might allow us to speculate on the nature of the Force.

We know that causes and effects are all around us. And we've learned to predict how objects will behave from observing some typical cause and effect interactions. But one thing that we learn from fantastical sci-fi inventions like the Force is that there could be kinds of causes and effects that are so foreign to us that we'd have no idea *how* they work, even though we'd recognize them *as* causes and effects. We thus have to ask ourselves what is required for something to be a real cause of an effect.

When we use the words "cause and effect," we refer to a specific kind of relationship between two or more objects, but just what do we mean by the word "cause" that makes it apply to both familiar and unfamiliar (sci-fi) cases? And if we can answer this, then we'll also have an answer to the question of what the difference is between a true cause of an effect and a mere coincidence.

We might say that since causes and effects are part of our scientific vocabulary, then we should look to science to answer this question. After all, who would know more about causes and effects better than the people who deal with them professionally? And surely a scientist can tell the difference between a true cause and a mere coincidence!

While this is a natural response, I should point out that even though scientists talk of cause and effect, the concept of causation itself is a philosophical one. What it means to say that some event *caused* another event has to be determined *before* the scientist can employ the term "cause" in any theory; for the meaning of "cause" is not understood as the result of experimental data or any amount of measuring. Rather, since experiments and measurements are means of identifying or understanding the causes of specific phenomena, the term itself must be understood before we can make any measurements or experiments.

How, then, has philosophical analysis helped us understand what the term "cause" means? This very question was addressed by both the Scottish philosopher David Hume and the German philosopher Gottfried Leibniz. Indeed, their attempts to analyze the concepts of "causation" and "force" led them to conclude that we cannot possibly possess scientific knowledge of these concepts. The reasons why will take us to the heart of why the Force in *Star Wars* so thoroughly captivates our imagination; we seem to recognize causes even if we have no way of explaining how they work. But in order to see how we arrive at this startling conclusion, we must begin by looking at what we think causes are and why the Force is a cause.

"Size Matters Not"

The Force is a special power that allows the Jedi to act on parts of the world without being in physical contact with those objects. It allows them to move rocks, spaceships, lightsabers, and droids, apparently by using only the mind. And unlike physical and mechanical forces in our world, the size of the objects moved doesn't matter; as Yoda puts it, "Size matters not." These objects, we suppose, wouldn't behave that way without the Jedi being there and willing them to behave that way. So the

Force is part of the cause of these events. But the question remains, "What is a *cause?*"

When we think of a cause, we usually think of an object or event that produces some kind of change; the cause of Alderaan's destruction is the Death Star. But causes also explain non-changing states as well; we speak of the cause of one's health or the cause of the world's existence. So causes are part of our explanations for why things are the way they are, and why things undergo the changes they do. But what makes some event a case of causation rather than mere chance? There has to be some set of conditions that must be met in order to be a true cause. Here's where David Hume comes in.

David Hume (1711–1776)[1] points out that a true cause has three features: temporal priority—the cause comes before the effect; contact—the cause must be in physical contact with what it effects; and there must be a *necessary connection* between the cause and effect—some law-like connection or reason why the event we call "the cause" *must always* produce the event we call "the effect."

A necessary connection between cause and effect is the kind of connection that would not only rule out coincidence, but would show why the effect *must* be the result of the cause; so that if we knew everything about the cause, we could deduce with perfect accuracy exactly what the effect would be. For example, if the motion in the cue-ball is the cause of the motion in the two-ball that it hits, then there must be a necessary connection between the motion of the cue-ball and the resulting motion in the two-ball. So if we knew what that necessary connection was, then we could tell long before it happened exactly how and why the cue-ball would affect the two-ball, even if we'd never seen any billiard balls collide before. If there were a necessary connection between Luke's willing for his lightsaber in the ice cave on Hoth and the motion of the lightsaber to his hand, then, if we had a knowledge of that connection, we would know (prior to seeing it happen) how and why the lightsaber would fly to his hand. Necessary connections are part of the explanations of how and why causes produce their effects.

---

[1] See David Hume, *Treatise on Human Nature*, edited by L.A. Selby-Bigge and P.H. Nidditch (Oxford: Clarendon, 1992), Book I, Part iii, §§ii–vi.

Hume then asks, "What observations do we have of necessary connections between events?" None. According to Hume, we have no knowledge of causes and effects because we have no knowledge of the most important ingredient: the necessary connection between them.

What we observe when we see, for example, a moving cue-ball approaching a stationary billiard ball, is the motion of the cue-ball, followed by contact between the balls, and then the motion in the second ball. But no matter how closely or frequently we examine these events, we'll never observe the necessary connection between them. We never observe that feature of their interaction that makes it so that the second ball *must* move when contacted by the moving cue-ball—it's entirely possible that the second ball won't move at all after the collision.

The lack of knowledge of any necessary connections means that, no matter how many times we observe the same thing, we can still imagine the second ball not moving after the collision. As Hume puts it, "From the mere repetition of any past impression, even to infinity, there will never arise any new original idea, such as that of a necessary connexion."[2] All we observe is that one kind of event is constantly followed by another kind of event; and so we develop a habit of expecting some kinds of events from the observation of others. Yet there's no absurdity or impossibility in the typical effect not occurring when the familiar cause does. (Quantum physics tell us that the same causal conditions can have different effects at different times.)

Since, according to Hume, we never observe the necessary connection between cause and effect, we have no knowledge of causation, just a habit of expecting certain kinds of events to be followed by other kinds of events. Causation is thus a mysterious concept. After all, how does the mass of the earth cause the moon to stay in orbit, or cause earthly objects to fall? How does a magnet attract iron to it? Describing the causal mechanism in these kinds of interactions as a *force* fails to explain *how* that force does what it does. And in these cases, not only is the necessary connection unobserved, but contact between the objects appears to be missing too!

---

[2] *Ibid.*, Book I, Part iii, §vi.

No matter how many times we see Jedi toppling legions of battle droids with the flick of their hands, we'll never observe the necessary connection between the motion in the Jedi's hands and the toppling of the battle droids. We'll only observe that the one kind of event is followed by the other. But this doesn't show us that they are necessarily connected. After all, experience tells us that hand-flicking and the toppling of objects at a distance is not typical!

The Force in *Star Wars* violates our expectations because it too operates in ways quite mysterious to us. It's by the use of the Force that Luke draws his out-of-reach lightsaber to his hand in the wampa's ice cave on Hoth. This kind of attractive force is just as mystifying to us as some of the causation we regularly experience, like gravity. So why can't we lift a spacecraft from a swamp with our minds alone? What prevents that in our universe?

The Power that Keeps On Giving

We learned from Hume that no observation can amount to observation of a true cause. All we have is the habit of expecting things to behave in a certain way. But what if we decided that Hume is wrong? What if we said that "the reason causes produce their effects in the case of the billiard balls is that the cue-ball transfers its motion to the ball it hits"? The problem with this, however, is that, as Gottfried Leibniz (1646–1716) shows us, this concept of transferring motion is just as problematic as the alleged necessary connection. Leibniz, one of the inventors of calculus and a contributor to the scientific revolution of the seventeenth century, argued that the concept of causation between distinct substances is incoherent.

Since Aristotle, one of the fundamental philosophical and scientific concepts has been "substance." To be a substance is to be a *thing* with properties. For example, we might describe Yoda as a substance because he is a thing that has properties, such as being old and green, and a thing that moves, talks, is conscious, has a body, and is capable of moral reasoning. These properties depend on the existence of a *thing* which has them. If the substance of Yoda were annihilated, then there would be nothing to have these "Yoda" properties; there must be something to *be* old, green, in motion, conscious, and so on.

So substances are things that have properties, and properties depend on substances for their existence.

According to Leibniz, the concept of causation includes the transfer of motion or other properties from one substance (a cue-ball) to another substance (a two-ball). This means that causation is a kind of giving. So, in addition to the concept of substance, we need the further concept of *causation as giving*. We often think of a cause as an object giving its own properties to another object—the particles in a lightsaber give some of their motion to the particles of metal in a blast-door causing it to heat up. It follows then that causes must have the properties they give to their effects; a lightsaber cannot cause a blast-door to be hot unless it has heat itself.

Now, as Leibniz argues in his *Monadology*, one body cannot cause a change in another:

> There is also no way of explaining how a [substance] can be altered or changed internally by some other creature . . . [Properties] cannot be detached, nor can they go about outside of substances . . . Thus, neither substance nor [properties] can enter a [substance] from without. [3]

If one physical object, say a cue-ball, were to have a property, say motion, and if that cue-ball were to cause motion in a (presently) stationary eight-ball, then the cue-ball would have to transfer some of its motion to the eight-ball. But how does one substance transfer one of its own properties to another substance? As we've said, since properties are properties *of* something—they're not free-floating, but attached to substances—then the property of motion can't be given from the cue-ball to the eight-ball without some part of the cue-ball's substance moving from the cue-ball to the eight-ball as well. But this doesn't happen; bodies don't cause motion in other bodies by giving up part of themselves. When Luke causes C-3PO to rise in the air, he doesn't transfer any of his own substance to C-3PO's chair. So causation as the giving of properties from one body to another, Leibniz argues, can't happen.

---

[3] G.W. Leibniz, *Monadology*, in *G.W. Leibniz: Philosophical Essays*, edited by Roger Ariew and Daniel Garber (Indianapolis: Hackett, 1989), §7, pp. 213–14.

The Force, however, is not this kind of causation. When a Jedi knocks over a line of battle droids, he doesn't transfer some of his motion to the droids. And certainly we don't think that all causation includes the transfer of properties in this way. What's being given to the glass by the diamond that cuts it? What property of the earth is given to the falling body? But if we reject this model of causation, then we're stuck with the problem of figuring out exactly what all instances of causation have in common, by virtue of which they are causes.

"There's [Not] One All-Powerful Force Controlling Everything"

If Hume is right, we have no knowledge of causation because we lack any observations of the main component of causes: the necessary connection between the cause and the effect. And if the account of causation he examines is correct, which requires that causes be limited to bodies in contact with each other, then things like gravity and electromagnetic force don't obviously count as causes. On the other hand, if Leibniz is right, the problem is how we account for causes in a way other than substances transferring properties. So the concept of causation is in deep trouble; there seems to be no way to clearly understand how an alleged cause produces its alleged effect.

This conclusion, however, seems to be too much to swallow. Most of us believe that there's a difference between a true cause and effect and a mere coincidence. But what's that difference? One likely candidate would be natural laws. One of the features we tend to include in our concept of cause, which seems to help us exclude explanations like coincidence, is *law-guided uniformity*. The principle of uniformity says that similar causes produce similar effects. A better way to put it is that changes or interactions between objects are governed by general laws so that every time an event of a certain type occurs, the laws dictate that effects of a certain type will follow.

So, in the *Star Wars* universe, the laws could be such that every time a Jedi desires to draw his lightsaber to his hand from across the room, the Force makes it happen. Of course, this doesn't solve the problem because it doesn't tell us why it happens, or what makes this law able to produce these kinds of interactions; only that in this kind of universe the laws make it happen. If one of the lessons we learned through Hume and Leibniz is that explaining *how* causes do their work is too diffi-cult, then maybe we ought to think of causes and their effects as somehow *correlated* (we assume that the two events are related to each other, for example, whenever Darth Vader gets frustrated, another admiral bites the dust) in what seems to be a law-governed way and give up trying to figure out whether or how they are necessarily connected.

There are, however, two features of this suggestion that we ought to notice. First, the fact that we describe these causal interactions as law-governed presupposes that there's some nat-ural connection between certain events, so that whenever an event of one kind occurs, it'll be followed by an event of another kind. And secondly, even if we thought that causes and effects were merely *probabilistically* related, so that whenever some kinds of events occur, then it's *likely* that an event of a cer-tain kind will follow, that still would presuppose that there's a natural and law-governed connection between the events; oth-erwise, we wouldn't have a reason to think of these events as *causally* related. But what evidence could we have of such a law-governed connection?

memory The obvious answer is that we have the evidence of a long train of past observations. Whenever Darth Vader exerts pres-sure on the throats of people, as many Imperial officers have discovered, they choke. And this happens every time Vader exerts pressure on their throats. So the cause of the choking is the pressure on the throat. So, we may infer, that next time Vader exerts pressure on someone's throat, it will cause them to choke too. This appears to be a reasonable inference based on experience, and one that incompetent Imperial officers ought to keep in mind!

And if there are such law-governed connections, they would allow us to make accurate predictions based on past evidence. So the earmarks of a natural causal law include observations that whenever events of a certain type (Darth Vader willing the asphyxiation of an Imperial officer) occur, they're followed by events of a certain type (the choking of the officer), and these observations will typically allow us to make accurate predic-tions of similar events employing the described conditions. Hume, however, argues that this kind of argument is deeply flawed. We can't generalize from past experience that there's a law-governed connection between events unless we use circular reasoning—that is, we assume the truth of what we want to prove in order to prove it.

Laws of nature are general descriptions of how all matter behaves all over the universe whether we observe it or not. But how are such laws ever justifiable? How are we to justify a claim about how all matter must behave all over the universe at all times? We can't—at least not by observation. So is there an argument to show that there are laws of nature?

Well, we might argue that since the suns of Tatooine have always risen and set in the same way everyday, and they seem to be behaving in their typical way now, it's reasonable to infer that they will continue to do so in the future because there is a law of nature guiding their motion. But, Hume points out, this argument only works if we have reasons for thinking that past regularity is evidence of future regularity. There are lots of things that were true in the past, and are true now, but will not be in the future; that's why people buy insurance. In *The Empire Strikes Back*, it might have been true to say that Darth Vader had always obeyed the Emperor, and is now obeying the Emperor. But can we infer that he will always obey the Emperor in the future? Not unless tossing him down the second Death Star's reactor shaft counts as obedience![4]

The only way to justify our belief that the future will resemble the past, such that things that were true in the past will remain true in the future, is if we had reasons for thinking that nature is orderly. But nature is orderly only if there are laws of nature. That is, past regularity is only evidence of future regularity if there are laws of nature, but this is what the conclusion of the argument is supposed to establish. This argument would be circular because we can't assume that there are laws of nature in order to prove that there are laws of nature! So, Hume concludes, there is no non-circular argument which shows us that there are laws of nature.

---

[4] In this example, I'm using the actions of a person, whom we might reasonably believe makes his own decisions and acts autonomously, so the analogy with inferences about causes in general wouldn't make sense in this case. But the main point still holds; in any series of events, from the fact that they've always been observed to behave in a specific way, it doesn't follow that they *must* continue to behave that way unless we have an independent reason for making that judgment.

Failing to specify how causes and effects are correlated allows things like coincidence, magic, wishful thinking, and the Force to count as true causes. But that's not something we can tolerate as a scientific society. It's precisely the account of *how* the laws regulate events that distinguishes true causes from non-causes. But if we can't legitimately establish that there are laws of nature, then we're in no position to claim that these laws explain what is required to be true causes. So laws of nature can't ground our distinction between true causes and non-causes.

In sum, while we deeply believe that there are differences between real causes and pseudo-causes, precisely articulating and justifying those differences has eluded us. What this leaves us with is experiment and probability. In our search for an account of specific cause and effect relationships we must experiment to provide reasons for thinking that the correlations we observe between specific kinds of events isn't merely coincidental. And while we may never be absolutely certain about the truth of our conclusions, we need not embrace Han Solo's famous words: "it's all a lot of simple tricks and nonsense."

"May The Force Be with You"

This discussion doesn't show that there are no causes or laws of nature, nor does it show that inquiry into the meaning of "causation" is fruitless. But it does seem to show that our thinking about causation isn't yet precise enough to do the kind of work we'd like it to. Indeed, our term "cause" probably doesn't pick out any single kind of interaction, but rather refers to a whole host of different kinds of interactions. Moreover, like causation, the Force remains a deeply mysterious concept to us; neither one is easy to define and explain, but we have no trouble recognizing them. And what's more disconcerting is that, from how we use the term, the Force qualifies as a kind of cause, even though we remain deeply puzzled by *how* the Force does what it does!

What makes this distressing is that most accounts of what makes science *scientific* is its ability to identify and explain true causes and distinguish them from pseudo-causes such as magic or mystical powers. This is probably what prompted England's Nobel laureate and philosopher Bertrand Russell in 1929 to say that we should eliminate the word "cause" from our vocabulary. As he puts it: "The Law of causality, I believe . . . is a relic of a bygone age, surviving, like the monarchy, only because it is erroneously supposed to do no harm."[5]

In the end, this essay is a plug for science fiction; after all, science fiction and fantasy allow us to examine possible ways this world could've been different, compelling us to analyze our scientific and philosophical concepts in a way that helps us get clear about what our concepts mean. What we mean by "cause" is a very important question, and one that the fictional reality of the Force allows us to examine more deeply than we would otherwise.

---

[5] Bertrand Russell, *Mysticism and Logic* (New York: Norton, 1929), p. 180.

12

The Force Is with *Us*: Hegel's Philosophy of Spirit Strikes Back at the Empire

JAMES LAWLER

Central to the unfolding plot of *Star Wars* is a question and a mystery: What is the Force? In *A New Hope*, Obi-Wan Kenobi tells Luke Skywalker that his father was betrayed and murdered by Darth Vader, a Jedi Knight who "turned to evil . . . seduced by the Dark Side of the Force." "The Force?" asks Luke. Obi-Wan replies: "The Force is what gives the Jedi his power. It's an energy field created by all living things. It surrounds us and penetrates us. It binds the galaxy together."

All living beings create the energy field of the Force, and at the same time this energy field is essential to living beings, binding the entire galaxy—ultimately the entire cosmos—in a unified whole. The Force has both Dark and Light sides, but there is not a Dark Force and a Light Force, not Evil over against Good. Such a conception of good versus evil is understandable in the context of Episodes IV through VI, dominated by the malevolent Lord Vader. Even when we learn that Vader is actually Luke's father, the news only deepens our sense of repulsion for the evil servant of the Dark Side, which we maintain until the very last moment when Vader unexpectedly turns against his Master—Darth Sidious, the Dark Lord of the Sith and Emperor of the Galaxy—and dies reconciled to his son.

In the absence of the background trilogy of Episodes I to III, this ending to the entire story lacks depth and a sense of conviction. However, as the background story emerges, not only is the final ending fully justified but our understanding of the nature of the Force becomes more profound. We learn why there isn't a Dark Force and a Light Force, a Good opposed to an Evil, but only one Force whose two sides must be brought into *balance*. And we understand how it is that Darth Vader, formerly known as Anakin Skywalker, is the Chosen One whose destiny it is to bring about this balance.

Thanks to the background story, Vader's death-bed conversion to the acknowledgement of love is no artificial happy ending, but the outcome of what Georg Wilhelm Friedrich Hegel, at the conclusion of his *Phenomenology of Spirit,* calls "the Calvary of Absolute Spirit."[1] All life· goes through transformations in which what at first appears to be evil turns out to be good, while the good must be crucified, as Jesus was on Mount Calvary, in order that a higher good be achieved. This transformation of light into dark and dark into light is the pathway of Spirit—Hegel's philosophically probing conception of what George Lucas calls "the Force."

Mythic Journey of the Hero

Star Wars provides an unparalleled modern account of the archetypal journey of the hero into the nether world of darkness as a means of discovery and knowledge, of power and freedom, of love and fidelity. The Force is Lucas's distillation of religious thought and feeling throughout human history.[2] In his understanding of this history, and at the core of *Star Wars*, the divine is no separate deity controlling events from the outside, but the inner God-force that impels the hearts and minds of all of us as we seek to fulfill our inner truth. Connecting with the Force gives the hero within each of us the insight and energy to rise to new levels of fulfillment.

Such an understanding of human destiny is clarified by the contrast between the religion of the Force and the secular view

---

[1] Georg Wilhelm Friedrich Hegel, *The Phenomenology of Spirit*, translated by A.V. Miller (Oxford: Oxford University Press, 1977), p. 808.

[2] Lucas relates that in preparing for *Star Wars* he read fifty books on the religions of the world, but of these he mentions only one, Joseph Campbell's *The Hero with a Thousand Faces*. Campbell's book details the many myths and tales of the hero's adventures as essentially a journey of self-transformation. Based on this reading, Lucas says that he "worked out a general theory for the Force, and then I played with it." (Laurent Bouzereau, *Star Wars: The Annotated Screenplays* [New York: Ballantine, 1997], p. 35).

that the primary means for achieving human goals are provided by science and technology. The opposition of science and technology to the religion of the Force is presented from the start in *A New Hope*. Obi-Wan is training Luke with the aid of a robot ball that hovers in front of him, shooting laser beams as Luke attempts to defend himself with his lightsaber. Han is skeptical. "Hokey religions and ancient weapons are no match for a good blaster at your side, kid." Luke comments, "You don't believe in the Force, do you?" "Kid," says Han, "I've flown from one side of this galaxy to the other. I've seen a lot of strange stuff, but I've never seen anything to make me believe there's one all-powerful Force controlling everything. No mystical energy field controls my destiny. It's all a lot of simple tricks and nonsense." In the face of this skepticism, Luke demonstrates the reality of the Force by blocking the laser attack with his eyes covered. Han calls this luck. "In my experience," says Obi-Wan, "there's no such thing as luck."

There's no doubt in the minds of the audience that the Force is something real, and that Han's reliance on empirical evidence and technological force is missing the deeper picture. But how seriously should we ourselves take this idea of a mystical Force? When we think objectively about it outside of the film, when we ask ourselves what is really real, don't we live most of our lives as Han Solo does, relying on external technologies of power and control to achieve our goals, with little or no confidence in the inner power of our own consciousness? With his idea of the Force as an external controlling deity, Han fails to understand its profound connection with the inner power of the human spirit.

For both the scientifically minded and conventional religious viewers who believe in such an external deity, the Force is magic and make-believe, not something to be taken seriously outside the realm of film and fantasy. However, this understanding of the Force only pushes the question of its nature to a deeper level. What is the appeal of this magic? How does the fantasy of *Star Wars*, with its magical drama of the Force, cast its own spell on its audience? If we dismiss this force of fantasy itself, aren't we too acting like the skeptical Han Solo, dismissing in our minds as inessential and irrelevant the power of imagination that we nevertheless can feel—a power that holds us in its thrall throughout the many hours of artistic wizardry that makes up *Star Wars*? In his lightsaber training lesson, Obi-Wan tells Luke: "let go your conscious self and act on instinct . . . Your eyes can deceive you. Don't trust them ... Stretch out with your feelings." It isn't by thinking that we understand the Force. It's by feeling. But feelings too are real.

Each episode of *Star Wars* begins with the same opening lines: "A long time ago in a galaxy far, far away . . ." We're put in mind of the opening lines of the fairy tale, "Once upon a time." Under the surface of a technically advanced galactic society, we're invited to enter a deeper realm of myth and magic and ancient religion. With *Star Wars*, George Lucas has created a myth for our time, the germ, in fact, of a new religion—one clothed in the garb of the future and the ancient spirit quest of the hero. As the civilizations of our own time clash over rival theologies inherited from the past, mankind is in need of an empowering belief for our time, one that provides a unifying distillation of all the world's religions. To appreciate the way in which *Star Wars*, with its heroic drama of the Force, responds to this need, we must first of all to let go of our conscious minds and all dependence on empirical evidence, and stretch out with our feelings and imagination. We need to let ourselves be captured by the spell of magic.

Spirit: Hegel's Distillation of the History of Religion

Like Lucas, Hegel attempts to distill the essence of religion in his *Lectures on the Philosophy of Religion* and other works. Religion, he argues, is distinguished from science and philosophy in being a matter of feeling and "picture thinking," rather than of rationality and conceptual thought. The object of religion may be called God or Absolute Spirit, but for the religious person such terms are labels for a peculiar object of feeling and imagination, not concepts for rational inquiry. The ultimate goal of the philosophy of religion is to justify the truth of religious feeling by explaining the reality that it taps into—the all-encompassing and dynamic reality of Spirit.[3] Each civilization has its own religious picture of the ultimate nature of reality, the divine, the God, the Absolute Spirit. This picture reflects the

---

[3] See G.W.F. Hegel, *Lectures on the Philosophy of Religion*, Volume I, edited by Peter C. Hodgson (Berkeley: University of California Press, 1984).

kind of civilization it is, and the stage of humanity's self-development that it represents. A scientific-technological civilization that puts Matter in place of Spirit is no exception to this rule.

Hegel traces a developmental pattern in the historical succession of religious beliefs, one that produces in effect a distillation of divinity. In the succession of basic religious orientations, what one religion calls "good" another religion denounces as evil or darkness. But for the final distillation to appear it's necessary for the human spirit, on its heroic journey to self-fulfillment, to find the balance between these opposites.

Human history begins with the divine in nature, as human beings living off plants and animals in the wild are immersed in the natural world. For such people there is no separation between the divine and the human. Like the spirits of nature, human beings too wield magical power in controlling the world around them by their wishes and in their dreams. This is the childhood of humanity, Hegel says. The mindset of the child, who willingly enters the fantasy of "once upon a time," is the general outlook of the culture itself. As Yoda remarks in *Attack of the Clones*, "Truly wonderful the mind of a child." This is also the general outlook of all the ancient nature-centered cultures of the East, as exemplified in the Daoism of China. Giving expression to this history, *Star Wars* appropriately culminates with the battle between the monstrosities of the most advanced technological civilization and the slings and arrows of the nature people, the Ewoks in *Return of the Jedi,* who take C-3PO as a god. As a product of the advanced civilization, though, the gentleman droid cannot accept this worship: "It's against my programming to impersonate a deity."[4]

In the next major stage of human history, which takes place primarily in the West, no one could mistake a physical object for a god. As human beings develop greater technological powers over nature, together with mighty systems of economic, social, and political power in which a small number of people have immense control over the lives of the majority, the divine is conceived of in the image of the rulers—a power radically separate from and ruling over the world. The progress of such separation between the higher realm of the gods and the lower world of

---

[4] For further discussion of the depiction of technology and nature in *Star Wars*, see Chapters 7 and 9 in this volume.

nature and humans culminates in the slave empire of the ancient Romans. This slave state, which subjects all conquered peoples to an order based on the might of the Roman army, reduces everything sacred in life to an object of utility for political purposes. *Star Wars*, with its portrayal of the slide from Republic to Empire, borrows liberally from this Roman history—while suggesting parallels with our own time.[5]

To the individual trampled under by the overwhelming machine of deadly imperial force, the divine inevitably recedes to an "unattainable Beyond." Hegel calls this dark but necessary moment of the journey of mankind "the Unhappy Consciousness."[6] All the childlike magic of life is gone. The Stoic sage of the time of the Roman empire preaches detachment from emotional involvement in the surrounding world, because the individual is thought to be powerless to change matters governed by forces that are wholly outside of our control. Epictetus advises: "If you kiss your child, or your wife, say that you only kiss things which are human, and thus you will not be disturbed if either of them dies."[7] The Stoic recommends acquiescence to external powers in the belief that whatever inscrutable plans the gods have orchestrated for humanity, there must be good in them. But the Skeptic delights in refuting such beliefs as infantile by pointing to the empirical testimony of hard realities. There's no all-powerful Force that masters the universe, including the power of the Emperor himself. There's only my own cunning, and the power of a good blaster, as the rebel Han Solo says.

We therefore see two opposite forms of religion in early world history. From the earliest societies and the East, there is the divine as an all-pervading natural force capable of emerging in the most unexpected objects, as in the Ewoks' vision of a divine C-3PO. From the beginnings of Western civilizations the contrary concept emerges of an external divinity that supposedly controls all, yet dwindles to being an "unattainable

---

[5] For further discussion of this political transformation in *Star Wars,* see Chapter 14 in this volume.

[6] Hegel, *The Phenomenology of Spirit*, p. 131.

[7] Epictetus, *Enchiridion*, #3. Available at http://classics.mit.edu/Epictetus/epicench.html. For more discussion of Stoic philosophy, see Chapter 2 in this volume.

Beyond." If there is to be a distillation of the essence of religion as the core of a new myth for our time, it must combine these two opposite conceptions of the divine. Just such a synthesis, Hegel argues, is represented by the "Consummate Religion" of Christianity with its story of a God who becomes a human babe, grows up with a family, enters upon his mission, and accomplishes this mission only by dying the ignominious death on Mount Calvary of a criminal nailed to a cross.[8]

What is this mission? To teach a people plunged in the darkness of a world ruled by pitiless physical force that God is not a menacing power ruling over us, but the deepest inner reality of each person. It's the inner Holy Spirit that binds us all together in a powerful unity that is the irresistible Force by which we can resist and overcome all inner darkness and every outer unjust form of rule. Thus, at the peak of the imperial power of Rome, intrepid bands of Christian rebels, believing that divine Force has merged with the human spirit, began the long climb from a world of Empire whose principle is that only one person is completely free, the Emperor, to a world whose dominant inspiration is that all should be free to rule themselves. Hegel calls this evolution of the state from tyranny to freedom "the march of God in the world."[9] Similarly, defenders of liberty can justly say, in the language of *Star Wars*, that the Force is with us. It is with *us*—a people united in the spirit of creative freedom and mutual love. For this is the nature of Spirit, according to Hegel. It's the Force that runs through us all together. It's truly understood only when we overcome the darkness that we ourselves cast by our separation from one another, our egotism—only when we learn the ultimate and unconquerable power of love.

Anakin Skywalker as the Chosen One

Anakin's mother, Shmi, tells Qui-Gon in *The Phantom Menace* that her gifted son was conceived without a father. "He is the chosen one," the child of prophecy, Qui-Gon later tells the Jedi Council. The same prophecy that foretells the growth of the Dark Side also tells of "the one who will bring balance to the

---

[8] See G.W.F. Hegel, *Lectures on the Philosophy of Religion*, Volume III, edited by Peter C. Hodgson (Berkeley: University of California Press, 1985).

Force." All these echoes of Hegel's Consummate Religion of Christianity, from prophecy to Virgin Birth to a mission of liberation from darkness, set up certain natural expectations. And yet Anakin is no clone of the Christian Savior as Jesus is conventionally understood. Upsetting the standard Christian paradigm, the prophesied savior of *Star Wars* becomes the archetype of modern villainy, the evil Lord Darth Vader, a machine as much as a man, whose every breath sounds with menace. And yet the prophecy is fulfilled. Anakin-Vader indeed brings balance to the Force, striking down the Emperor, and then dying in the loving embrace of his son.

Giving reason to this reversal of conventional Christianity, Hegel is sharply critical of a theology according to which Jesus is the sinless savior whose mission is to redeem a humanity sunk in darkness. He is the light, the *Gospel of John* says, "and the light shines in darkness, and the darkness does not comprehend it" (*John* 1:5). If he is the light, Hegel effectively argues, he nevertheless himself enters into the darkness. The Christian God enters the very darkness through the paradigmatic journey of the Son of God to the cross on Mount Calvary, where Jesus experiences utter abandonment, crying out, "My God, my God, why have you forsaken me?" (*Mark* 15:34).

The essence of sin, Hegel argues, is the belief that one is an isolated individual, an ego separated from the All—all other human beings and the rest of reality.[10] In his sense of abandonment Jesus too experienced such a condition of sinfulness. He plumbed the Dark Side of reality to demonstrate "that the human, the finite, the fragile, the weak, the negative are themselves moments of the divine, that they are within God himself, that finitude, negativity, otherness are not outside of God and do not, as otherness, hinder unity with God."[11]

If we seriously accept the Christian conception of Jesus as both God and man, then the Christian religion is truly the story of the hero's journey in which the Son of God descends from

---

[9] G.W.F. Hegel, *Elements of the Philosophy of Right*, edited by Allen W. Wood (Cambridge: Cambridge University Press, 1991), p. 279, paragraph 258.

[10] See G.W.F. Hegel, *Lectures on the Philosophy of Religion*, Volume II, edited by Peter C. Hodgson. (Berkeley: University of California Press, 1987), pp. 740–41.

[11] Hegel, *Lectures on the Philosophy of Religion*, Volume III, p. 326.

his exalted heights into the darkness of an oppressive epoch of earthly life, and so is able to connect the darkness to the light in a renewed balance. Only in this way does God *realize himself* as God.[12] Just as we understand light only through its opposition to darkness, so God truly appreciates himself as God only by becoming something other than God—a finite human being subject to despair and death. God becomes human in every human being, for, as Hegel's contemporary William Wordsworth writes, "trailing clouds of glory do we come, From God who is our home."[13]

The emerging human ego soon separates itself from this original divinity experienced in childhood—that is, identifies itself as a separate being in opposition to everything else—to the Infinite reality outside of itself. Thus begins the war of the separate human ego with the All, our infinite home becomes the Dark Side of God. Through the Son, which represents every solitary human being, the God within us enters into the darkness of separate, finite, ego-centered existence. The inexorable outcome of this journey finds tragic expression in the solitary despair of Jesus's cry from the cross.

But if there's full comprehension of the divine nature of this journey, of the unity of the light with the dark, such a death is the death of death itself, and the return of the Son to the Father in the unity of the Holy Spirit. Then, the empowered individual sees with the very eye of God. Hegel cites with approval the thought of the medieval Christian mystic Meister Eckhart (around 1260–1328): "The eye with which God sees me is the eye with which I see him: my eye and his eye are the same." With such a vision, the individual shares in the divine substance: "If God did not exist," Eckart argues, "nor would I; if I did not exist, nor would he."[14]

Hegel thereby shows how both things can be true, as Obi-Wan says: the Force is both "an energy field created by all liv-

---

[12] *Ibid.*, pp. 327–28. See James Lawler, "God and Man Separated No More: Hegel Overcomes the Unhappy Consciousness of Gibson's Christianity," in Jorge J.E. Gracia, ed., *Mel Gibson's Passion and Philosophy* (Chicago: Open Court, 2004), pp. 62–76.

[13] William Wordsworth, "Ode: Intimations of Immortality from Recollections of Early Childhood." Available at http://www.bartleby.com/145/ww331.html.

[14] Hegel, *Lectures on the Philosophy of Religion*, Volume I, pp. 347–48.

ing things"—it's our own energy, infinitely magnified for the one who knows how to connect consciously with all living things—as well as the Force that "binds the galaxy together." For Hegel, Jesus's crucifixion begins the destruction of the old paradigm of separate human egos at war with one another. It's the birth of a new kind of community, bound together in the spirit of love. Overcoming ego-separation and re-connecting through love with all living things, the empowered individual actively participates in the God-force, the Spirit, that binds the galaxy together.

The Force of Love

Reality is ultimately "Spirit," Hegel argues. And Spirit is "'I' that is 'We,' and 'We' that is 'I.'"[15] Our deeper nature is not to be an "I" separate from other "I"s by the confines and distances of our material bodies. Wherever there is one such separate "I" there are others, and each of these egos struggles against the others. Where every "I" asserts itself against every other "I," there's murder and mayhem—that perilous life of mankind described by philosopher Thomas Hobbes as "solitary, poor, nasty, brutish and short."[16]

If the human species is to survive, Hegel argues, some individuals must surrender to others. Out of surrender of the weak to the strong, there emerges the world of Masters and Slaves, until finally everyone is subservient to the one Emperor—the Dark Lord of the separate ego that is the deepest potential and ultimate aspiration within every separate ego.[17] Here is the Dark Side of the Force, which for Hegel is the negative being of God. But the true nature of God, which Hegel calls Spirit, is not that of a separate power ruling over a universe of dominated creatures. This is an idea of an outmoded religion, as Han Solo recognizes. Such an all-controlling God is really the ultimate Dark Lord of unlimited egotistical power.

On a psychological plane, the "I" that is "We," or Spirit, is discovered most vitally in the experience of *love*. The true mean-

---

[15] Hegel, *The Phenomenology of Spirit*, p. 110.

[16] Thomas Hobbes, *Leviathan*, Part I, Chapter XIV, in *Great Books of the Western World*, Volume 23 (Chicago: Encyclopedia Britannica, 1952), p. 85.

[17] For further discussion of Hegel's master-slave dialectic as depicted in *Star Wars*, see Chapter 13 in this volume.

ing of the sacred journey of the hero, exemplified in the life and death of the Christ figure, is infinite love.[18] But, as Diotima teaches Socrates in Plato's *Symposium*, the path to infinite love begins with the love of one person.[19] A crucial moment in Hegel's *Phenomenology of Spirit* is the love of the intellectual and magician Faust for the young maid Gretchen, a love that is made possible only through Faust's bargain with the devil—to give up his soul in exchange for the intense experience of life that can only be found through love. This is indeed what the power of love seems to be for the separate ego—the very loss of one's soul. Such love, which Faust obtains by giving himself over to the powers of darkness, brings about death to Gretchen as well as peril to the immortal soul of the lover. But for Hegel passionate love in which body and soul are totally at stake is the only way to achieve a higher level of vitality and wholeness.

Hegel thereby helps us appreciate a central problem with the Stoic philosophy of the Jedi Knights. Their ideal of detachment from emotional involvement with others seeks to forestall the descent into the darkness of a Faustian love, but in doing so it leaves no room for the higher vitality that only comes through deeply personal connections with particular individuals. It's this unnatural Stoic detachment that leaves a lovelorn Anakin no alternative, and so precipitates his Faustian bargain with the devil.

In a debate with the Jedi Council in *The Phantom Menace*, Qui-Gon defends Anakin's candidacy for Jedi knighthood despite his age. Anakin has spent the first nine years of his life living alone with his mother. Yoda explains to Anakin why his attachment to his mother is dangerous for a Jedi warrior: "Afraid to lose her, I think." "What's that got to do with anything?" Anakin protests. "Everything," Yoda tells him. "Fear is the path to the Dark Side. Fear leads to anger. Anger leads to hate. Hate leads to suffering." Qui-Gon disagrees with the negative assessment of Anakin. He tells the Jedi Council, "Finding him was the will of the Force. I have no doubt of that." Indeed, for the devotee of the Force, as Qui-Gon says to Shmi earlier in this episode, "Nothing happens by accident." Only the mysterious operation

---

[18] See Hegel, *Lectures on the Philosophy of Religion*, Volume III, p. 128.
[19] See Plato, *Symposium*, in *Great Books of the Western World*, Volume 7 (Chicago: Encyclopaedia Britannica, 1952), pp. 167, 210.

of the Force could explain the series of events that led from the Naboo cruiser's leaking hyperdrive, to an emergency stop on an obscure planet, to the discovery of the slave boy Anakin with his remarkable abilities. As skeptical here as Han Solo, the Jedi Council would rather put this all down to accident, for accepting Anakin means confronting their own deepest fears. If it's possible to be seduced by the Dark Side, it must also be possible to be overly attached to the light—and overly fearful of the dark. The Jedi too are afraid—afraid of real human love, afraid of connection with the other person, afraid of the loss of self-control that comes to the "I" of passionate love which is at the same time a "We."

Padmé asks the grown-up Anakin in *Attack of the Clones*: "Are you allowed to love? I thought that was forbidden for a Jedi." Anakin replies: "Attachment is forbidden. Possession is forbidden. Compassion, which I would define as unconditional love, is central to a Jedi's life. So you might say we are encouraged to love." But such compassion without attachment, without possession and being-possessed, is a superficial, abstracted, intellectualized form of love. Attachment and possession are forbidden because such connections to particular things and people lead to fear for them and fear of losing them. And fear leads to the Dark Side. Therefore, the love of the Jedi Knight must be a detached love—if it can indeed be called love with its willingness to sacrifice friends and loved ones for the perceived higher good. Anakin rejects this detached love of the Stoic sage, as does Luke in *The Empire Strikes Back* when he spurns Yoda's declaration that his training is more important than the life of Han and Leia. Giving an ironic twist to the deeper unity of the light with the dark, the Emperor echoes Yoda's counsel in *Return of the Jedi*, when the Dark Lord tells Luke that his faith in his friends is his great weakness. The Jedi fears what the Sith Lord despises, the power over the ego wielded by human love.[20]

Anakin's eventual declaration of love in *Attack of the Clones*, in the most sexually seductive scene in the whole of *Star Wars*,

---

[20] In the climactic battle of *The Matrix Revolutions*, Agent Smith, with characteristic disgust, similarly tells Neo that "only a human mind could invent something as insipid as love." See James Lawler, "Only Love Is Real: Heidegger, Plato and the *Matrix* Trilogy," in William Irwin, ed., *More Matrix and Philosophy: Revolutions and Reloaded Decoded* (Chicago: Open Court, 2005).

is worthy of Shakespeare: "I'm haunted by the kiss you should never have given me. My heart is beating, hoping that kiss will not become a scar. You are in my very soul, tormenting me. What can I do? I will do anything you ask." Such passionate, personal love indeed leads Anakin to the Dark Side. He kills indiscriminately out of rage against his mother's murder. From the beginning of their relationship, Anakin and Padmé sense that their dark, secret love will ruin them.

With such an understanding of the background story, we finally come to appreciate why Luke recognizes the good in his father. It's because Anakin doesn't fear to go where love takes him, both when his love of Padmé takes him into the darkness and when his love of Luke brings him back again. We understand that his destiny, subtly and beautifully orchestrated by the will of the Force and the magic of George Lucas's art, has all along been to love. By loving in a way that's truly unconditional, without fear of the darkness into which his love leads him, he fulfills his destiny, destroys the Emperor, and so brings balance to the Force.

Part IV

"There's Always a Bigger Fish"

Truth, Faith, and a Galactic Society

13

"What Is Thy Bidding, My Master?": *Star Wars* and the Hegelian Struggle for Recognition

BRIAN K. CAMERON

Star Wars, as the name suggests, is about struggle and conflict, hope and renewal, war and death. On the one side, there are the Rebels, whose struggle for freedom from Imperial domination and fear motivate their supporters and give life to the movement. On the other side, there is the Emperor and his minions who, driven by what philosopher Friedrich Nietzsche (1844–1900) refers to as the "will to power," willingly sacrifice entire planets and their populations in a ruthless attempt to achieve their goals. Art really does imitate life or, at the very least, it illuminates an important feature of it—namely, the exercise of a certain kind of power.

It isn't difficult to explain how this kind of power arises; fear is the mechanism that accounts for its existence and strength. It is fear of losing his sister that moves Luke to do the Emperor's bidding and strike down his father. It is fear that motivates the Senate to form the clone army that ultimately brings about its own demise. And, it's the fear of losing his mother that sends the young Anakin Skywalker down the path to the Dark Side and prompts the ancient Jedi Master, Yoda, to voice the mantra of his religion: "Fear leads to anger . . . anger leads to hate . . . hate leads to suffering."

Fear illuminates the path to slavery and suffering, the path that leads to the Dark Side. At the same time, though, it reveals a certain mode of exercising power—the way of the Sith Master. The Master rises to his station and maintains his dominance over his apprentices or slaves by evoking and playing upon their fears. And the apprentice or slave maintains himself as a slave by allowing those fears to determine his being. This interplay between power and fear is what the nineteenth-century German philosopher Georg Hegel (1770–1831) called the "master-slave dialectic." By looking at the *Star Wars* saga through the lens of Hegel's master-slave dialectic we will not only better understand the nature and limits of the Emperor's power, but also why— apart from the Hollywood impulse to give audiences a happy ending—that power failed. And, as an added bonus, Hegel's analysis forces us to look most carefully at the personal exercise of power, bringing into sharper relief the various characters within the Star Wars galaxy and their motivations.

Masters and Slaves: Who Rules Whom?

Thales, the very first philosopher in the Western tradition, was once asked, "What is most difficult?" He replied, "To know thyself." Indeed, Thales was not far off the mark: coming to understand ourselves and the value and meaning of our experiences really is one of the most difficult things any of us can do. Similarly, coming to understand how self-knowledge is itself possible, how it arises, and in what it consists is one of the more challenging problems philosophers grapple with. In *Star Wars*, two of the most compelling themes are Luke's journey of self-discovery and his father's redemption as the result of his own coming to a new self-identity at the end of *Return of the Jedi*.

As unlikely as it may sound, it's the problem of self-knowledge that ultimately leads Hegel to examine the relationship between master and slave. For Hegel, knowledge about ourselves as individuals, knowledge about the value and meaning of our projects and experiences, necessarily implies a relationship to other people. Our individual self-understanding does not arise independently of others; rather, it emerges in the context of a relationship with other people. Their recognition (or lack of recognition) of us as having valuable, independent projects and experiences shapes how we perceive ourselves. Not surprisingly then, the type and quality of our relationships to others will have a direct influence on our capacity to know and value ourselves. Some relationships can enhance our capacity for self-knowledge while others, like the relation between a master and a slave (or between the Emperor and his subjects), distort the picture we have of ourselves. But, what's really interesting about this is, the fact that it is the *master*, and not so much the slave, whose self-understanding is distorted by the relationship. Let's see why.

From the standpoint of self-knowledge, the individual becomes aware of herself as an individual (she becomes self-conscious) at the moment when she confronts another like herself, a subject capable of interpreting and understanding the world.[1] In this meeting, the two are aware of each other, but that awareness carries with it a certain tension. Insofar as the other is a co-interpreter of the world, she is a subject for whom the world presents itself. On the other hand, insofar as the world remains an object to her, the other is likewise an object within that world.[2] When, for instance, Luke and Vader first meet in *The Empire Strikes Back,* Vader is torn. On the one hand, he regards Luke as a trophy, a mere object of conquest. On the other hand, he also sees Luke as a potential rival to the Emperor, an equal and partner.

In any case, at this point the individual is only aware of herself in terms of her capacity to interpret and understand the world. What she lacks is an understanding of herself as an active creator, that is, as a being with meaningful projects and goals. Yet in order to know herself in this way, the individual must somehow fashion a world according to her own will; she must, in other words, make for herself a human world. Then and only then will her individuality emerge and itself become something to be interpreted and understood by another. The problem is that being creative in this sense requires that we impress our will on others by ordering our world. In this respect, we are all like the Emperor, attempting to remake the world in our own image.

The struggle begins! Each refuses to see the other as a co-equal subject, and each sees in the other the means to create a world of their own design. Both risk all in the life-or-death struggle for supremacy, for it is by such a struggle that, Hegel thinks, we come to know and value life with all its creative

---

[1] G.W.F. Hegel, translated by A.V. Miller, *Phenomenology of Spirit* (Oxford: Oxford University Press, 1977) §178–184. All other Hegel citations will be from this edition, with the relevant sections in the text.
[2] *Ibid.*, §186

possibilities.[3] In the end, one reaches the brink of terror and backs down, only to become the slave of the other. This, in simple terms, is how Hegel understands the historical emergence of the relation between masters and slaves.

It's tempting to think that at this point the master has what he wants. As master, he can command the labor of the slave and make the world into what he wills. Freed from the drudgery of mundane work, the master can live in lavish surroundings, indulge in fabulous pleasures, and do pretty much as he pleases (think Jabba the Hutt). It certainly looks as if the master has what he wants, just as it looks as if the Emperor, with his crimson-clad guards and fawning courtiers, has what he wants; but appearances can be deceiving.

It was to be recognized by another, an equal, that the master risked everything to become master, not to live a life of pleasure. The slave is a human being, but as long as he remains a slave he cannot give the master the recognition he desires—the recognition of an equal. Why does this matter? Hegel expresses it this way: "Self-consciousness exists in and for itself when, and by the fact that, it so exists for another; that is, it exists only in being acknowledged."[4] Although I am surely something independently of others, the understanding I have of myself, of the value of my projects, of the meaning and sense of my experiences, is dependent upon the way others see me. Naturally, I must trust in and value the judgments of those who evaluate me. If I judge them to be unequal, incapable of understanding or passing judgment upon the value of my life, then their opinions are worthless to me. Only an equal is capable of understanding me in the way I understand myself. Thus, if I am to gain the recognition I desire as a self-conscious being, if I am to understand the truth about myself and my possibilities as a human being, then I must seek out an equal.

But this is impossible for the master. By definition, the master "prefers death to the slavish recognition of another's superiority."[5] And it is only through death, his death or that of his adversary, that the master achieves what he wills—lordship. The

---

[3] *Ibid.*, §187

[4] *Ibid.*, p. 111.

[5] *Hegel's Dialectic of Desire and Recognition: Texts and Commentaries*, edited by John O'Neill (New York: State University of New York Press, 1996), p. 55.

possibility of peaceful co-existence with co-equals—with other masters—is likewise foreclosed. The original struggle for (a one-sided) recognition is merely transplanted to a new site. For as long as the master refuses to recognize the other as a co-equal subject, for as long as he wills that he be master, his most important human aims are, and will forever be, frustrated.

Of course it goes without saying that the slave's aims are likewise frustrated. Being a slave is only a happy state of affairs in bad histories. In reality slavery is a brutal and inhuman institution, and the brief glimpse of slavery on Tatooine that we get in *The Phantom Menace* is tame and whitewashed. Nevertheless, the situation for the slave is also not what it might at first seem.

To begin with, it is the slave whose labor creates the world of things, and through that labor he comes to experience himself as a creative being. This is certainly the case for young Anakin working in Watto's shop. While the master cannot in the end be satisfied with himself—for he can choose only to live a life of animal pleasure or fight anew and die in the field of battle—the slave can go beyond himself and his situation by overcoming his fears. In *The Empire Strikes Back*, Luke's experience in the cave and his subsequent Jedi training symbolizes his own struggle with, and overcoming of, fear. His fear at first enslaves him and prevents him from acting as a Jedi Knight. Although Luke claims that he is not afraid, Yoda knows better and warns, "You will be . . . you will be." His overcoming of that fear in turn constitutes an important part of his maturation and in their duel on Cloud City, Vader praises Luke for overcoming his fear. Consequently, it is the master who represents an historical dead end. He can never go beyond what he is and realize himself as a free self-conscious subject. The slave, on the other hand, has nothing to lose but his fear; he can and will go beyond what he is because his desire is not to be master, but to be free. Hegel says that he finds this freedom in his work, a space in which he controls his small, limited world and recognizes the freedom of having a "mind of one's own."[6]

An Empire of Fear and Trembling

The management of fear is the business of the Empire, and fear is the coinage of power that must make itself visibly terrible in

---

[6] Hegel, *Phenomenology of Spirit*, p. 119.

order to rule.[7] The Emperor, precisely because he is unequal in relation to his subjects, cannot exert his power at all times. Within such a system it's the exceptional, the example or spectacle, which must circulate and demonstrate power. The decision to destroy the planet Alderaan, for instance, was made not because it constituted a threat, but because its visibility made it a useful show of force. "Dantooine," Grand Moff Tarkin announces, "is too remote to make an effective demonstration." True, the exercise of power is excessive, but it isn't indiscriminate—its use is calculated to maximize fear and render unnecessary the actual deployment of force elsewhere: "Fear will keep the local systems in line, fear of this battle station."

Like all weapons of mass destruction, the Death Star's military function cannot be easily separated from its political and policing functions—its purpose as a method of *domestic* control. Its objective power lies not in its actual use, but in the threat of its use, and herein lays the secret of its political function of justifying the exercise of power. "This station," says one overly zealous commander, "is now the ultimate power in the universe, I suggest we use it." The suggestion can be ignored, but not the implication. By its very existence, the Death Star invites use and seemingly justifies the extension of Imperial power to every corner of the galaxy. The power to destroy a planet is the power to render obedient entire populations. When wielded by the master, it shows who his enemies are, and in doing so it explains and justifies the master's power by revealing its strength.

The Death Star is the most spectacular display of a power that is not afraid of being seen as terrible; but it isn't the only display of that power, nor the only way by which that power makes itself felt. The Emperor's control over individuals, unlike that exercised over entire populations, must be managed with a degree of flexibility that corresponds with the interest he has in extracting ever more useful labor from them. In order to make those individuals useful and cooperative, the Emperor may replace the specific dread of a well-defined threat like the Death Star with the more constant terror of the unknown. "The Emperor is coming here?" a surprised commander asks at the

---

[7] See Chapter 14 in this volume, which also discusses the Emperor's use of fear in governing.

beginning of *Return of the Jedi.* "Yes," Vader replies, "and he is most displeased with your apparent lack of progress." The threat is undefined and left to play upon the commander's imagination. Almost without hesitation he responds: "We shall double our efforts!" And then a second ill-defined threat is voiced and left to hang in the air: "I hope so, commander, for your sake. The Emperor is not as forgiving as I am." Vader's "forgiveness" is legendary, after all.

In still other cases, the threat is defined but its meaning left unclear. In his confrontation with the Emperor, Luke's fear of seeing the Rebellion fail, of becoming like his father, and of seeing his sister turned to the Dark Side all become real. But what would it mean to become *like* his father? Does the end of the Rebellion mean the end of all rebellion; what exactly does it signal? If the Rebel fleet is destroyed, are his friends necessarily killed? Can the Emperor find Leia and if so, what would it mean to turn her to the Dark Side? In no case is Luke confronted with a specific and implacable sign of what's to come. Rather, a web of fear is spread by the Emperor's taunting in order to elicit Luke's anger and call forth that all-too-human power to override reason and give in to hate.

If the mechanism of fear explains how it is the Emperor rules his Empire and primarily relates to his subjects, it is hatred that explains his relation to his closest advisors and minions—Darth Maul, Count Dooku, and most especially, Darth Vader. Neither equality nor recognition, but instead hatred ties each to the other, because hatred is the primary way by which each makes sense of themselves and the world. Each is driven by his own hatred of life, of all things good, and (it is likely) of himself. Not surprisingly, then, each sees in the other a reflection of himself: something to resent and hate perhaps, but also something intelligible and understandable, a kind of common ground.

Earlier we saw that the master seeks after equals with whom he can relate as a self-conscious being. If Hegel is right and the master can never be satisfied with himself and his life, then it's not surprising that the Emperor should come to hate life and himself. In other words, it's reasonable to think that hatred will become the primary way by which the master understands his experience of the world and himself. Consequently, that same hatred will constitute the sole means by which the master relates to others as self-conscious beings, that is, as relative equals.

Naturally those relations will be seriously impoverished and deficient, as indeed they are. Even so, because those relations are
formed around the principle focus by which each understands
himself (in this case hatred), those relationships will be more personal, stronger, and more enduring than any other relation each
might have. More than anything else, this explains the Emperor's
power over his minions and their respective allegiances to him.
As Vader confides in Luke, "I *must* obey my master."

We might see this most clearly if we think carefully about the
evolution of Darth Vader and his eventual betrayal of the
Emperor. Vader starts off, in *A New Hope*, as a dark embodiment
of everything evil. In his first cinematic act, he crushes a man's
neck while questioning him about the whereabouts of some
stolen plans. From there, things only get worse: with the hind-
sight of the later films, we know he allows the death of his step-
family, Owen and Beru Lars; interrogates and tortures his own
daughter; kills his old friend and mentor, Obi-Wan; and nearly
kills his son in the Death Star trench. In *The Empire Strikes Back*,
Vader does no better—in a number of instances he simply kills
those subordinates who fail him in a kind of idealized form of
corporate downsizing. And so by the time we reach the last
installment of the saga, *Return of the Jedi*, and are aware of
Luke's parentage, we're given almost no reason to think that
Luke is anything more than deluded in believing there is "still
good in him." On the contrary, the so-called struggle Luke senses
in his father is buried so deeply that, up until the point where
Luke lays prostrate before a murderous Emperor, we're given no
indication that Vader is anything more than a willing servant of
evil. Then, and only then, does Vader act to save his son.

So why does he do it? Or, better yet—how does Vader sur-
mount the Emperor's hold over him?

There's really only one possible answer: Vader overcomes
the Emperor by overcoming his hate and achieving a new self-
consciousness. Confronted with his son's unshakeable belief in
his goodness, Vader comes to realize the truth about himself—
he isn't a pawn of evil, but a man of inherent goodness and
nobility.[8] Vader turns on the Emperor when he becomes aware

---

[8] For a discussion of Luke's faith in his father and its effect on Vader, turn to
Chapter 17 in this volume.

of himself as something other than a hate-filled man, something other than a slave. And, that awareness comes at precisely the moment when Vader comes face-to-face with the possibility of watching die the only person who saw goodness in him, his son Luke.

Luke and Vader's personal struggle with their own fears is at the heart of the larger story about struggle and conflict between the Rebels and the Empire. The resolution of that personal struggle represents a moment of self-discovery for both characters, a moment when each comes to understand, in virtue of their relation to one another, who they really were. And the same can be said for the larger struggles that are taking place within the saga. The Ewoks, for instance, prove who and what they are in their confrontation with the Empire. Similarly, the Naboo and the Trade Federations reveal something of themselves in their responses to the collapse of the Republic and the rise of the Sith. This, it seems, is what Hegel was trying to tell us—in the relation between masters and slaves, it is the slave, and not the master, who is in a position to reveal something about our possibilities as human beings. Fear may create and sustain relations of inequality, but the desire to know who and what we are will, in the end, likely triumph.

14

By Any Means Necessary: Tyranny, Democracy, Republic, and Empire

KEVIN S. DECKER

Palpatine—the weasel-like Senator from Naboo, the rapidly wrinkling Supreme Chancellor, and ultimately the cackling, loathsome Emperor—is reviled universally by fans as the epitome of evil. Still, you've got to give him credit for his political savvy. After all, Palpatine's career is a textbook case in how the unceasing desire for power can change something like democracy, or rule by the many, into a tyrannical dictatorship. Using the constant threat posed by the Dark Side of the Force, the Sith—Palpatine and his protegé, Darth Vader—use the hyper-technological Imperial military to keep iron-fisted, monochromatic control over the galaxy. How different this vision is from the diverse and colorful, if conflicted, Old Republic of the prequel trilogy!

This same kind of political one-hundred-eighty degree turn has occurred in human history, too. Politicians, political scientists and theorists over many centuries have grappled with how this could have happened, in most cases in order to prevent it from happening again. But the story of the road to tyranny isn't just of historical interest, even though democracy and tyranny date back to ancient Greece. It also embroils us in heady debates of today about the source of political authority, whether the needed expertise of politicians is a good trade-off against the possibility of their corruption, and how much power can safely be concentrated in the hands of a few.

These arguments often boil down to the question of who rules versus who *should* rule. This isn't an easy question, because it presumes that we've settled on what kind of government is best—democracy, republic, aristocracy, or some other? Also, it presumes that we know whether rulers need some virtue or expertise in order to rule, or could everyone simply rule themselves? Political life in the *Star Wars* galaxy provides us a jumping off point in approaching these central questions of political philosophy.

Galactic Politics for Dummies

Despite their lukewarm reception by the fans, Episodes I–III in the *Star Wars* saga tell us the most about the political forces that fundamentally drive its episodic stories and overall narrative. With the blockbuster episodes made in the late 1970s and 1980s, there wasn't much to say. The Cold War-style political message of *Star Wars* at that time was fairly simple: big, evil empires that rely on soulless technology and dominating control over their populations are bad, and rebellion against such empires is justified. By contrast, Episodes I–III deliver a more complex message about the human failings and weaknesses that help to undermine a huge, declining federation of civilizations.

To answer the question of how a democratic form of government could slide into empire, we have to define a few terms and make a few guesses about the nature of the Republic. In our galaxy, the word "republic" originates from the Latin *res publica*, the realm of public life outside of private affairs. The term's meaning is roughly equivalent to what we would call the "commonwealth" or "common good." Palpatine's government may be a republic in this simple sense alone: it recognizes and works for the common good. In *Attack of the Clones*, Anakin voices an idea of what a good republic ought to do. "We need a system where the politicians sit down and discuss the problem, agree to what's in the best interest of all the people, and then do it," he says to Padmé.

But some might argue that "republicanism" means more than just recognition of the common good. Government should be built on the idea that the freedom of its citizens is essential, they say, but their freedom depends on their *taking part* in government. Their participation includes *protecting themselves* from the arbitrary influence of others.[1] Such protection can be secured in

---

[1] See Philip Pettit, *Republicanism* (New York: Oxford University Press, 1997).

lots of different ways, perhaps most importantly through justifiable restrictions on the power of both government and certain collective interests like corporations and special-interest groups. However the republican tradition in political thought also stresses that citizens must be active participants in political life according to moral or civic duty. Rather than simply defining what republics have been historically, this way of thinking has *moral* importance—it makes a statement about how political life contributes to the good life, and what we ought to do to achieve it.

"The problem," writes Jean-Jacques Rousseau in the eighteenth century, "is to find a form of association which will defend and protect with the whole common force the person and goods of each associate, and in which each, while uniting himself with all, may still obey himself alone, and remain as free as before."[2] Rousseau poses the thorny question of how to balance the group needs that we all share and that can't be served without collective action with the dignity and autonomy (or self-rule) of the individual.

The Republic also seems to have certain features of a democracy. Democracies need two ideals as essential ingredients of their laws and institutions: self-government and equality. Since every inhabitant of Naboo, Coruscant, Dantooine, Kashyyk and all the others can't be expected to vote on every issue before the Senate, they interpret "self-government" the same way we do in America—in terms of a *representative* democracy. This is the preferred option for any large, heavily populated democracy for obvious reasons. There have been *direct* democracies, though, in which individual citizens do vote on everything. We can't conclude that simply because the Republic seems to be a democracy, every planetary system within it is also ruled by the people. Naboo, for example, democratically elects its queen, but it's implied in *The Phantom Menace* that the Gungans haven't had a say in the larger political affairs of the planet for some time.

So, is the Republic founded on the ideal of equality as well? By this we can't suggest that in a democracy everyone is born

---

[2] Jean-Jacques Rousseau, *The Social Contract and Discourses*, translated by G.D.H. Cole (London: Dent, 1973), quoted in part in Michael Rosen and Jonathan Wolff, eds., *Political Thought* (New York: Oxford University Press, 1999), p. 62.

equal in terms of their talents, capacities, social or economic status. Obviously the set of our natural endowments is virtually unique to each individual. Instead, equality in a democracy usually means equal rights, equal opportunity, and equal standing under the law. Civil rights laws, welfare systems, public education, and trial by a jury of one's peers have all been used to promote this kind of equality. But in the *Star Wars* galaxy, it's clear that this kind of equality isn't treated as a *universal* standard. Certain societies, such as the Jedi Order, seem to function based on hierarchical, not democratic principles. There are planets like Tatooine where slavery is not only legal, but also the basis of the economy; but as Shmi Skywalker points out, Tatooine isn't part of the Republic. And there's also the controversial issue of whether droids are persons, have rights, and thus deserve to be treated equally with "organics."[3] These are all reminders that in reality democracy has both an *ideal* meaning and a *real* landscape, as the examples of the civil rights and women's voting movements of the twentieth century show. In both cases, only moral arguments and public protests enlarged our conception of what equality meant, even as large numbers of citizens held that opportunities ought to be restricted to white men.

Let's assume that the Republic is a democratic republic in more than name only. How do we get from that to the tyranny of the Empire? Aristotle provides us with a suitable definition for *tyranny*: it's the "arbitrary power of an individual which is responsible to no one, and governs all alike, whether equals or betters, with a view to its own advantage, not to that of its subjects, and therefore against their will."[4] So the idea of a ruler who acts in blatant defiance of the laws, or perhaps in the absence of laws, is central to the definition of tyranny. Ancient Greek tyrants and Roman dictators were often voted into power by means of the laws they later defied, in order to respond to an external challenge to their state, like imminent invasion, or in some cases because of internal threats, such as civil war.

---

[3] You can read a defense of the idea that droids are deserving of equal treatment in Chapter 10 of this volume.

[4] Aristotle, *Politics* 1295a20–23, translated by B. Jowett, in *The Complete Works of Aristotle*, Volume 2, edited by J. Barnes (Princeton: Princeton University Press, 1984), p. 2056.

In his own route to tyranny, Palpatine and his *alter ego*, Darth Sidious, have taken a path like the one expressed in the lyrics of an old German song: "against democrats, only soldiers help." The Sith Lord's alliance with the Trade Federation and his commissioning of the Kaminoan clone army through the Jedi Sifo-Dyas both paved the way for the Clone Wars ten years later. Lust for power, not high ideals, is Palpatine's primary motivation. Palpatine wants to transform the Republic to obtain power, and he realizes that the only way to establish power over such a large, diverse group of peoples is through the use of military might. One snag: the mainly pacifist Senate won't allow such an army to be mustered, even when they find out that they have the Kamino clones at their disposal. Palpatine can't let this stand in his way, but fortunately his long-term scheming has paved the way for a solution. In *Revenge of the Sith*, we finally see his plan revealed in its awful magnitude, and its keystone is the power of the clone army to destroy most of the Jedi, allow Palpatine to dissolve the Senate, and suppress any opposition to his declaring himself Emperor. Why did the Senate vote in favor of giving Palpatine dictatorial authority, thus allowing him to harness the power he would eventually use to crush them? The answer is a familiar and simple one: fear.

Fear as an Ally

"Fear is my ally," hisses Darth Maul in the exciting ad campaign that led up to the much-anticipated release of *The Phantom Menace*. Maul's sentiment is echoed by Grand Moff Tarkin, who in *A New Hope* says that the finished Death Star will have a deterrent effect against rebellion, since "fear will keep the local systems in line." Both agree about the political value of fear with Palpatine, who is positively Machiavellian in his scheming toward the Empire, in the way he later controls his domain, and even while he taunts Luke to use his fear and anger as a means to bring him over to the Dark Side. In this, he is the paradigm of "the Prince," the unscrupulous ruler envisioned by Niccolò Machiavelli (1469–1527), a Renaissance political thinker who advised Italy's Borgia and Medici families. Machiavelli famously declared that if a prince has the choice between being loved and being feared by his subjects, he ought to choose fear. Ever the realist, Machiavelli held that this is because "love is held by a chain of obligation which, men being selfish, is broken whenever it serves their purpose; but fear is maintained by a dread of punishment which never fails."[5]

Machiavelli amends this statement, though, by saying that a good ruler ought to avoid those things that inspire hatred rather than fear, such as taking the property or wife of a subject. Today, we can hear echoes of Machiavelli's dictum when our leaders convince us to elect them or support their initiatives, not by offering us good reasons, but by playing on our emotions and sympathies. This tactic is held by many to be anti-democratic as it both disrespects and clouds our ability to make informed, rational decisions. Real democracy is based on our ability to make good decisions, since democratic political authority issues from the will of the people. We're rightly suspicious of such Machiavellian tendencies in our own leaders as a result.

Machiavelli's suggestion that clever politicians balance the happiness of citizens with uncertainty about their security has a very old pedigree. A prime example is found in ancient Athens, some fifty years before the advent of direct democracy there in 508 B.C.E. At the time, the Athenians were divided into three regional factions. The leaders of all three vied for political power, not to institute equality between citizens, but so that the classes they represented would gain by certain changes. Into this powder keg stepped the legendary Greek legislator Solon, held by later Greeks as "the greatest of statesman and the wisest of men" who had already saved Athens from civil war in 594 B.C.E.

Attempting to broker a settlement, Solon was suspicious of the attitude of Pisistratus, the leader of the disaffected working class, who "had an affable and engaging manner, was a great friend of the poor, and behaved with generosity even to his enemies."[6] This fooled many Athenians, but not Solon. Pisistratus cemented his place in the people's hearts by wounding himself, then driving a chariot into the Athenian marketplace to denounce an assassination attempt by his enemies to

---

[5] Niccolò Machiavelli, selections from *The Prince*, in Michael Curtis, ed., *The Great Political Theories*, Volume 1 (New York: Avon, 1981), p. 222.

[6] Plutarch, *Parallel Lives*: "Solon," quoted in *Readings in Ancient History: From Gilgamesh to Diocletian*, second edition (Lexington: Heath, 1976), p. 151.

his followers. Like the anonymous, red-robed guards that constantly accompany Palpatine, bodyguards were granted to Pisistratus, who used them to seize the Acropolis and establish himself as a tyrant, a single ruler who consults the laws only when it suits him. His position, effectively similar to the old Greek kings of the *Iliad* and *Odyssey*, passed to his two sons before the tyranny was ended. Solon, although allowed to live under the tyranny, was powerless to challenge the power of the Pisistratids.

In the later Roman political tradition, special powers and single-person rule made up the role of the dictator, which did not have the same negative meaning then as it does now. Dictators were often figures with military power—Julius Caesar for example—and were appointed indirectly by the Roman senate for specific purposes like commanding an army, holding elections, or suppressing sedition. Dictators were to resign their title and powers as soon as their task was completed and the emergency was over. But Caesar, whose appointment to the unheard-of position of *dictator perpetuus* perhaps gave us the first hint of the modern meaning of the word, used his powers to effectively destroy the Roman Republic and establish a hereditary Empire. Palpatine would have been proud.

Was George Lucas unconsciously thinking of his ancient history class in high school when he penned Palpatine's speech accepting radical "emergency powers" in order to combat the political Separatists lead by Count Dooku in *Attack of the Clones*? There, the future Emperor declares gravely:

> It is with great reluctance that I have agreed to this calling. I love democracy. I love the Republic. The power you give me I will lay down when this crisis has abated. And as my first act with this new authority, I will create a Grand Army of the Republic to counter the increasing threats of the Separatists.

The "reluctant" acceptance of the power he has been secretly hoping for, his noble words in defense of popular rule, and his solemn promise to lay down power when it's no longer needed would not have sounded inappropriate coming from Pisistratus or Julius Caesar. So the irony in this important scene, both in this sense and given what happens in *Revenge of the Sith*, is palpable (excuse the pun). It's an essential part of the tragedy of the prequel trilogy, however, that fear exposes the clay feet of the Republic's stone giant.

Palpatine's gambit puts a new spin on Machiavelli. Palpatine realizes that an adversarial relationship between himself and the rest of the Republic won't go his way: sometimes it's better to be loved than feared. But fear can still be his ally as long as he's poised, shoulder-to-shoulder with senators and citizens, against some *external* force. Long before the events of *The Phantom Menace*, Palpatine must have struggled with the same question as Pisistratus did: "How can a threat be *manufactured* that will unite the people behind me, and lead to their granting me special powers and a military force?" Palpatine's scheming is all the more in-*sidious* because, through the Neimoidian Trade Federation, Count Dooku, and their allies, he manufactures the threat. But modern democracies in our world have faced real threats to their existence, both external (like war and terrorism) and internal (like crime and political corruption).

After Obi-Wan reports in from Geonosis about the genuine threat represented by the Separatists, a senator from Malastare loyal to Palpatine claims, "The time for debate [about the Military Creation Act] is over. Now we need that clone army." Since the Senate won't use the clones pre-emptively, the "hawks" among them decide that the threat justifies granting Palpatine emergency powers, an act that is the beginning of the end for democracy in the Republic. Like these fictional senators, we need to ask ourselves the difficult questions, "What measures can be justly taken to defend a democracy in troubled times?" and "Is democracy undermined if undemocratic measures are taken in its defense?" These are questions as relevant and controversial today as they were a long time ago in a galaxy far, far away.

Power in the Hands of the Virtuous Few

There's an important scene in *Attack of the Clones* that contrasts two major answers to these questions we just posed about the defense of democracy:

ANAKIN: I don't think the system works. We need a system where the politicians sit down and discuss the problem, agree to what's in the best interest of all the people, and then do it.

PADMÉ: That's exactly what we do. The problem is that peo-
    ple don't always agree.
ANAKIN: Then they should be made to.
PADMÉ: By whom? Who's going to make them?
ANAKIN: Someone ...
PADMÉ: You?
ANAKIN: No, not me.
PADMÉ: But someone . . . ?
ANAKIN: (*nods*) Someone wise.
PADMÉ: I don't know. Sounds an awful lot like a dictatorship
    to me.
ANAKIN: (*after a long pause*) Well, if it works . . . ?

Anakin's thoughts reflect Palpatine's distrust of the politics of the
Republic, which were expressed more subtly in *The Phantom
Menace* over the Senate's handling of the Naboo trade embargo.
By this point, Anakin seems clearly under Palpatine's charis-
matic influence, if not of the Dark Side itself. Anakin voices the
view of his mentor that the bureaucratic aspects of a democratic republic hinder it when swift action is needed. Because of
this, the Republic may be unable to handle internal or external
challenges unless it leans on the leadership of its best, wisest,
and most virtuous citizens. Padmé seems to recoil at his "great
man" solution to political dissent, perhaps by maintaining that
democracy has the resources necessary to survive. Their debate
is reflected in the confrontation between the very different ideas
of two recent political philosophers, Leo Strauss (1899–1973)
and John Dewey (1859–1952). Both of them were concerned
with the problems and prospects of a kind of democracy we
haven't really looked at yet: modern *liberal* democracy. But
Strauss and Dewey understood the term "liberal" in very different ways.

    Strauss thinks that political thinkers of the past, particularly
Plato and Aristotle, provide timeless questions about the good
life and the just state that today's political philosophers should
still be concerned about. But, he would say, modern politics has
somehow gotten off the right track, taking its cues from
mediocre mass culture, mob democracy, and moral relativism
(the belief that no moral view is inherently superior to any
other). It's true that these seem to be characteristics of modern
culture, but Strauss calls our attention to the ideals that animate

the "philosopher-king" of Plato's *Republic* and the contemplative sage of Aristotle's *Nicomachean Ethics*. Both figures are beacons of virtue and wisdom as well as natural leaders. Their search for absolute and ultimate truth in political life, as in all other areas, has been abandoned for the most part, he thinks. So his sense of "liberal" attempts to recapture what was at the heart of Platonic and Aristotelian political thought: it expresses our inner impulse toward human excellence as being the end of all our efforts. Strauss says:

> The liberal man on the highest level esteems most highly the mind and its excellence and is aware of the fact that man at his best is autonomous or not subject to any authority, while in every other respect he is subject to authority which, in order to deserve respect, or to be truly authority, must be a reflection through a dimming medium of what is simply the highest.[7]

Strauss's way of thinking treats democracy as a "universal aristocracy" in which all are free to find their proper purpose and place in society, but society itself is structured by the insight that our wisest leaders have into what is essential, most real, or "the highest" in human nature.

John Dewey, called in his time "America's philosopher," would agree with Strauss's key idea that an ideal democracy is a universal aristocracy. But much depends on whether we put the stress on "universal" or "aristocracy," Dewey argues. For him, the "liberal" in liberal democracy means faith "that every human being as an individual may be the best for some particular purpose and hence be the most fitted to rule, to lead, in that specific respect."[8] He also stresses that we should see democracy as merely a way in which those with the greatest political expertise find their way into power. Democracy is more than a kind of political system involving voting and majority rule. It's a way of living that extends farther than politics, one that demands that individuals have the greatest freedom—in terms of

---

[7] Leo Strauss, "The Liberalism of Classical Political Philosophy," in *Liberalism Ancient and Modern* (New York: Basic Books, 1968), p. 28.

[8] John Dewey, "Individuality, Equality and Superiority," in *John Dewey: The Middle Works, 1899–1925*. Volume 13 (Carbondale: Southern Illinois University Press, 1983), p. 297.

equality of opportunity—to continue to grow as individuals and express their individuality. Democracy in this sense is a struggle: it requires our commitment to continually criticize and revise educational, political, and other means for providing opportunities for individuals. Sometimes these commitments may get in the way of traditional beliefs and values, and cause conflicts. But, Dewey says, it is also the best path for the attainment of excellence by a democratic citizenry *as a whole*. But Dewey's view of excellence is not like Strauss's because it is not solely dependent upon our accepting the wisdom of great and virtuous leaders. Instead, he says that democracy involves "faith in the capacity of the intelligence of the common man to respond with commonsense to the free play of facts and ideas which are secured by effective guarantees of free inquiry, free assembly and free communication."[9]

Anakin, particularly in his admiration for Palpatine and other "great men" and by his distrust of popular participation in democracy, holds a view comparable to Strauss's. For both of them, greater concentration of power in the hands of a few is justified by the natural ability of those few to lead and their virtues in assessing, judging, and responding to difficult and complex situations. To Strauss, these are "the wise," and Anakin sees wisdom and virtue not so much in Obi-Wan or the Jedi Council, but in figures like Palpatine who promise both the power and the license to correct injustices quickly and immediately. But the common person is apparently not fit to rule herself according to Strauss or Anakin, and the Straussian statesman is empowered to utilize many means, including deception, the stirring of patriotism, and manufactured threats in order to keep power.[10]

Padmé may represent a view closer to Dewey's. Although she agrees with Anakin in part when she claims in frustration in *The Phantom Menace* that the Republic is broken, she seems to have changed her mind in *Attack of the Clones* when she agrees with Queen Jamilla of Naboo's assertion that "the day we stop

---

[9] John Dewey, "Creative Democracy: The Task Before Us" in *John Dewey: The Later Works, 1925–1952*. Volume 14 (Carbondale: Southern Illinois University Press, 1988), p. 227.
[10] See the interview with Shadia Drury: http://www.opendemocracy.net/debates/article-3-77-1542.jsp.

believing democracy can work is the day we lose it." By opposing the Senate's Military Creation Act from the beginning, Padmé may have seized on a version of Dewey's central idea that democratic *ends* can be reached only by democratic *means*. Measures that threaten or clearly violate the republican and democratic principles we looked at earlier may create the *façade* of democracy, but they line the foundation of the democratic house with coercion, deception, and the establishment of aristocracies of all kinds—of wealth, of influence, or even those of higher education and virtue as Strauss suggests. Democracies can and should still value virtue and ability, but they should also put their trust in healthy checks and balances on the abuse of power, all at the reasonable cost of lessening the efficiency of democratic leadership. Of course, it's this loss of efficiency that future strong leaders like Anakin Skywalker deplore. When Palpatine seizes ultimate power, Anakin wins, but at the cost of his own soul. For the rest of the denizens of the Republic, the importance of balancing security and democratic principles is a lesson learned the hard way.

Palpatine's Legacy

Palpatine's rise from democratically-elected Supreme Chancellor to Emperor is a gripping, if ultimately tragic tale of how democracy may be destroyed from within by its own weakness when security is pursued by non-democratic means. It also exposes a flaw in the Straussian thinking of even well-meaning people like Anakin: "Who watches the watchers?" Strauss's virtuous statesmen don't ultimately answer to the common person but to a higher truth to which only the statesmen are privileged to. What checks are put on their obtaining power and who is to say that they are virtuous in their efforts?—only other members of "the wise."

The bitter truth raised here may stem from the fact that we have become more cynically distrustful of centralized authority, but there is also a deeper point to be made. Virtue is good, we agree, but our vision of human excellence today is much more diverse and plural than it was with Strauss's beloved Greeks. There are many goods worth pursuing, and perhaps some conflict with one another: the democratic challenge for now is to explore how to balance or reconcile these conflicts in order to maximize virtue, not concentrate it in figures of authority. As Senator, Supreme Chancellor, and ultimately Emperor, Palpatine's example throws light on the path from democracy to empire, a path paved with fear and insecurity, the illusory end-point of which is freedom and peace. In some ways, it may seem unsatisfactory to say that democracy is an "unfinished project" in which we all still have a part to play. In the end, however, admitting this might be the best guard against our own Palpatines, present and future.[11]

---

[11] I am grateful to Jason Eberl, Keith Decker, Robert Arp, Bill Irwin, and Suzanne Decker for reading and commenting on this chapter. This wise "Jedi Council" helped to improve it in crucial ways.

15

Humanizing Technology: Flesh and Machine in Aristotle and *The Empire Strikes Back*

JEROME DONNELLY

The philosopher Walter Benjamin (1892–1940) once remarked that in an age of technology the copy takes on greater importance than the original. The Sony Corporation's mechanical dog created a sensation that illustrates Benjamin's insight.

George Lucas's *The Empire Strikes Back* achieves its powerful effect in a very special way, by making the mechanical and bionic world of science fiction preferable to nature's flesh and blood. Lucas captivates his audience by combining ultra-realism and familiarity with the content of its predecessor, *A New Hope*. Together, these provide *The Empire Strikes Back* with an unusually powerful appeal in drawing the viewer into Lucas's strange new world. This compelling verisimilitude lends plausibility not only to the film's action but also to its underlying themes, especially the theme of *humanizing technology*, that is, treating the mechanical products of technology as if they possessed life, a capacity for thought and feeling, and rational and emotional interaction with people. In the course of celebrating technology, Lucas develops an opposition between technology and nature and, at crucial moments, ennobles technology at the expense of nature. Because the theme operates so subtly in a film of otherwise forceful, gripping plot and effects, analysis requires bringing the theme to the surface in order to realize fully its meaning and implications.

The attitude expressed in *The Empire Strikes Back* represents a break with the dominant philosophical tradition of Western culture, one with roots in Aristotle and usually referred to as

181

"philosophical realism." For Aristotle, the natural universe is shot through with order, meaning, and value. Nature is not only the principle of order and growth in the universe; it is purposive and serves as a guide for human activity. Things in the world are composed of *matter*, for example, the flesh, blood, and bone of human beings, and *form*. Aristotle defines form as "that which makes a thing what it is."[1]

Form is what makes living things develop into what they become; acorns develop into oak trees, and chicken eggs into chickens, all the while transforming food and water into the different matter of wood, leaf, feather, and flesh.[2] Aristotle observes a hierarchy in nature, extending from the inanimate through vegetable, animal, and human life. The vegetable form (or soul) has the capacity for such activities as nutrition and reproduction, while the animal soul adds to these powers with others, such as locomotion and perception. Human beings combine these powers with the greater powers of language and rational thought, and are thus at the apex of the natural hierarchy.[3]

Artificial products, including technology, can complete "what nature is unable to carry to a finish," but Aristotle insists on a basic distinction between things that exist as part of the natural world and those made by human skill, which include art and technology. Art can be wonderful but is subordinate to nature, which is both prior to it and its source. Aristotle's sharp distinction between the natural and the artificial would apply to Luke Skywalker's bionic hand, since the limb is produced from a pre-existing form and matter (or material). All manner of products—clothes, ladders, glasses, prostheses—extend or enhance nature, enabling human beings to keep warmer, reach higher, see better, or even replace damaged or missing natural body parts.

---

[1] Aristotle, *Physics*, translated by Richard Hope (Lincoln: University of Nebraska Press, 1961), 194b12.

[2] *Ibid.*, 193b9–12.

[3] Aristotle, *De anima*, translated by J.A. Smith, in *The Complete Works of Aristotle*, edited by Jonathan Barnes (Princeton: Princeton University Press, 1984), 414a28–b20.

"I Am Fluent in Six Million Forms of Communication"

In *The Empire Strikes Back*, Lucas implies that the world is mostly artificial, a world made up simply of interchangeable parts, a view reinforced by the constant tinkering and fixing of all the intergalactic gadgets used in space travel. Nature is depicted as little more than a nuisance, and technology is superior and necessary to repair the mess that nature continually finds itself in, whether it is a lost limb or repeated threats to the safety of the body and the potential extinction of life. This is in sharp contrast to Aristotle's view of the relationship of art (which would include technology) and nature. While everything in both art and nature consists of form and matter, they do so in very different ways.

Aristotle emphasizes that nature works from within, while art and technology are produced from outside, whether in making a statue with limbs or prostheses to replace them. Art and technology fall outside of the order of nature and aren't alive. Pygmalion, the ivory statue, which in Greek legend was brought to life by the goddess of Love, is only a story. In the real world, statues don't live or love; only people do. And anyone who fell in love with a statue would be wasting both time and affection. Technology is not only lifeless; it depends on nature as the basis of both its forms and matter. In his *Metaphysics*, Aristotle uses the example of a bronze sphere to make this point: "the production is from bronze [matter] and sphere [form]—the form is imported [from outside the matter] into this stuff and the result is a bronze sphere."[4] In nature, form operates from within matter, as, for example, an acorn grows from within to become an oak tree. The difference is that between Sony's mechanical dog and a real dog. C-3PO is a more sophisticated version of Sony's mechanical dog. Neither grows from within; both are produced artificially from without.

The issue is not simply one of looking at modern technology with a new admiration. Both real and fictional heroes have famously felt affection for the tools of their trade, admiring the

---

[4] Aristotle, *Metaphysics*, translated by Hugh Lawson-Tankred (London: Penguin, 1998), 1028b33–1029a7.

beauty and craft of their weapons, and occasionally speaking to sword or arrow in hoping aloud for victory or a sure hit in the "Don't fail me now" tradition. Yet, when technology is accorded the capacity to behave in human terms, the relationship between man and tool changes considerably. The transformation is striking in *The Empire Strikes Back*, as Lucas substitutes robots for some of the traditional secondary adventure characters, and in so doing shifts audience responses by directing affections away from human characters to these ingenious (often cute) products of technology. The human emotion generated on behalf of technology becomes accentuated by the absence of strong feeling for what should be emotionally charged relationships. Despite the inclusion of traditional adventures from epic and romance, along with a budding love relationship between central characters Han Solo and Princess Leia and the depiction of loyal bonds between comrades, the film repeatedly deflects attention and feeling away from these human relationships, particularly by constant deflation of the incipient love story.

Aristotle would take an entirely different approach to droids, clearly distinguishing them from nature and people (who are at the apex of nature's hierarchy). He would classify R2-D2 or C-3PO as "instruments of production." In the *Politics*, Aristotle seems to anticipate the likes of *Empire*'s futuristic robotics, imagining how an "instrument" (or robot) "could do its own work, at the word of command or by intelligent anticipation like the statues of Dedalus or the tripods made by Hephestus."[5] Clearly, Aristotle does not conceive of them as loveable creatures or like members of a family—something that Lucas is inclined to do.

Placing *Empire*'s robots in familiar human roles radically alters the nature of the audience experience by blurring the distinction between life and technology. To illustrate the extent to which Lucas preserves the experience of robots as characters, it's instructive to compare the composition of his group to a set of counterparts in the film version of *The Wizard of Oz*. The whining, worrying C-3PO is reminiscent of the lachrymose Tin Woodsman, who himself has all the appearance of a robot; the

---

[5] Aristotle, *Politics*, translated by Ernest Barker (Oxford: Clarendon, 1946), 1253b35.

meddlesome R2-D2 sniffs out mischief like Dorothy's Toto; and, as if to emphasize these similarities, Chewbacca the Wookiee has a mane and a sentimental roar like the Cowardly Lion. And when C-3PO is shattered and then put back together, it scolds its mender in just the exasperated tones of the Scarecrow when Dorothy patiently replaces his straw.

The parallel points up important differences in the way the characters appear to the audience; Frank Baum's story uses Dorothy's dream as a framework to distinguish fantasy from reality, as opposed to Lucas's depiction of a science-fiction fantasy as real, even to the point of eschewing the usual preliminary credits. Instead of framing off the adventure as a fantasy, Lucas goes in the opposite direction by obliterating the frame and drawing the audience into the film's galaxy—dodging meteorites that fly off the screen, ducking explosions from stereo speakers surrounding them. However real the Tin Woodsman seems, he remains framed off within a dream, one calculated as a reminder that the relationship between Dorothy and her friends, however delightful, remains clearly an imaginative experience from which Dorothy and the audience awake. *The Empire Strikes Back* strives for the opposite effect, which gives the robots and their human functions and relationships a strong sense of validity—often at the expense of real humans and real human relationships.

"I Thought They Smelled Bad on the Outside"

This background of parallels only highlights the differences in attitude, and nowhere more clearly than in Lucas's theme of humanizing technology. The theme builds gradually so that through the course of the film the technological marvels—at first so vast and various in this strange new galaxy—seem finally as familiar and indispensable as the family car. Indeed, Han and Chewbacca spend much of their time acting like mechanics tinkering with spaceships as if they were jalopies parked in the driveway. And, like real driveway mechanics, their grease-monkey antics often end in comic frustration and failure.

The function of these comic moments is to give the objects of their tinkering a sense of the familiar and the ordinary. In the film, familiarization promotes acceptance of this futuristic technology, which ushers in an actual humanizing of its products, achieved with spectacular effect in R2-D2 and C-3PO. No longer simply handy pieces of technology, they become more than robots; sometimes Mutt and Jeff comic figures, sometimes endangered and unsuspecting children, they arouse feelings at one moment of amused affection and at the next of concern. Apparently programmed to meddle and fret, C-3PO engages the audience's emotions in the very act of being an annoyance. It's as if technology has breathed the breath of life into its products, and not only in the robots. From a distance, what appear to be approaching monsters turn out to be AT-AT walkers, the elephantine troop-transports of the Imperial army. Even their destruction has a curious animal quality as they resist the most sophisticated rocket assault, only to be tripped up at their metal ankles and fall heaving and shuddering on the ground.

With the AT-ATs, technology imitates nature; in the robots, technology evokes responses enabling it to replace the flesh and blood of organic nature. Technology fills the vacuum created when real, living nature gets dramatically shoved aside early in the film, in a scene in which Han Solo, mounted on a tauntaun, rescues the wounded Luke Skywalker.

Realizing that without heat, they won't survive the night in Hoth's frozen waste, Han sacrifices his mount by slicing it open so that Luke can use the creature's body heat by nestling in its opened guts. The sudden unexpectedness of Han's slashing into the animal's flesh seems brutal, yet the act is presented as necessary for survival and perfectly proper that man sacrifice beast to save a human life. This attitude accords with Aristotle's hierarchy of the natural order.

The incident offers a possibility for making a dramatic use of the tradition of great steeds from classics to cowboys—from Alexander the Great's historic Bucephalus to the Lone Ranger's fictional Silver. Such horses are justly seen as objects of admiration, and their riders would be saddened to lose them. Yet, Han expresses a curious lack of feeling toward a living thing, and one that has served him without fail. His only response is sarcasm as he slices open the animal's belly, remarking, "I thought they smelled bad on the outside."

At this point, the film turns away from creaturely flesh to the wonders of technology. How different is this view of animal flesh from that of Aristotle, who acknowledges that "there are some animals which have no attractiveness for the senses" and that "it is not possible without considerable disgust to look upon the blood, flesh, bones, blood-vessels, and suchlike," but who, nonetheless, encourages the study of all animal life, "knowing that in not one of them is Nature or Beauty lacking."[6]

"Luminous Beings Are We . . . Not This Crude Matter"

The disdain for creaturely flesh and blood illustrates a view that repeatedly crops up in Lucas's film: the display of an absence of value placed on physical life or on the goodness of nature, which is replaced by a predilection for technology.

Yoda, though separated from the technological action, speaks for many of the values expressed in the film, and his views give a clue to the basis for this preference. His initial, physically repugnant appearance soon becomes a kind of corroboration for his status as a guru. He has something of the Eastern mystic about him. His isolation appears to be a backdrop for a life of ascetic contemplation, rather than a sign of alienated withdrawal. Yoda is seen finally as an embodiment of unselfish goodness and thus a perfect mentor, under whose guidance Luke achieves a heightened consciousness. But there is something more to Yoda's isolation; he seems to live in a world devoid of human emotion. Yoda warns Luke against the self-destructiveness of hate, but nowhere does he advocate love. The fruit of Yoda's training bears this out; though Luke shows loyalty (a quality he has demonstrated before becoming Yoda's pupil), nowhere does he come to the sort of compassionate insight one might expect from an enlightened mind.

Yoda's is a life without joy. World weary, perpetually exhausted, he takes no pleasure in reflecting that he has been training Jedi Knights for eight hundred years. Apparently, none of that has given any cause for celebration; he shows no inclination for song or delight in any form. His spirit of renunciation—"You must unlearn what you have learned"—implies a rejection of emotion and comes close to the sort of Buddhist injunction, "Give, sympathize, control," familiar to modern readers of T.S. Eliot's *The Waste Land* or in its more recent and pop-

---

[6] Aristotle, *Parts of Animals*, translated by A.L. Peck (Cambridge: Harvard University Press, revised edition 1945), 645a29–31; 645a23.

ular Zen manifestations.[7] Such an implicitly dualistic attitude has closer affinities with the legacy of the Puritan suspicion of life embodied in flesh, a view filtered through to the modern world via American Transcendentalism, than it shares with the sense of a unity of mind and body as well as the unity of being, as it does in Aristotle or in the work of J.R.R. Tolkien.

Aristotle takes a holistic approach in conceiving of the relation of body and soul (or mind). In his philosophy, matter and form are indivisible, except for purposes of analysis. Unlike Plato, he doesn't depreciate matter (or flesh) or denigrate it as a source of trouble or pain. Instead, Aristotle argues that matter joined with form actualizes *being*, and being is good. Aristotle would have no trouble answering the question posed by an agonized Hamlet, "To be or not to be?" Without matter, form cannot be individualized, that is, there can be no individual beings without it, while matter without form doesn't even exist.

The same split between mind and matter in Lucas's film is a familiar feature in much of the thinking about science going at least as far back as Francis Bacon (1521–1626). Science and technology, in this post-Renaissance view, emphasize discovery as a source of power over nature rather than as a discovery of truths about nature and man's relation to the rest of the universe. Seeking power over nature easily becomes a kind of combat, with man pitting himself against the material universe. Yoda's teaching Luke to levitate a rock while standing on one hand demonstrates more than training in concentration; perhaps it even shows the same will to overcome matter and gravity that appears in the modern impulse to balance massive skyscrapers on slender fingers of steel and concrete.

More importantly, it's in keeping with the spirit of nature as an obstacle to be overcome that the robots exhibit mind overcoming the limitations of flesh, and the comic re-building of C-3PO after having been blown apart by an enemy shot only dramatizes the implied insignificance of the relation of body to mind. In the same scene where C-3PO is reconstructed, the body becomes a series of interchangeable parts. Even as C-3PO comically scolds Chewbacca for getting its head on backwards,

---

[7] For further discussions of Yoda as a "Zen master" and a "Stoic sage," see Chapters 2 and 3 in this volume.

the robot evokes pity, as if it were a human patient in an operating room.

Clearly lacking real flesh and life, lacking even that artificial life of a Frankenstein monster patched together from the flesh of unwitting donors, the robot has assumed a completely human role.[8] Its dialogue with human characters and their paternalistic feelings toward the incessantly gabbing machine conspire to evoke smiles at one moment, pity and fear at the next, and so confuse the human and the technological. Having taken on the capacity for human interaction, R2-D2 and C-3PO operate like minds severed from organic bodies and installed in machines. As fleshly sense disappears, body is reduced to the status of an automobile—albeit one capable of absorbing and processing data—whose parts are as interchangeable and as valuable as the springs on a car. Aristotle's inseparability of body and mind disappears. Watching C-3PO's parts being tinkered with carries the conviction that body no longer has any integral relation to thought, any more than a car can be said to participate in the experience its driver is having. Thus, separating mind and body, and rejecting the latter as insignificant to humans and irrelevant to thought, blurs a proper distinction between humanity and technology and so advances the theme of humanizing technology, giving it plausibility it wouldn't otherwise have.

Similarly, humanizing technological puppets makes it easier to think of human beings as something like robots with interchangeable parts. *The Empire Strikes Back* develops this theme to such an extent that in the closing moments when Luke's bionic hand replaces the real one he has lost in battle, the new appendage appears not only identical with and equal to the original, but even preferable to the flesh and blood hand. This bionic hand, so the film suggests, can be replaced by any number of similar devices. Luke's expression of admiration as he flexes his new technological fingers marks a triumph over nature. In contrast, Aristotle lavishes several pages of his *Parts of Animals* to the wonders of natural, human hands. He emphasizes elsewhere that just as a stick in the hand cannot be the source of movement, neither does a hand move itself; instead,

---

[8] For further discussion of the "personhood" of R2-D2 and C-3PO, see Chapter 10 in this volume.

its movement has its source and co-ordination in the soul. In *The Empire Strikes Back*, flesh does not really matter, and the expression of revulsion toward the stink of real flesh actually assists in encouraging a preference for an odorless, mechanical substance. Nature does everything for the sake of something, says Aristotle, for whom nature is the norm.[9] In *The Empire Strikes Back*, that attitude is reversed. Technology exists not only as a subject; technology becomes the norm.

While body parts can be replaced, that isn't true of the person. For Aristotle—and, indeed, for an entire tradition in Western philosophy that includes Cicero, Thomas Aquinas, and their modern counterparts such as Etienne Gilson, Peter Geach, and Henry Veatch—each person is unique.[10] The primary feature of the person is so obvious that a description of a person might well overlook it: a person is unique and thus irreplaceable. The basis for the individual self is in what Aristotle calls "primary substance." Each person is thus like a fingerprint—unique to that individual in a world in which all individuals share in having fingerprints. However many parts are interchangeable, persons, as persons, are never interchangeable. Human beings share in a common nature; they continue to beget and replace other human beings—all having in common their humanity, as well as physical features like arms and legs. Yet, while limbs can be lost (and artificially replaced), the uniqueness of the person remains.

Rejecting technology as a substitute for human norms and rejecting the converse—that humans are the equivalent of machines or computers—doesn't entail a rejection of the value of technology. *The Empire Strikes Back* attacks the distinctiveness of human beings by encouraging a view of humans in which the inseparability of mind and body no longer exists. Technology is proffered instead as having the potential for becoming human. Where popular culture has given us a Tin Woodsman who longed for a human heart, technology has now given us a tin heart as a substitute, thus fulfilling that dream in reverse. To regard technology as a contribution to

---

[9] Aristotle, *Physics*, 199b10.

[10] See Etienne Gilson, *The Spirit of Medieval Philosophy* (New York: Scribner's, 1937); Peter Geach, *God and the Soul* (London: Routledge, 1969); Henry Veatch, *Rational Man* (Bloomington: Indiana University Press, 1962).

human life is one thing; to think of technology as the means of raising the status of human nature is to repeat the mistake of Jonathan Swift's Lemuel Gulliver, who returns from his last voyage having discovered a society of beings that look like horses but display a rational understanding that far surpasses anything that Gulliver has experienced in human company, and develops a loathing for the human species. Totally misanthropic, he rejects his wife and children and chooses the company of horses in the barn. A preference for the products of technology must surely have the same result: an actual demeaning of the truly human and a consequent rejection of the company of people in exchange for the barn and the company of horses (or mechanical dogs). The capacity for reasoning and feeling, for choosing and valuing, is distinctly human. Insofar as it blinds us to this human distinctiveness, humanizing technology ultimately results in *dehumanization*.

16

"A Certain Point of View": Lying Jedi, Honest Sith, and the Viewers Who Love Them

SHANTI FADER

Not long after our second (or was it third?) viewing of *Attack of the Clones,* my boyfriend and I became involved in one of our not-uncommon debates about Lucas's galaxy in general and the Jedi in particular. As we argued the finer points of Jedi philosophy and mindset, he commented, "Isn't it interesting how the Jedi lie so much more than the Sith, and yet they're supposed to be the good guys?"

Jedi enthusiast that I am, I automatically leaped to their defense—only to be stopped by the realization that he was right. The Jedi do an awful lot of lying and shading of the truth for a religious order that's supposed to be on the side of virtue. Obi-Wan Kenobi lies to Luke about his father; Yoda misleads Luke when he arrives on Dagobah; and Mace Windu covers up the fact that the Jedi are losing their powers. By contrast, the Sith do a surprising amount of truth-telling for villains. Count Dooku tells a captive Obi-Wan flat-out that the Senate has been infiltrated by a Sith. Senator Palpatine, *aka* the Sith Master Darth Sidious, worms his way into power without speaking a single literal untruth.[1] And, of course, in one of the most famous moments in Lucas's entire epic, Darth Vader tells Luke the devastating truth that Obi-Wan had withheld.

---

[1] The big exception would appear to be the speech he gives to the Senate in *Attack of the Clones*, which certainly seems to contradict the facts. I'll discuss this shortly.

The more I thought about it, the more it baffled me. Honesty is generally seen as a virtue (except when someone asks you "Does this make me look fat?"), and lying as a terrible, hurtful vice. Why, then, would Lucas have his Jedi lie and his Sith tell the truth? As far back as Plato and Socrates (fifth and fourth centuries B.C.), philosophers have been wrestling with the puzzle of truth and falsehood, in the process coming up with a varied and fascinating array of ideas. I certainly don't pretend to have the answer to what truth really is, but in this chapter I'll explore several possibilities raised by philosophers and reflected in Lucas's intriguing paradox.

Just the Facts

The search for truth is as old as the first human being who wondered about the meaning of existence, and as modern as the movies playing in today's multiplex. One of the primary purposes of mythology and religion is to seek the truth about our purpose in this life. "What is truth?" Pontius Pilate famously asked Jesus—and philosophy itself might be seen as an endless search for an answer to that question.

But what, exactly, *is* truth? On the simplest and most literal level, truth is what corresponds to the facts—to be true, a statement has to correctly represent the way things really are. I can say, "The ticket line for *The Phantom Menace* stretched all the way around the block." This statement is true if the ticket line did stretch all the way around the block, and false if I'm exaggerating due to my sore feet. George Lucas envisioned the *Star Wars* movies, Carrie Fisher played Princess Leia, and John Williams wrote the score: these are all facts and therefore when I make these statements, what I say is true.

But is truth really this simple? I believe there's far more to it. Factual truth is certainly necessary for a society to function. Merchants and craftspeople need to represent their products accurately if they want to keep their customers. No legal system can function without factual honesty—witnesses in court swear to tell "the truth, the whole truth, and nothing but the truth," and are punished if caught in a lie. On a more personal level, trust is one of the most important ingredients of relationships.

But telling the truth isn't as easy as simply reporting facts, as anyone who's had to deal with an opinionated boss, an insecure friend, or nosy in-laws can confirm. People lie for many reasons: to make themselves look better, avoid blame for something they've done, protect a loved one who's fallen afoul of the law, or gain something they can't (or won't try to) get through honest means, among others. This is particularly true when a society's leaders fail their people or commit a wrongful act. Those holding power are usually unwilling to relinquish it, and seldom hesitate to cover up their error. This drama manifests in *Star Wars* as the decline and fall of the Old Republic-era Jedi Order.

In *Attack of the Clones*, the Jedi have found themselves in a terribly awkward position: they're losing their connection to the Force. The Jedi are peacekeepers, an order of religious knights not unlike the Templars of European history or the Round Table of Arthurian legend, and if it became known that their powers were fading, they would also lose the awe and respect previously accorded them. (That the Jedi are indeed viewed this way is established by the Trade Federation officials' reaction to Obi-Wan and Qui-Gon Jinn in *The Phantom Menace*.) In order to carry out their duties as the "guardians of peace and justice," they feel they're forced (no pun intended) to break their own moral code. How long the Jedi would've been able to maintain this pretence is uncertain; the illusion of power seldom lasts very long with nothing to back it up. Later, we'll examine whether or not this deception is justified; but it's unquestionably a lie in the simplest and most straightforward sense.

Then there are the Sith. The German philosopher Friedrich Nietzsche (1844–1900), who was very interested in both truth and power, and enjoyed questioning traditional morality, could easily have had Palpatine in mind when he wrote:

> The intellect . . . unfolds its chief powers in simulation; for this is the means by which the weaker, less robust individuals preserve themselves . . . In man this art of simulation reaches its peak: here deception, flattery, lying and cheating, talking behind the back, posing, living in borrowed splendor, being masked, the disguise of convention, acting a role before others and before oneself—in short, the constant fluttering around the single flame of vanity is so much the role and the law that almost nothing is more incompre-

hensible than how an honest and pure urge for truth could make its appearance among men.[2]

Here we begin to see that truth is not so simple. While Palpatine for the most part doesn't tell direct falsehoods, his words are always layered with hidden meanings, most of them for the benefit of the audience members who know exactly what he's really after. (So much of what Palpatine says in Episodes I and II seems directed at the audience, rather than his fellow characters, that I'm tempted to suspect that his Sith powers include the knowledge that he's fictional and the ability to read ahead in the script!) The best example of this, interestingly, is his acceptance speech upon being granted "emergency powers" by the Senate in *Attack of the Clones*—the very speech that appears to be his most blatant lie.

"I love democracy," Palpatine proclaims. Of *course* he loves it! Democracy is the tool that granted him a smooth and bloodless rise to absolute power. Just because he discards the tool when it's no longer necessary doesn't mean it didn't please him while he was using it. As for his pledge to lay his power down once the crisis was resolved, clearly Palpatine wasn't thinking of the same crisis as the rest of the Senate. As late as *Return of the Jedi*, Palpatine (now the Emperor) still sees threats to his power and to the Empire he rules. If he doesn't consider his "crisis" resolved, he's being true to the letter of his speech; and if the Senate heard something other than what Palpatine secretly believed, we in the audience know better. Like Obi-Wan, Palpatine lied only "from a certain point of view."

"Judge Me by My Size, Do You?"

One of the pleasures I took from my first viewing of *The Phantom Menace* was hearing scattered horrified gasps from the audience when Queen Amidala first addresses that helpful, gray-haired man as "Palpatine." The kindly Senator is a façade designed to deflect suspicion away from himself while he

---

[2] Friedrich Nietzsche, "On Truth and Lie in an Extra-Moral Sense" (1873), in *The Portable Nietzsche*, edited by Walter Kaufman (Princeton: Princeton University Press, 1954), p. 43.

maneuvers everyone around him (including the Jedi, who really should've known better) into liking him, trusting him, and giving him exactly what he wants. Palpatine takes control of the Senate without personally spilling a single drop of blood because he conceals the fact that he's really a ruthless, power-hungry, and vengeance-seeking Sith Master. The few times we see him as Darth Sidious, his face is hidden beneath a heavy hood.

Then there's Yoda. When we first meet him neither Luke nor the audience has any idea that this comical, wizened little chatterbox could be the great Jedi Master whom Luke was sent to find. Yoda doesn't reveal his identity, but keeps up the game until Luke figures it out on his own. How is this any different from Palpatine's actions?

The difference can be found not in *what* the two characters are doing but in *why*—in the intention behind their actions (and of course, their ultimate consequences). The reasons behind a person's actions can be every bit as important as the actions themselves. And while many philosophers, such as Immanuel Kant (1724–1804), would say that lying is never defensible, others, including *utilitarians*, believe that there are times when lies are harmless or even beneficial, that is, when they would produce the greatest good for the greatest number of people. Nietzsche goes even further, dismissing conventional morality altogether and declaring that truth is nothing but the specific set of lies accepted by a particular society.[3]

Turning briefly away from Palpatine and Yoda, we can now look at the Jedi Council's decision to conceal the waning of their powers and ask: what was their intention? They may have honestly thought their lie served the greater good, letting them continue to act as peacekeepers and negotiators. Certainly the galaxy becomes a harsher place once the Jedi are eradicated or forced into hiding. In the end, though, however altruistic their intentions might have been, the Jedi certainly appeared to be lying to hold onto power.

Palpatine's intentions have no such shades of grey about them. He wants to take over the Senate, overthrow the Jedi, and make himself the single, supreme ruler of the entire galaxy; he wants power for its own sake and uses deception to gain it.

---

[3] *Ibid.*

Yoda, on the other hand, doesn't deceive Luke for power or personal gain (with the possible exception of Luke's flashlight, with which he stubbornly refuses to part). His motives are similar to those of the Tibetan Lama Marpa the Translator, who misled and toyed with his would-be student Milarepa for years—demanding near-impossible physical labor and repeatedly refusing to give him instruction or initiations—before finally relenting and taking on the incredibly patient youth.[4] A more modern example would be the old karate master Mr. Miyagi from *The Karate Kid*, who commands his baffled student Daniel-*san* to perform endless chores before revealing that they were actually cleverly disguised lessons (with the side benefit of giving Mr. Miyagi a clean house and shiny cars). To understand Yoda, we need to realize that he, like Marpa and Mr. Miyagi, is playing the Trickster.

Tricksters are found in myth and story throughout the world. They're usually wise and powerful beneath a playful or even foolish exterior. Tricksters disguise themselves and play pranks in order to test people, disrupt their preconceptions, or jolt them into a new way of thinking. Yoda's behavior tested Luke, exposing the young man's faults—his impatience, impulsiveness, and incomplete understanding of the Force—faults which Luke would've tried to hide, consciously or not, if he'd known he was facing a Jedi Master.

Yoda's primary lesson is that in order to use the Force, one must look beyond appearances. Palpatine embodies the negative side of this lesson, with his kindly face and hidden lust for power. Yoda, powerful and enlightened beyond what his wizened exterior would suggest, embodies the positive.[5]

Truth and the Marketplace

Truth, then, is less obvious than it initially seems. People aren't always what they appear, and words that sound honest can be colored by hidden meanings. But this hardly explains or solves the paradox of the lying Jedi and honest Sith, particularly not in the case of Obi-Wan Kenobi, whom we first meet as a wise

---

[4] For the story of Milarepa and Marpa, see http://www.cosmicharmony.com/Av/Milarepa/Milarepa.htm.

[5] For further philosophical analysis of Yoda's character, see Chapter 2 in this volume.

desert hermit and mentor figure. Why would such a person lie to Luke? From one perspective, this is a terrible act—a betrayal of young Luke's trust, a way to manipulate him into joining the battle on the Jedi's team. When Obi-Wan's lie is exposed, Luke is shattered to the point of very nearly choosing death. But from another perspective, Obi-Wan wasn't trying to manipulate Luke, but to protect him.

"You can't handle the truth!" Jack Nicholson shouts at the climax of *A Few Good Men*. Not all truths are pretty or easy to face. And just as some forms of entertainment are too intense for young children, some truths are simply too much to handle for people at an early stage in their emotional and intellectual development. The Greek philosopher Socrates (470–399 B.C.) compares the seeking of truth to shopping in a marketplace: an inexperienced shopper, who can't tell good merchandise from bad, may find herself swindled into buying food that's spoiled, unwholesome, or even poisoned—or, like Luke's Uncle Owen, buying a droid with a bad motivator.[6] Nietzsche makes the uncomfortable point that we only actually want truths that are pleasant or that help us, and we're quite tolerant of lies that do us no harm.[7]

The Luke that Obi-Wan meets on Tatooine is young and sheltered. He knows nothing more complex than his aunt and uncle's farm, and sees the Jedi as perfect, shining heroes out of legend, not real people with frailties and human weakness. Obi-Wan feels that this Luke isn't ready for the ugly truth about his father. As Socrates would put it, he doesn't yet have the wisdom to keep that knowledge from poisoning him. Most likely, if Luke hadn't rushed off to face Vader half-trained, he would've eventually learned the complete story in a gentler way. But for the time being, Obi-Wan offers the young Jedi a version of the truth that he could handle.

"Unexpected This Is, and Unfortunate"

If Obi-Wan uses a lie to protect, the Sith use truth as a weapon. Vader tells Luke the truth about his parentage at the worst possible time, and in a way that inflicts as much pain as humanly possible: truth without compassion is brutality. In *Attack of the*

---

[6] See Plato, *Protagoras*.
[7] Nietzsche, *op. cit.*

Clones, Yoda's renegade apprentice Count Dooku picks a similarly bad situation in which to tell young Obi-Wan that a Sith has infiltrated the Senate. Dooku even echoes Vader's dialogue as he invites the Jedi to join him, knowing that he'll either be believed and gain an ally, or disbelieved, in which case telling the truth actually covers it up.[8]

Neither Vader nor Dooku is telling the truth because he wants to increase anyone's knowledge or understanding, or lead them toward a more authentic life. Instead, they both use truth in an attempt to break a Jedi's faith in something they know and trust—in Obi-Wan's case, the Senate, and in Luke's case, Obi-Wan himself—and in doing so to make them question their loyalty. This, of course, works better in the case of the vulnerable, half-trained Luke. Despite his initial words of disbelief, Obi-Wan passes Dooku's information on to the Jedi Council (where it's largely dismissed). But even Luke doesn't give in entirely. Though shattered in body and spirit, he lets himself drop into the abyss below Cloud City rather than join Vader.

Later, Luke returns to Dagobah, where Vader's story is reluctantly confirmed first by a dying Yoda, then by the spirit of Obi-Wan in a dialogue that raises the question: was Obi-Wan's lie really a lie at all? In a strictly literal sense it is—Darth Vader can't have killed Luke's father if he *is* Luke's father. But as we've seen in this chapter, truth is seldom as simple as the literal facts make it seem.

Obi-Wan says, "Luke, you're going to find that many of the truths we cling to depend greatly on our own point of view." This isn't necessarily the evasive self-justification it appears to be. It could certainly be argued, as Obi-Wan does, that the good man and Jedi who was Anakin Skywalker was destroyed when he chose the path of the Sith and became Darth Vader. Vader says as much when Luke calls him Anakin: "That name no longer has any meaning for me." To which Luke responds, "It is the name of your true self. You've only forgotten." Changing one's name is a near-universal way to signal a new identity, dying in a metaphorical sense to one's old self and being reborn. There's no denying, however, that Obi-Wan didn't orig-

---

[8] In other words, hiding it in plain sight. For an interesting exploration of this idea, see Wendy Doniger, *The Woman Who Pretended to Be Who She Was* (New York: Oxford University Press, 2004).

inally intend Luke to understand his words in this metaphysical sense—any more than Palpatine expected the Senate to see through the layers of meaning in his acceptance speech. That intention makes it a deception even if truth was buried in his words. It also brings the virtuous Jedi Knight uncomfortably close to the wicked Sith Master, one of the shadings into grey of previously one-sided characters that helps make the *Star Wars* films so interesting.

The question of whether or not Obi-Wan really lied is less important than *why* he said what he said—his intentions. A parallel can be found in the Parable of the House on Fire, which the Buddha tells to his disciple Shariputra. A wealthy man's house catches on fire. His children are oblivious to the fire and the danger it poses. They ignore their father's warnings and continue to play with their toys as the house burns around them. The father finally tells his children he's got wonderful carts outside for them, carts driven by each of their favorite animals. Delighted, the children run outside. The promised carts are not there, but in their place are carriages that carry them safely away from the fire. Buddha then asks his disciple whether or not the father in the parable is guilty of falsehood. Shariputra says no:

> The elder is not guilty of falsehood, for he has only enabled his children to avoid the calamity of fire, and has thereby saved their lives . . . If that elder had not given them even so much as a single small cart, he still would not have been speaking falsely. Why? Because the elder previously had this thought, "I shall use expedients to lead my children out."[9]

So when deception is used to attain noble ends, to assist someone whose awareness and understanding are incomplete, it isn't really deception. This is surprising, coming as it does from the Buddhist tradition in which one of the basic tenets is "right speech," which includes honesty. Perhaps Shariputra overstates his case and the elder has indeed told a falsehood, but nevertheless is not "guilty" as no one would argue that lying to save an oblivious child from death is wrong.

---

[9] *Lotus Sutra*, Chapter 3: "Parable of the House on Fire" http://www.buddhistdoor.com/bdoor/0112/sources/lotus7_p1.htm.

Obi-Wan's intentions are very much the same as those of the elder in the parable. He sees Luke in danger of falling into a life in which his spiritual potential will be squandered or corrupted, or quite possibly even losing that life before it had really begun. He sees as well that Luke is blind to that danger, so he uses "expedients" to lead the young man toward a more authentic life. Plato touches on a similar idea when he relates the story of Socrates and the "Noble Lie."[10] Socrates is faced with the task of explaining to the people of his hypothetical Republic why they've been divided into social classes of craftspeople, guardians, and leaders. To convince them, he invents a fantastic tale of their having been formed, educated, and nurtured within the earth along with their weapons and tools, and that precious metals have been mixed into them—metals that equip each man for one specific task in life. Socrates himself acknowledges that this is a falsehood, and seems reluctant to have told it:

GLAUCON: It isn't for nothing that you were so shy about telling your falsehood.

SOCRATES: Appropriately so.

Nevertheless, he feels, as Obi-Wan did, that it was a lie necessary for the greater good of his students. If reality fell short of Obi-Wan's hopes, it's as much the fault of the impatient student as of the teacher's lie.

"Trust Your Feelings"

Truth can also mean a spiritual understanding and awareness that's not provable by cold, hard facts. In *Indiana Jones and the Last Crusade*, Harrison Ford's Dr. Jones draws a sharp line between the two when he tells a classful of adoring students that archeology is "the search for facts. *Not* truth." He then directs any students who are after truth to a philosophy class down the hall. Obi-Wan's "certain point of view" comment may sound like a bald-faced attempt to cover his former lie; Luke certainly seems to think so. It is, however, an important

---

[10] Plato, *The Republic*, Book III, 414d–415d. For more on this subject, see Chapter 14 in this volume.

reminder not to cling too blindly to a literal, mechanistic truth.

According to Joseph Campbell, a mythologist who influenced Lucas, one of the central conflicts in *Star Wars* is that of man versus machine.[11] The Empire, with its bland uniforms, faceless white-armored stormtroopers, a Sith Lord who's half-robot, and of course the "technological terror" of the Death Star, represents a loss of humanity and with it the ability to see truth from any perspective other than their own—a cold, mechanistic, power-driven perspective that sees no truth beyond bare facts.[12] Machines can't see shades of meaning and are incapable of intuitive understanding; everything is black or white, right or wrong. Furthermore, by refusing to acknowledge the viewpoints of anyone but themselves, the Empire renders outsiders less than human, mere things to be exploited and conquered.

This is why the Sith are no better for their honesty. Not only is their version of truth a narrow, limited one, but they speak it only to serve their own purposes. Truth-telling for the Sith has nothing to do with increasing wisdom and understanding; it's just another tool to help them gain power or hurt their opponents. Ironically, in speaking more literal, factual truths, they lose the higher spirit of truth—that integrity that comes when honesty is practiced for the sake of illuminating the human soul. The Jedi try to hold this integrity. When they fail, valuing power above honor, they fall from grace and are nearly eradicated. Yoda tells Luke, "A Jedi uses the Force for knowledge and defense, never for attack," and the same could be said about truth. Even if the intention toward a higher truth sometimes fails (as it did in the case of Obi-Wan and even more so in the Old Republic Jedi), it still serves a different and more noble end. Vader's truth brings Luke nothing but darkness; the same truth, from Yoda and Obi-Wan, brings understanding and compassion.

Luke is finally the one who must sort out these layers of truth and deceit. In *Return of the Jedi*, he rejects both versions of who and what his father is, and constructs his own truth—one that is

---

[11] Joseph Campbell with Bill Moyers, *The Power of Myth*, PBS (Mystic Fire Video, 1988).

[12] For further discussion of the de-humanizing nature of technology depicted in *Star Wars*, see Chapter 9 in this volume.

at once stronger and more compassionate than either Vader's or Obi-Wan's truth.

The symbol of the lightsaber helps illuminate this idea. Lightsabers are one of the most striking and memorable images to come out of the *Star Wars* films. Obi-Wan describes them as "the weapon of a Jedi Knight," "not as clumsy or as random as a blaster," and "an elegant weapon for a more civilized age." They're futuristic high-tech swords, and the sword has long been a symbol of truth—the weapon of knights and samurai, in many cases a physical manifestation of their honor. In the Tarot, the Suite of Swords represents knowledge and the intellect, and the Ace of Swords in particular is often interpreted or even depicted outright as a blade of truth cutting through layers of deception and confusion. "The Battle Hymn of the Republic" speaks of "His terrible swift sword . . . His truth is marching on." Like truth, a sword can be used for good or evil, to protect or harm. The only difference between a Jedi's lightsaber and that of a Sith is the blade color.

In *A New Hope*, Luke is given his father's old blue-bladed lightsaber; he accepts it as willingly and unquestioningly as he accepts Obi-Wan's story. In *The Empire Strikes Back*, Vader slices off the hand holding that blade, an action as harsh and brutal as the truth he then speaks. Instead of joining Vader and constructing a new lightsaber under his instruction, Luke chooses to build one on his own and (presumably) without instruction. Luke's choice of a green blade (representing life and growth), rather than a red blade as the Sith all use (representing blood and death), is certainly not accidental.

Later, Luke confronts the spirit of Obi-Wan, who finally tells him the full story behind Anakin Skywalker's fall and transformation. Interestingly, Luke's response (once past his initial bitterness) is to insist that there's good left in Vader. Obi-Wan disagrees: "He's more machine now than man. Twisted and evil." But Luke is through with accepting the words of others unquestioningly. Obi-Wan and Vader have given him only part of the story. The rest comes from his own intuition, the "feelings" that Jedi are told to trust above everything else.

This is the truth of the heart, a truth beyond mechanistic facts or even shades of meaning, the final step in the path Luke chose when he turned off his targeting computer on the Death Star run. Luke seeks to build his own truth, trusting what he feels above what anyone tells him, and as a symbol of this truth he builds and wields his own lightsaber. For this reason, he alone is able to move beyond words, appearances, and the dizzying kaleidoscope of individual perspectives. He not only sees the spark of Anakin Skywalker flickering within the mechanical shell of Darth Vader, but redeems him and thereby helps bring down the Empire and the Sith against all expectations. In doing so, he redeems the fallen honor of the Old Republic Jedi and restores their truth to what it should have been.

Philosophers in *this* galaxy have been debating the question of what truth is from "a long time ago" to this day, and if history is any indication, they aren't likely to agree on it anytime soon. But at least we finally have an answer to the question of the lying Jedi: they lie because truth isn't simple, and because they know that truth told without compassion can be brutal. Claiming that truth should always be told, regardless of other ethical considerations, is like claiming that there's nothing left of Darth Vader to be redeemed—true on only the most superficial level. Fans may not like to see their heroes as less than honorable, but the lesson of the lying Jedi is that truth depends on perspective, on intention, on intuitive understanding, and finally on a compassion that's willing to see the whole picture and not just a single "point of view."

17

Religious Pragmatism through the Eyes of Luke Skywalker

JOSEPH W. LONG

In a memorable scene from *A New Hope*, a skeptical Han Solo tells the idealistic Luke Skywalker, "Kid, I've flown from one side of this galaxy to the other. I've seen a lot of strange stuff, but I've never seen anything to make me believe there's one all-powerful Force controlling everything." Nevertheless, Luke becomes a hero because of his faith in his friends, his father, and most importantly, the Force, a mystical energy field in which he believes but which he cannot empirically verify.

The question of when to believe something and when not to believe is very important in the *Star Wars* galaxy and in our own. In fact, this is one of the central questions in the crucial branch of philosophy known as *epistemology*, the study of the theory of knowledge. Epistemology is important to all of us because clearly some things should be believed and others not. It seems, for example, somehow right to believe in the existence of black holes and wrong to believe in the existence of unicorns.

In this chapter, we'll explore the important matter of "when to believe" by first looking at the skeptical position of the nineteenth-century philosopher William Clifford, and then putting this position to the test with the help of arguments from the famous pragmatist philosopher William James. A pragmatist is a person who is committed to a practical and human view of the world and of epistemology. Pragmatists like James argue that in addition to reasons that show the truth of what we believe, there are also practical reasons to believe in something. We'll call the former reasons *truth-conducive* and the latter *pragmatic*. We'll see that William James's position, that a pragmatic faith belief can be a positive thing, indeed our salvation, is exemplified well by Luke Skywalker.

"A Lot of Simple Tricks and Nonsense"

In his 1874 article, "The Ethics of Belief,"[1] William Clifford tells us that faith is "wrong always, everywhere, and for anyone."[2] It's easy to see how one could maintain that faith, or believing upon insufficient evidence, is wrong in an epistemic sense (that it may not lead to knowing a truth); but Clifford believes it is also morally wrong. To explain why he thinks faith is immoral, Clifford tells us this story: A shipowner is about to send a ship full of immigrants to the new land. The shipowner is warned that the ship is old and weathered and not overly well built at the start, and may not make the long journey. Although he could have the ship inspected and repaired if necessary, the shipowner decides to trust in Providence. "It has made many voyages," he reasons. "Surely, it will make this one also." Ultimately, the ship sinks and the immigrants all perish. Now, we can see why Clifford believes faith is morally wrong. It can lead to disastrous consequences. But what if the ship had made it to the new land successfully? In that case too, says Clifford, the shipowner would be guilty, "because he had no right to believe on such evidence as was before him."[3]

When Luke turns off the targeting computer of his X-wing fighter and "uses the Force" to blow up the Death Star, he is guilty of the sin of faith. What makes holding a belief immoral is not simply a matter of whether that belief is true or false, or even whether it is fruitful or unfruitful, but rather of how it originated. The danger of faith is not only that we might have a false belief or even that we should pass on a false belief to others, although this is bad enough. Still worse, if we should be in the habit of not seeking justification for our beliefs, we may become

---

[1] William Clifford, "The Ethics of Belief," in *Lectures and Essays*; reprinted in William L. Rowe and William J. Wainwright, eds., *Philosophy of Religion: Selected Readings*, third edition (Harcourt Brace, 1998), pp. 456–461.
[2] *Ibid.*, p. 460.
[3] *Ibid.*, p. 456.

overly credulous and thus, savage, like the barbarous Sand People of Tatooine.

Han Solo, at least the Han that we meet at the beginning of *A New Hope*, seems to be a skeptic like Clifford. Although he congratulates Luke on blowing up the Death Star, we can imagine how vexed he would have been if he were privy to Luke's unorthodox method. He believes the Force is nothing but "a lot of simple tricks and nonsense," and "no match for a good blaster at your side." We've all known people who adhere blindly to what they were taught as a child, never exposing themselves to experiences which might make them doubt. Clifford tells us that the life of such a person "is one long sin against mankind,"[4] and I believe he has a good point. We'd hardly respect Luke if he had refused to enter the cave on Dagobah where he faced his doubts and the knowledge of the Dark Side within himself. But does this mean that faith is always wrong?

"I Find Your Lack of Faith Disturbing"

Of course, faith is not always advisable. In *The Empire Strikes Back,* Luke has unwarranted faith in his abilities as a Jedi and foolishly leaves his training with Yoda to try to help his friends. This faith backfires and costs him dearly, as he loses his hand in an imprudent showdown with Darth Vader. But under certain conditions, William James argues that faith can be not only morally permissible, but even salvific or hero-making. Luke Skywalker's actions ultimately help demonstrate this. James discusses the importance of hero-making faith in "Ethical Importance of the Phenomenon of Effort":

> The world thus finds in the heroic man its worthy match and mate; and the effort which he is able to put forth to hold himself erect and keep his heart unshaken is the direct measure of his worth and function in the game of human life. He can *stand* this Universe. He can meet it and keep up his faith in it in presence of those same features which lay his weaker brethren low. He can still find a zest in it, not by "ostrich-like forgetfulness," but by pure inward willingness to face it with these deterrent objects there. And hereby he makes himself one of the masters and lords of life. He must be

---

[4] *Ibid.*, p. 460.

counted with henceforth; he forms a part of human destiny. Neither in the theoretic nor in the practical sphere do we care for, or go for help to, those who have no head for risks, or sense for living on the perilous edge . . . But just as our courage is so often a reflex of another's courage, so our faith is apt to be a faith in some one else's faith. We draw new life from the heroic example.[5]

What are these conditions that must obtain for faith to be morally acceptable? First, it is acceptable to have faith only when the choice is *intellectually undecidable*. If a little bit of thinking could decide the issue one way or the other then we cannot simply choose to have faith. Also, the decision in question must constitute a *genuine option*. A genuine option is a choice which is *living, forced,* and *momentous*. A living option is one where there exist at least two real possibilities that may be chosen between. As a teen, Luke had few live career options. Perhaps he could be a moisture farmer like his Uncle Owen. Perhaps he could go off to the Imperial Academy next season after the harvest. But before meeting Obi-Wan Kenobi, being a Jedi Knight was not a real live possibility. It became a live possibility only after Obi-Wan told Luke about his father and after his aunt and uncle were killed by Imperial stormtroopers. Likewise, Han Solo's live choices are to be a mercenary or a smuggler before his adventures with Luke and Leia. Only later could he realistically choose to be an officer of the Rebel Alliance. In addition to being live, a genuine option must be forced. A forced option is one where a decision must be made, or where choosing not to decide amounts to choosing one way or the other. Luke and Leia's decision to swing across the retracted bridge on the Death Star in *A New Hope* was a forced option. Choosing not to decide would be identical to choosing death (or at least surrender.) Finally, a genuine option must be momentous. That is, it must be important and unique. Deciding to go to the grocery store to buy paper towels is not momentous. Nothing very important hinges upon the decision and the decision could be made again at any time in the future. Obi-Wan's decision to respond to R2-D2's message from Princess

---

[5] William James, "Ethical Importance of the Phenomenon of Effort," in John J. McDermott, ed., *The Writings of William James* (Chicago: University of Chicago Press, 1967), p. 716.

Leia, however, is momentous. A great deal hangs upon it and a decision must be made immediately for as Leia pleads, "You're my only hope."

Luke's decision to have faith in the Force seems to fit all of James's criteria. It seems clearly intellectually undecidable. How could Luke empirically test the power of the Force?[6] One must believe in the Force in order to act through it. Thus, he could hardly have the scientific skepticism necessary to set up an appropriate experiment and still control the Force. His decision is living. Either believing or not believing is a real possibility. The choice is forced. If he chooses not to decide, then for all practical purposes, he has chosen against putting his faith in the Force. And finally, it is momentous. Trusting in the Force opens for Luke unique and important opportunities. So, does this prove that Luke's faith in the Force is advantageous? Not yet, it seems. First, we must show that the advantage Luke could gain by believing a truth is greater than the disadvantage he could have by believing a falsehood.

"I Don't Believe It" . . . "That Is why You Fail"

James and Clifford agree that believing truths and avoiding falsehoods are our "first and great commandments as would be knowers;"[7] but these are two different things. For instance, one could avoid error by believing nothing, but it seems clear there is value in believing some things, particularly true things. So which is more important, or does each have same worth? Clifford stresses the avoidance of error, but it seems to me that James is correct when he says that believing what's true is equally or even more important than weeding out false beliefs.

Furthermore, some truths cannot be realized without faith. In *The Empire Strikes Back,* when even Han has become a bit of a believer, he intentionally flies the Millennium Falcon into an asteroid field to lose the Imperial TIE fighters chasing him. Han's

---

[6] The only empirical test I can think of that might be performed is the blood test for "midi-chlorians" that Qui-Gon performs on Anakin in *The Phantom Menace*; but as far I know, this test is not available to Luke.

[7] William James, "The Will to Believe," reprinted in *Philosophy of Religion: Selected Readings*, p. 466.

belief in his ability as a pilot despite great odds (3,720 to one against, by C-3PO's calculations) helps create the fact of his (and his crew's) survival. By choosing to believe in spite of a lack of justification, Han may actually help create a truth, the truth of his survival. And this hardly seems morally wrong.

In some cases, it seems we can create truths through our beliefs. Take the often heard story of a man confronted by dangerous criminals in a dark alley. Instead of running from the criminals or fighting them, which would be futile, the man appeals to the good in the criminals, treats them as if they were loving people. And by treating the criminals as if they were loving despite better evidence, the criminals are made loving. This is perhaps what happens when Luke confronts Darth Vader on the second Death Star at the end of *Return of the Jedi*. The Emperor, meanwhile, tells Luke that his faith in his friends is his weakness. But Luke's faith proves to be his saving grace. After Luke surrenders on Endor, he reminds his father there is still good in him, that he is still Anakin Skywalker. He does this with no justification, only faith, for Obi-Wan has told him Vader is lost: "He's more machine now than man, twisted and evil." Eventually, Luke's faith saves him, as Vader kills the Emperor before the Emperor can destroy Luke. But Luke's faith is not only beneficial for himself. It also saves his father, for his faith turns Anakin back to the Light Side of the Force before he dies. It thus seems that there are certain circumstances under which it is not only morally acceptable to have faith (to believe without sufficient evidence), but it can also be salvific for oneself and perhaps even for others.

"A New Hope"

Faith is an important element of the *Star Wars* galaxy, but it is also important in our own. As a college teacher, I have learned the value of faith in the classroom. Before meeting a new class, I have no good evidence about whether my students will be good students or bad students. By "good" I mean intellectually honest critical truth seekers who are enthusiastic about philosophy. In fact, one could argue that I have inductive or circumstantial evidence that at least some of my students will not be good. After all, in the past I always have had some students that lack enthusiasm or honesty or are not committed to finding truth. Nevertheless, when I walk into a new class, I choose to believe that all of my students are good students and I treat them as such. Although I could be wrong, I believe that my decision to believe in the goodness of my students helps bring about the virtues of enthusiasm and honesty and commitment to truth in them. My reasons for believing in the goodness of my students is not "truth-conducive," that is, I don't hold this belief based on good evidence. Rather, as a pragmatist, I believe that there are practical reasons why one might be justified in believing something. For example, I believe in the goodness of my students because I think some good will come of it and no harm will be done.

Yoda and Obi-Wan lack good evidence that Luke can become a Jedi and vanquish the Emperor and Vader. In fact, they have good reason to doubt Luke's success because of Anakin's failure. Like Anakin, Luke is "too old to begin the training," lacks patience, and has "much anger in him." Clifford would agree with Yoda's initial reluctance to train Luke.[8] James, however, would recognize the potential for a great good that could come from doing so. And as we all know, James's pragmatic faith wins out in the end.

A better example of pragmatic thinking from our own galaxy can be found in Reverend Martin Luther King, Jr.'s famous "I Have a Dream" speech. In spite of a lack of truth-conducive evidence and in opposition to the prevailing social conservatism, Reverend King chose to believe that his dream of whites and blacks standing hand in hand as equals could become a real possibility. Although the struggle is not yet complete, his dream seems to be coming true in twenty-first-century America, and this could not have happened without his faith and the faith of

---

[8] Yoda and the other members of the Jedi Council had the same reluctance to train Anakin. It's interesting to speculate about James's attitude towards the justification of Qui-Gon's faith to take Anakin as his padawan. Initially, it seems that Qui-Gon's faith is unjustified since Anakin turns to the Dark Side. Nevertheless, it appears that in the end Anakin fulfills the prophecy by killing the Emperor, and thereby restoring balance to the Force. So perhaps Qui-Gon's faith was justified after all.

others like him. Because of this faith, we are in a better world today. The example of Reverend King demonstrates how faith can allow us to find a good and a truth outside of ourselves and give us all "a new hope."[9]

─────────

[9] I wish to thank Kevin Decker and Jason Eberl for their helpful comments on earlier versions of this paper. I would also like to thank Seetha Burtner and C. Joseph Tyson for fruitful discussions about *Star Wars* and philosophy, as well as my mentor, Professor Charlene Haddock Siegfried, Donald Crosby, Wayne Viney, and William Rowe from whom I learned so much about William James. Additionally, I would like to thank Andrea (Cummings) Gerig who caused me to begin thinking about the ethics of faith "a long time ago."

Masters of the Jedi Council

JEROLD J. ABRAMS is Director of the Program in Health Administration and Policy, and Assistant Professor of Business Ethics at Creighton University. He has published several essays on semiotics, ethics, and continental philosophy. It's true that he's getting older, and his skin is getting greener. But when nine hundred years old *you* reach, look as good *you* will not. Hm?

ROBERT ARP received a Ph.D. in philosophy from Saint Louis University. He has published articles in philosophy of mind, ancient philosophy, modern philosophy, phenomenology, and philosophy of religion. He's calculated that his chances of successfully making any money doing philosophy are approximately 3,720 to one against.

JUDY BARAD is Professor of Philosophy at Indiana State University. She has published several books, including *The Ethics of Star Trek*, and is currently completing *Michael Moore: The American Socrates*. In addition to teaching courses in ancient and medieval philosophy, she teaches a course on philosophy and *Star Trek*. She uses both mind melding and Jedi mind tricks to move back and forth between the *Star Trek* and *Star Wars* worlds.

CHRISTOPHER M. BROWN is Assistant Professor of Philosophy at the University of Tennessee at Martin. He has published in metaphysics and medieval philosophy and teaches courses in metaphysics, ethics, the philosophy of religion, and the history of philosophy. Inspired by Obi-Wan Kenobi, and fearing that Western civilization as we know it is soon coming to an end, he has found a safe place in northwest Tennessee to hide out with his family until "a new hope" arises.

BRIAN K. CAMERON teaches philosophy and other Jedi mind tricks at Saint Louis University. For a living, he bets on podraces, builds droids in his spare time, and engages in blind conformity.

ELIZABETH F. COOKE is Assistant Professor of Philosophy at Creighton University. She has published several articles in applied ethics and American philosophy, particularly on Charles S. Peirce and Richard Rorty. She currently trains with the Rebel forces to fight the Evil Empire, although she knows that if they strike her down she will become more powerful than they can possibly imagine.

KEVIN S. DECKER teaches philosophy at Saint Louis University and Webster University. He writes on American philosophy, ethics, and social and political thought, and is active in progressive politics. These days, he's got a bad feeling about this.

RICHARD DEES is Associate Professor of Philosophy at the University of Rochester, with secondary appointments in neurology and medical humanities. He writes on political philosophy and has just published a book on the social and conceptual foundations of religious toleration, *Trust and Toleration*. He also works in medical ethics, and is particularly interested in technologies that enhance neurological functions. With his colleagues in neurology, he is currently looking into ways to increase midi-chlorian levels.

JEROME DONNELLY has taught at the University of Michigan (Ann Arbor), the University of Wisconsin (Madison), and the University of Central Florida (Orlando) from which he recently retired. He has published criticism ranging from neoclassicism to popular culture and maintains that many great works of literature and art have been popular, but that mere popularity isn't what makes works great. That includes *Star Wars*.

JASON T. EBERL is Assistant Professor and Co-Director of the Master's degree program in Philosophy at Indiana University–Purdue University Indianapolis. He has published in metaphysics, bioethics, and medieval philosophy. He was once involved in a duel at point-blank range, but foolishly waited until the other guy shot first—Thankfully, he missed.

SHANTI FADER received a B.A. in English from Mount Holyoke College in 1993. She is currently the associate editor of *Parabola* magazine (a journal devoted to the study of myth and religious tradition), which has published a number of her essays, stories, and reviews. She can use her own hair to make the Princess Leia buns, and has won awards for her recreation of Padmé's "picnic dress."

RICHARD HANLEY is from Australia, where they make the good movies these days, and is Assistant Professor of Philosophy at the University of Delaware. He is the author of *The Metaphysics of Star Trek*, as well as articles on *The Matrix*, time travel, and more. Rumor has it he's a protocol droid.

JAN-ERIK JONES is Assistant Professor of Philosophy at Southern Virginia University. He has published on metaphysics and early modern philosophy, and has been known to subject innocent bystanders to hours of detailed discussions of why lightsabers are impossible—Light doesn't just stop three feet from its source!!

JAMES LAWLER teaches philosophy at SUNY–Buffalo. He has written *The Existentialist Marxism of Jean-Paul Sartre*, and a book on IQ theory that criticizes biological determinism: *IQ, Heritability, and Racism*. He has edited a book on the U.S. Constitution, *The Dialectic of the U.S. Constitution: Selected Writings of Mitchell Franklin*, and participated in a debate on socialism in *Market Socialism: The Debate Among Socialists*. His current book, *Matter and Spirit: The Battle of Metaphysics in Early Modern Philosophy before Kant*, will be published by University of Rochester Press. Recognized at the age of two as being strong with the Force, Jim was nevertheless rejected for being "too young." He never forgave the Council, and chose philosophy instead. This was no accident.

JOSEPH W. LONG holds a Master's degree in philosophy from Colorado State University and is expecting a Ph.D. in philosophy from Purdue University in 2005. He has published articles on epistemology and critical race theory and currently makes his home in northwest Iowa where it is only slightly colder than on Hoth.

WALTER ROBINSON, whose Buddhist name is Ritoku (which means "Gathering Virtue"), is a Zen monk and teaches East-West philosophy at Indiana University–Purdue University Indianapolis. The focus of his academic interest is Buddhist philosophical psychology, and his fantasy is to discourse with Yoda on Zen koans.

WILLIAM O. STEPHENS is Associate Professor of Philosophy and Chair of Classical and Near Eastern Studies at Creighton University. He has published on fate, love, ethics and animals, the concept of the person, sportsmanship and the Cubs fan, and various topics in Stoicism. He can easily be mistaken for a Wookiee when he rouses in the morning.

The Phantom Index

The Journey of Luke Skywalker
An Analysis of Modern Myth and Symbol

STEVEN A. GALIPEAU

So many years after *A New Hope* burst upon the world in 1977, why is The Force still with us? Why do the *Star Wars* movies continue to haunt the imagination of young and old alike?

The Journey of Luke Skywalker is the classic depth-psychological study of the *Star Wars* epic, uncovering a wealth of symbolic meaning embedded in this seemingly simple tale of adventure. Luke Skywalker's journey, from his early life on a desert farm to his act of redemption that helps transform an entire galactic civilization, captures the struggles of the modern psyche.

"In Galipeau's view, the Star Wars *sequence, whose narrative he examines in amazing and often quite subtle detail, serves people in the way our other eternal stories do."*

> — LENNY KOFF,
> University of California, Los Angeles

"A masterly study of a modern myth in the grand heroic tradition."

> — CLAIRE DOUGLAS
> editor, *The Visions Seminar*

'The Journey of Luke Skywalker *reveals that, at a time when the fate of the world demands that each of us see through the evil of uncompassionate empire-building, popular film has managed to become an effective vehicle for the instruction of the soul."*

> — JOHN BEEBE
> author of *Integrity in Depth*